Fight for Old DC

FIGHT FOR OLD DC

George Preston Marshall, the Integration of the
Washington Redskins, and the Rise of a New NFL

ANDREW O'TOOLE

University of Nebraska Press | Lincoln & London

For Mia and Mateo,
with a whole lot o' love

Contents

Preface

George Preston Marshall—this name kept popping up as I researched the life of Art Rooney for an earlier project. Marshall—well, all I knew of him previously was that his Washington Redskins were the last major sports franchise to integrate.

Indeed "Marshall the bigot" is an enduring legacy, but there was much more to the man than this unfortunate memory. He was a showman, a sportsman, a man of great foresight and imagination. The more I learned, the more intrigued with him I became. But was Marshall worthy of a full-scale biography? Perhaps, but in Marshall I saw something else. He reminded me of the great baseball folk figure Bill Veeck. Like Veeck, Marshall seemingly popped up whenever a significant issue confronted his sport. He was there at the ready, with an opinion and a solution to whatever problem might arise.

I began to envision a story in which Marshall played the lead, a role as an individual who finds himself immersed in every vital issue confronting his sport. Previously I have chronicled some of the sports world's great characters, including Branch Rickey, Paul Brown, and Rooney. Those figures are tough acts to follow indeed, but Marshall's intrinsic pomposity and unflappable verbosity make him a writer's dream.

But Marshall is just a part of the tale told here. Interwoven throughout the narrative are the stories of numerous players who crossed his path. Commissioners Bert Bell and Pete Rozelle—two men essential to the rise of the National Football League—are here. So are Shirley Povich and Sam Lacy, two journalists who wielded the power of the pen to poke and compel. There is the politician Stewart Udall, who used his position of authority to make this country more democratic. And then there's a football player, Bobby Mitchell, who wanted nothing more than an equal opportunity to ply his skills in his chosen profession.

This story plays out against a backdrop of a changing social landscape. The *Brown v. Board of Education* decision was handed down by the Supreme Court of the United States on May 17, 1954; this monumental event was followed three years later by the Little Rock Nine and the integration of Little Rock's Central High School. And in 1960 the election of John F. Kennedy as the country's thirty-fifth president offered promise of a more progressive society.

Change was indeed in the air, but this change was met with great resistance on the streets, in the schools, and on the playing field.

I was born into this world Irish, Catholic, and a Pittsburgher—three circumstances one can never escape. I'm three generations removed from the Old Country, a long since lapsed Catholic, and nearly four decades gone from the Iron City. Still, if asked, I would describe myself as an Irish-Catholic Pittsburgher. That and a Steelers fan.

My heritage played a direct part in several of my earlier works. Art Rooney and Billy Conn were natural subjects for me, and I enjoyed every moment I spent with them.

Paul Brown, however, was not a likely fit for me. The founding father of the Browns and Bengals was certainly deserving of a full-scale life study, but there was one aspect of his career that intrigued me more than any other: his role in ending professional football's unofficial ban on black players. The story of Marion Motley and Bill Willis drew me in. Much has been written about Jackie Robinson's historic arrival in Brooklyn, and deservedly so, but the pioneers in football have been virtually overlooked in comparison.

How was it possible that sixteen years after Willis and Motley the Redskins still remained an all-white outfit? This disturbing fact fascinated me, and I began to look into the events that surrounded the integration of the Redskins. Bobby Mitchell and George Preston Marshall were the leading stars in the tale, but the backstory was brimming with equally captivating characters.

Today the NFL is a behemoth. Practically twelve months a year the league pervades the news. If it's not the college draft, it's the OTAs (whatever the hell those are) or free-agent season. The Super Bowl, the pinnacle of the football season, has become such a spectacle that the game is nearly unwatchable.

How did we get to this point? That is the genesis of this book.

Personally I have to say I agree with George Marshall's assessment of the NFL more than half a century ago: "The NFL can't encompass the world. It's not that important."

It may not be that important, but the NFL damn near encompasses the world. I have to believe that if George Marshall were still with us he would love every moment of this dominance.

Acknowledgments

A book of this nature would not be possible without the assistance and support of many, including Barbara Jones, George Preston Marshall Foundation; Jon Kendle, Pro Football Hall of Fame; Alexandria Caster, University of Arizona; Dave Kelly, Library of Congress; Paul Dickson (Paul, thanks for the advice and encouragement); Derrick Kenney, Capital Press Club; Zack Bolno, Washington Redskins; John Konoza; Michael J. Jones, Western Illinois University; Stephen Plotkin, John F. Kennedy Presidential Library and Museum; Michael Henry, University of Maryland; Forrest Gregg (thanks for your help and enthusiasm); Joseph D. Schwarz, National Archives; Beth Shankle, National Press Club; Jim Limpert, *Washingtonian*; Melissa Taing, John F. Kennedy Presidential Library and Museum; Roberta Saltzman, Dorot Jewish Division, New York Public Library; Amber McDowell and Donda Morgan, from Senator Tom Udall's office; and Michele Casto of the Martin Luther King Jr. Memorial Library in Washington (thanks for everything, Michele).

I owe a special debt of appreciation to Derek Gray, archivist of the Washingtoniana Collection at the Martin Luther King Jr. Memorial Library in Washington. Thanks, Derek, for your support and, even more important, your patience.

I owe special thanks to everyone who spoke with me about this particular era in Washington DC and NFL history, including Robert Ames Alden, Marti Barry, Upton Bell, Charlie Brotman, Mike Brown, Victor Gold, Steve Guback, Ron Hatcher, Dick Heller, Tom Hurney, Ed Kiely, Myra MacPherson, Thomas Nordlinger, Bill Nunn, Bill Peeler, Art Rooney Jr., Theodore Sorensen, John Thomas, Sterling Tucker, Senator Tom Udall, Dick Victory, Russ White, and Martie Zad.

And finally, my bride Mickie . . . thanks for the support and encouragement. You and me, it's a beautiful thing this life we have.

Prologue | Burgundy, Gold, and Caucasian

"I have nothing against Negroes, but I want an all-white team."

These words were spoken by George Preston Marshall to a *Pittsburgh Courier* reporter in 1950.

Marshall also famously once said, "I believe in states' rights, both in government and in football."

Years later, after every NFL team had integrated except his own, Marshall spoke with *Sport Magazine* for a 1957 profile. He carefully chose his words when discussing his all-white team.

"There has been so much pressure placed on us that it would appear as if we were trying to exploit the race angle," Marshall told the writer, Ed Linn. "I did exploit Indians in Boston. I'll admit that and the same kind of exploitation has taken place with the Negro in baseball. It's wrong. Anyway, Negroes play against us, so what's the difference?"

Marshall was nothing if not consistent.

The fact that the Redskins were an all-white operation was an open secret. There was a time, not so long ago, when such a sight wasn't so remarkable. For years the game was remarkably pale. George Preston Marshall had informed a writer in 1941 that a black athlete would never again play in the NFL.

"Negroes will never play in our league again because the white players would not stand for it," he said. "After a tangle on the turf every player would rise but the Negro. He would never rise, he would be dead."

And Marshall knew something of the subject. It was he who, following the 1933 season, sweet-talked league leaders into cleaning up their sport, which had been "stained" by the participation of several black players. Why men of substance like George "Papa Bear" Halas and Art Rooney could be swayed by Marshall is difficult to discern.

But that was then.

In the spring of 1947 Jackie Robinson burst into the national consciousness. He played the game of baseball with a fierce sense of purpose, and Robinson, with his indelible sense of self, prompted lines of demarcation to divide the spectators. Many were filled pride, others with outrage, and some sat silently entranced by the social spectacle before them.

Jackie wasn't the first breath of change, however. One year earlier, with very little hoopla, the Los Angeles Rams and Cleveland Browns had each welcomed black players—the first to play pro football in thirteen years.

No, it wasn't 1941 any longer. Circumstances had changed; people had changed. One look around the league, and any half-educated football fan could see what a Jim Brown, an Ollie Matson, or a "Big Daddy" Lipscomb could do for a team's fortunes.

In 1950 Chuck Cooper stepped on the basketball court as a member of the Boston Celtics. Cooper's arrival prompted barely a mention in the sports pages.

And so over the course of the next decade integration continued in the three major league sports. The change came in dribs and drabs, with each new barrier broken gathering less notice than the previous. By 1961 the circle was nearly complete. Every team in the National Football League, the American Football League, the National Basketball Association, and Major League Baseball employed at least one black player.

Every team, that is, with the exception of one.

The NFL's Washington Redskins remained the lone holdout, the last vestige of segregation in professional sports.

George Preston Marshall, according to Sam Lacy, columnist for the *Baltimore Afro-American*, was the "racist owner of the Washington Redskins and the only one of the thirty-eight operators of major league franchises who finds solace in the perpetuation of segregation." "Only in the capital of the nation," Lacy wrote, "in a stadium be-deckled by flags of freedom does the spirit of democracy get kicked in the pants."[1]

A favorite phrase used by Lacy when describing Marshall's team was "lily-white." This term was picked up by Shirley Povich, who, while writing for the *Washington Post*, had been poking the Redskins owner in print for some twenty years. His finely tuned literary jabs always found their mark. And when Povich began to focus on Marshall's intransigence the results were often poetic.

"George Marshall is still trying to restore the Confederacy, ninety-four years after everyone else has quit," Povich observed. "The décor Marshall has chosen for the Redskins is burgundy, gold, and Caucasian."[2]

It's been written that it was Corinne Griffith who encouraged her husband, George Marshall, to relocate his football team from Boston to Washington. At least that was her story. Whether it was true or not the Redskins and Washington were a natural fit. The Boston sports fan of the mid-1930s cared little for professional football. And Boston reporters were suspicious of the Redskins' owner, George Preston Marshall, who just happened to be a DC native.

Griffith came into her marriage with Marshall well acquainted with fame in her own right. During cinema's silent age she was a starlet of acclaim and fame. Griffith even had an Academy Award nomination on her résumé for her role in the 1929 film *The Divine Lady*. In her prime, before the Depression hit, Corinne could command up to $150,000 a picture. Her lasting legacy, however, is not her worthy work on the silver screen but a little ditty Griffith penned for the Redskins faithful.

Griffith's modest ode has been credited with being the first fight song for a professional team. Originally named "Fight on Redskins," with an assist from composer Barnee Breeskin, who wrote the music for the catchy tune (which was adapted from the hymn "Jesus Loves Me"), Griffith unveiled the song to a receptive public in the summer of 1938, when the Redskins were fresh off a World Championship:

Scalp 'um, swamp 'um, we will
Take 'um, big score
Read 'um, weep 'um, touchdown
We want heap more

Fight on, fight on, 'til you have won,
Sons of Wash-ing-ton
Rah! Rah! Rah!

Hail to the Redskins
Hail Victory!
Braves on the warpath
FIGHT FOR OLD DC.[3]

The "song," as it were, was embraced by Redskins fans. In time the tune became synonymous with the team and its lyrics, however primitive, protected by the faithful. And so, when Marshall opted to change the final line of the song prior to the 1959 season, it was a calculated decision. The Redskins were the southernmost pro football team, in a southern-minded city, and Marshall had longed marketed his Redskins as "Dixie's team." Over the previous few years pressure had been mounting for Marshall to integrate his club. These calls fell on stubbornly deaf ears. Columns were written decrying Marshall's hiring practices, and pickets were organized protesting the same.

Journalists and fans opened the 1959 team brochure and saw that the tag line of "Hail to the Redskins" had been changed to "Fight for Old Dixie."

Marshall's response to the changing times was a simple, defiant alteration to a line in his team's fight song.

1

"What's the Difference?"

Harry Wismer was running late for an engagement.

He was expected to address the Capital Press Club at noon, but it was nearly one o'clock when the Redskins official finally arrived at Washington's Twelfth Street YMCA.

Falling behind schedule was not an unusual predicament for Wismer, and quite often the cause of Harry's tardiness was his gregarious nature. It was often said that he didn't know a stranger, and as he strolled along the streets of northwest DC Harry couldn't take a step without bumping into a friend, maybe an acquaintance, or just an admirer offering a good word. And he couldn't just nod and keep moving; that wasn't Harry's style. He had an endearing and quite puzzling habit of greeting an acquaintance with a heartfelt, "Congratulations!"

"Congratulations!" Harry would boom in his recognizable baritone, while thrusting his right hand forward.

Why "Congratulations"?

Because, Wismer explained, "it makes people feel good."[1]

Behind the microphone Wismer was equally unreserved. His popularity stemmed from his years as the radio play-by-play man for the Washington Redskins. That role earned Wismer the moniker "Voice of the Redskins." His broadcasts would be peppered with a running commentary on the many dignitaries in attendance at the afternoon games.

"President Eisenhower is here today," Wismer would inform his listeners.

"Justice Clark is seated just below us."

"It seems as if Dick Nixon has just arrived."

Wismer didn't limit his on-air introductions to members of the Washington A-list. He frequently told his audience of the unknown as well as the known. It made no difference to Harry; he was a glad-hander to all, big or small.

A slight problem existed with Wismer's Griffith Stadium list of dignitaries; quite often he made it all up. This tendency to occasionally embellish sometimes bled over into his play-by-play accounts.

In one instance from years earlier Wismer was announcing an Army contest during the days of Glenn Davis and Doc Blanchard. In the course of the game Blanchard took a handoff and proceeded to break free on the way to a 75-yard touchdown run. Wismer erroneously believed the ball to be in the possession of Davis, and he animatedly described the great Glenn Davis dashing down the field and closing in on the end zone. "Davis" had reached the 20-yard line when Wismer recognized his mistake. Ever the professional, he adroitly adjusted the call.

"He's at the 20, . . . the 10, . . . and Glenn laterals to Blanchard—touchdown, Blanchard!"

Indeed a broadcast with Harry Wismer behind the mic was never dull.

His appearance before the Capital Press Club, however, was not related to his role as the Redskins' announcer. Harry hadn't served as play-by-play man for the Redskins for several years, but in the first days of 1957 he was in the news and in demand. The invitation to speak came in the wake of Wismer's public falling out with Redskins owner George Preston Marshall. Theirs was more than a simple disagreement. Wismer had in fact filed suit against Marshall charging that funds of the corporation "have been improperly used . . . for the maintenance and upkeep of a private residence for George Preston Marshall as well as for food, beverages, automobiles, and employment of chauffeurs, cooks, maids and other servants."[2]

This lawsuit was just the final straw in a disintegrating relationship. Five months earlier the Redskins' starting halfback, Vic Janowicz, had been severely injured in an automobile mishap. The accident occurred in Los Angeles while the Redskins were on the West Coast training for the upcoming season. The crash left Janowicz partially paralyzed, effectively ending his career as a professional athlete. Wismer believed that Janowicz should receive his full salary for the 1956 season. Marshall, however, had other thoughts. In his view the football club had nothing to do with Janowicz's unfortunate condition. That Wismer went public with his criticism splintered what was already a contentious association.

That third day of the new year of 1957 was cool but comfortable in the nation's capital. A bright sun burst through clear skies as Harry Wismer arrived at the Twelfth Street Y. Wismer's host, the Capital Press Club, had been founded in 1944 by the *Chicago Defender* columnist Alfred E. Smith. He had started the organization because the National Press Club excluded black journalists from membership, and Smith believed they needed a guild to call their own, a place where issues such as civil rights could be discussed. The location for this luncheon, the Twelfth Street Y, held its own significance in the community. The building in the northwest quadrant of DC was the first YMCA in the country that was built to serve a black community, but this YMCA served as more of a community center than a recreational facility. Just a few years earlier Thurgood Marshall, counsel for the NAACP, had prepared the *Brown v. Board of Education* case at the Twelfth Street Y.

Presiding over the affair was Lawrence Oxley, president of the Pigskin Club. The subject of the day's gathering, "The Negro Athlete in Pro Football," was a topic familiar to the writers gathered in the room. As head of the Pigskin Club, Oxley had a substantial interest in the subject. The Pigskin Club had been celebrating Negro athletes for a quarter century. Beyond bringing athletes recognition, however, the organization strove to achieve racial equality on the playing field. As Oxley stepped to the podium to introduce the tardy guest of honor, he hoped that Wismer would shed some light on an issue of importance to the luncheon attendees.

Wismer did not disappoint.

He came equipped with a pocketful of yarns, some born in truth and others stretching the bounds of believability. All of Harry Wismer's tales, tall or otherwise, entertained. It was when the subject turned to the role of the Negro in football or more specifically the conspicuous lack of a black player on the Washington Redskins squad that he captured the rapt attention of the Capital Press Club members. Once the question-and-answer portion of the luncheon program was under way, Wismer's candid responses to the attendees' pointed queries won the crowd over. He didn't arrive at the affair with the intention of stirring up a hornet's nest, but Harry never shied away from speaking his mind.

During the course of his comments before the Capital Press Club Wismer remarked, "What a grand job the Negro athlete is doing in professional football," but he added, "I have been squelched by President George Preston Marshall of the Redskins every time I have suggested that they hire a Negro player."

According to Wismer, Marshall's response to such a proposal was acidly succinct. "You mind your broadcasts," Marshall told the one-time announcer, "and I'll mind my football team."[3]

But the Redskins were George Marshall's club, and a vice president, no matter how much stock he held, had only so much power. Indeed he was but a "helpless minority stockholder," and he alone could not force a change in Washington, Wismer explained.

Wismer added, however, "In the light of the President's order on desegregation in Washington; and because it is the decent thing to do, George Marshall should end the discrimination against Negro players."[4]

Seated near the front of the room was Sam Lacy, sports editor of the *Baltimore Afro-American*. Armed with ideals and a passion for fighting against discrimination and injustice, Lacy had entered the profession of journalism in the 1920s. First at the *Washington Tribune*, and then later the *Chicago Defender*, Lacy was at the forefront of black sportswriters pushing the integration of Major League Baseball. When offered the opportunity to become the sports editor for the *Afro-American* in 1943, Lacy jumped at the chance.

He also leaped at the opportunity to question the former Redskins official.

Lacy stood and addressed Wismer. "Marshall is interested in big, fast backs. Why didn't the Redskins pick Syracuse's 212 pound half back?"[5]

Lacy was referring to Jim Brown, the first-round selection of the Cleveland Browns during the November 27 collegiate draft. In his zeal Lacy occasionally overlooked the facts. In this instance Brown was not available when Washington drafted, but his point was well taken nonetheless.

"Maybe Marshall is afraid of winning the championship," Wismer responded. "Maybe he's afraid he'd have to pay the players too much money."

Lacy wasn't finished. "How do the coaches feel about the lack of Negro players?" he asked.

"Well," Wismer began, "Ollie Matson played under Joe [Kuharich] at San Francisco and with the Chicago Cardinals. And I think Joe would have Matson playing for him here if he could. But Kuharich is helpless."[6]

From across the room came another query. "Can you confirm that Marshall has stated that there never will be a Negro on the Redskins?"

"I can only let the record speak for itself," Wismer replied.[7]

This report about Marshall's purported statement was not window-rattling news; that George Preston Marshall was incurably reluctant to integrate his Redskins was an acknowledged reality. It was an issue that had not yet been addressed in such a public forum, however. Wismer's candid comments inspired a rash of headlines in newspapers across the country, and several organizations quickly began discussing the possibility of boycotting the Redskins. Not surprisingly, reporters sought out Marshall in search of a response to Wismer's inflammatory comments. Marshall, however, was uncharacteristically quiet. He avoided the numerous interview requests. Marshall's only comment came in a personalized telegram to Sam Lacy, who was pushing for a boycott in his *Baltimore Afro-American* column. "Any citizen has the right to avoid any event he does not care to attend," Marshall wrote.[8]

Within a couple of days the Capital Press Club reached out to Marshall and offered him a forum in which to defend himself against Wismer's accusation of discrimination. He declined the invitation but wired to the Capital Press Club his response to Wismer's charges.

"Thanks for the opportunity, but I have no intention of having a public debate with Mr. Wismer on this or any other subject," Marshall replied. "The sentiments expressed by him have no connection whatsoever with this organization."[9]

Lacy wasn't the only voice promoting a boycott. The Red Rooster Sports Committee, a New York–based activist group that comprised thirty or forty fans and former Negro athletes, sent a letter to Tim Mara, owner of the New York Giants. The missive asked Mara to work with Marshall "in the interests of his securing qualified players on the Redskins regardless of color."[10]

The Red Roosters, who derived their name from that of a New York restaurant where the group often met to discuss the issues of the day, praised Mara and the Giants for their "own Democratic practice of hiring" but warned that unless Marshall "has a change of heart before January 31, you and other owners will be embarrassed by having to cross a picket line to get to the NFL draft in Philadelphia."[11]

The Red Roosters promised that the league meetings would be only the first protest, stating that "the pattern of discrimination practices by the Redskins is about to result in a league wide boycott, which would seriously affect the attendance at a Giants-Redskins game at Yankee Stadium."[12]

Tim Mara did not respond directly to the Red Roosters' letter. His son Wellington, who served as the team's secretary, did offer a quote to the press on the Giants' hiring practices. "Our team's position on this is clear," the younger Mara said. "We hire boys for their ability. We can't tell Marshall how to run his team any more than he can tell us how to run ours."[13]

John H. Young, chairman of and spokesman for the Red Roosters, talked with Marshall by telephone and asked for the opportunity to discuss the matter face to face. Young's request for a meeting was turned down flat by Marshall, who said he would meet with the Negro representatives only if instructed to do so by the NFL commissioner.

Young had no better luck when he contacted the commissioner, Bert Bell.

There was nothing in the NFL rules that would allow him to force Marshall into a meeting, Bell explained.

"Our policy to admit all players regardless of race, color, and creed has existed since the inception of the league in 1920," Bell told reporters. "At present we have something like forty or fifty Negro boys on our teams. We were the first of the professional sports leagues to hire Negroes. Players chosen by teams are selected upon the basis of individual ability. This is a matter for individual clubs to determine." Picketing the league meeting, Bell said, would be a "very foolish and blundering thing to do."[14]

Before concluding his impromptu press conference, the commissioner explained that he had never discussed the issue with Marshall nor did Bell ever ask Marshall's personal views on the hiring of Negroes.

"It is obvious from these actions both commissioner Bell and Mr. Marshall have entered into an agreement not to recognize our case or even give it the dignity of an audience," Young told a reporter with the *Philadelphia Inquirer*.[15]

This controversy was the last thing Bert Bell needed.

For more than a decade Bell had worked tirelessly to protect and advance the NFL. He would come home from the office at five or six o'clock in the evening only to spend the next six or seven hours working the phones. For Bert there was no down time; it was always business. He had once been a well-read man of wide interests, but now Bell rarely occupied himself with any activity that didn't pertain to football. In his youth he had been one of the country's finest golfers, but he hadn't played a round since being named commissioner. Bell devoted himself wholly to the betterment of the league.

Although he unquestionably had his own ideas and convictions, Bell made certain to speak with George Halas, Art Rooney, and George Marshall whenever the league faced a big issue. It was after all Halas who for all intents and purposes had created the whole damn thing in the early twenties. Marshall came aboard a decade later, a novice to the game but full of opinions and observations on how to make football a more spectator-friendly sport. Marshall and Halas became the best of friends, though their friendship endured numerous tussles big and small. Pittsburgh's Rooney was almost always a voice of reason, but Bell was the glue that held together an eclectic band of unlikely brothers.

Bell was the game's leader and believed by many to be the most powerful man in sports, but the NFL's strength lay in its many commanding personalities. Behind closed doors, and occasionally in full public view, these men would often fight. Verbal spats, certainly. Sometimes punches were even thrown, but in the end they would come together. The best interests of the league nearly always took precedence over individual interests.

As 1956 came to a close and the new year began, the affable Bell was routinely making the short trip from his Philadelphia base to Washington. Nearly once a week Bell would board a train bound for the capital with one purpose in mind: lobbying Congress. The commissioner wanted for his league what baseball had been given decades earlier: an antitrust exemption. And within the next few weeks the Supreme Court would be handing down a ruling that would determine if pro football would be granted protection under antitrust laws.

The National Football League was approaching a crucial epoch. Antitrust exemptions were just the tip of the commissioner's agenda. Bell was planning to unveil his latest idea at the upcoming league meetings, which were scheduled to begin on the last day of January. The commissioner wanted to pool all television money and divide it equally among the teams. The big-city teams and the small-market clubs would all have a uniform share of the revenue stream. When team owners gathered in Philadelphia, the groundwork for a new NFL would be chartered. Much to Bell's chagrin, however, Marshall's hiring practices overshadowed other important issues at hand.

At 10:30 a.m. on a blustery, rainy Philadelphia day a dozen pickets gathered outside the Bellevue-Stratford Hotel.

The meetings inside had already begun before the protesters arrived. All of the attendees, team owners and coaches as well as Marshall himself, had already entered the hotel before the protesters set up their pickets on Broad Street in front of the hotel's main entrance. As the day wore on the number of picketers dwindled until only a handful of marchers remained by late afternoon. Those who stuck it out huddled underneath the building's large canopy for protection from the elements. A report making the rounds in the press revealed that, truth be told, the Red Roosters were not a bona-fide association. In fact the group had no officers, and indeed they appeared to be nothing more than a conglomeration of men who enjoyed watching and following sports—a revelation that some believed negated the grievance altogether.

This "revelation" did not deter the determination of the demonstrators who battled the biting wind and rain with their signs:

Hitler banned Jews, Marshall banned Negroes.

George Marshall is against Negro players and a players union.

President Eisenhower wants every vestige of discrimination eliminated. This includes the Redskins.[16]

Members of the Red Roosters weren't the only ones applying pressure on Marshall. In addition to the picketers' protests Marshall received telegrams from James Roosevelt, a U.S. representative from California, and J. Glenn Beall, U.S. senator from Maryland, asking the Redskins' owner to reconsider his position on hiring.

Marshall read Beall's missive to reporters: "'Achievements of unsegregated teams in the Olympics and other sports events both professional and non-professional, demonstrate advantages of free competition regardless of race, color or creed and I therefore add my personal support to wide-spread opinion that sports profit by use of the best talent available on basis of skill alone.'"

Marshall offered a two word commentary, "I agree."

The normally expansive Marshall was fairly mum concerning the controversy. He did, however, make certain to address the lawsuit filed against him by Wismer earlier in the month.

Wismer's allegations were "ludicrous," Marshall stated, before adding, "Mr. Wismer was a director of the Redskins until last November and approved everything we did until then."[17]

But Marshall couldn't ignore what was happening in front of the hotel. If the protest and telegrams bothered Marshall, he hid his discomfort well.

"I came from Washington. Pickets are not unusual in the Capital," Marshall told a reporter. "I've seen them many times. As I recall, the picket lines in front of the White House protesting the Rosenbergs' sentences were much larger than the one outside for me. I only hope what happened to the Rosenbergs doesn't happen to me."[18]

The Rosenberg crack didn't slip past John Young. "What Marshall is trying to do is link our picket line with communism," Young said. "This is a typical, bigoted Marshall statement."[19]

Inside the Bellevue-Stratford's ballroom Redskins coach Joe Kuharich was standing with Cardinals owner Walter Wolfner. A bemused Kuharich offhandedly mentioned to Wolfner, "You could put a stop to all this if you would only make a deal with us."[20] Kuharich was dreaming. Ollie Matson was not on the market, and, even if he were, George Marshall would never permit such a deal.

While Marshall came under fire from civil rights activists and a handful of reporters, the league owners were conspicuously silent. Not a single word was publicly spoken concerning the controversy in Washington. Although every other club in the circuit had been integrated, not one individual passed judgment on Marshall. Prior to the evening session on Friday, February 1, with picketers marching outside the Bellevue-Stratford protesting one of their own, Marshall's brethren circled the wagons around their embattled pal. As the session began Commissioner Bell stood up before the group and began to speak.

"George Marshall, having completed his 25th year in professional football, is the greatest asset sport has ever known, with his honesty, integrity and his perfect frankness in expressing what he believes."

Coming in the wake of a well-publicized lawsuit brought by Harry Wismer, not to mention the muted response from his colleagues following Wismer's comments a month earlier, the tribute held special meaning to Marshall, who was obviously touched by the testimonial. Notorious for never being short of words and renowned for offering unsolicited opinions, a humble Marshall was moved to silence by this unexpected tribute.

"I think he was a bit shaken by the tribute," Bell said. "I've never seen him so quiet before."[21]

Two days later, in the *Washington Post* Shirley Povich remarked, "One wonders why it took them twenty-five years to decide that Marshall is their great asset. Perhaps they merely wanted to be completely sure."[22]

2

Pomp and Pageantry

George Preston Marshall was born in Mason County, West Virginia, to T. Hill Marshall and the former Blanche Preston Sebrell.

"Yes," Marshall acknowledged, "I was born in West Virginia, but I was conceived and everything else in Washington."[1]

And this matters.

This is who he was.

George Preston Marshall was a son of the South. His views of the world, as well as his core beliefs of wrong and right, were generated by the customs of Dixie. This is not spoken in judgment but stated in fact. George Marshall was proud of his heritage and his firmly held convictions. And never did he make excuses for these principles. As the 1950s came to a close Marshall's Washington Redskins remained the only franchise among the three major sports leagues to not have a single black player, a fact their owner dismissed as trivial.

"I have no racial policy," Marshall claimed with great authority. "I hire Negroes in many capacities.

"I was the first laundry operator to use all colored route men. How many do you see on laundry trucks today?

"I was the first to use colored ushers and vendors at Griffith Stadium athletic contests and at one time there were nearly five hundred colored persons employed in this very building when the [Palace] laundry plant was situated here."[2]

Marshall said these words with a straight face, the same expression he wore when saying he didn't want to "exploit" a "colored" player the way other teams around the league had done.

Marshall had a distinguished way about him—a debonair look, one could say. Not leading-man handsome but something more along the lines of a bit player, the kind of fellow who, on the silver screen, just might save a dame caught in a tight spot. His mug was topped by a full head of shining black hair. What really grabbed attention, though, was Marshall's undeniable sense of style. A favorite item was a full-length coonskin coat, which he wore on the street as well as on the sideline. That the look went out when the Roaring Twenties came to a close mattered not a bit to Marshall. He was also known to appear at league meetings in a dressing gown, silk pajamas, and slippers. His eccentric fashion sense stirred nary a ripple of notice at these gatherings. "It's just George," the other owners would acknowledge under their breath.

Marshall's idiosyncrasies extended beyond his wardrobe. He never drove a car or flew in an airplane during his lifetime. He did, however, enjoy being driven about in a chauffeured automobile—transportation fitting the aristocrat Marshall envisioned himself to be.

He was rarely awake before 10:00 a.m., and he always took a nap before dinner.

Whenever staying in a hotel suite Marshall insisted on rearranging the furniture. The bed was always placed within arm's reach of a telephone, so that Marshall could lounge about while conversing. He also wanted a second telephone situated next to a chair, and if the suite was supplied with a second, excess chair, Marshall placed it in a closet or in the hallway.

Marshall did nothing halfway—no matter the occasion, no matter the endeavor. He was obstinate, to put it mildly. He had opinions, and he was never too shy to spout them for public airing. More often than not Marshall needed no prompting to expound his views, only a forum.

He was pompous and possessed a volcanic disposition. These traits engendered the many feuds that checkered Marshall's volatile career. His coaches, front office personnel, and players were a favorite target of Marshall's fury, but he didn't limit his wrath to the Redskins family. Fellow owners, league officials, sportswriters, and even politicians were all on the receiving end of Marshall's invective.

"I know more about football talent than any man in this business," he once proclaimed, and as if to prove this point Marshall fired his coaches with a stunning frequency.[3] Ray Flaherty, Washington's first winning coach, a coach who led the Redskins to two championships, came back from serving his country in World War II to find he no longer had a job.

Although many outsiders believed Marshall preferred to be surrounded by sycophants, the opposite proved to be a more accurate depiction. He didn't like "yes-men," and Marshall actually preferred that his employees express their disagreements with him, as long as they backed their opinions with a well-presented argument. Sometimes he could even be swayed to change his mind, embracing the new viewpoint and presenting it as if it were a George P. Marshall original thought.

With his outsized personality Marshall dominated any room he entered. A sportswriter well acquainted with Marshall once described the irascible Redskins owner as "not always offensive, but he was never merely inoffensive. [Marshall] does not hold conferences, he holds court."[4]

Dutch Bergman served as the Redskins' coach for just one year, the 1943 season, in which his club won the East Division title. Bergman suffered the fate of many Redskins coaches who came before him and those who followed. One year of working with Marshall was more than enough to make a fair appraisal of the pros and cons that came with leading Marshall's Redskins.

"The trouble with coaching for Mr. Marshall," Bergman said, "was that you prepare two sets of defenses every game; one for the opposition, and one for Marshall."[5]

His was an ego born for the stage, and a life in the theater was indeed once a dream for young Marshall. Years before he entered the world of pro football Marshall had a walk-on part in a Broadway play; his was a short-lived career in the arts, however.

"I helped carry the star on stage in a sedan chair," Marshall would explain years later, "but I put too much enthusiasm into the role, and when I bounced the sedan chair, I got bounced, too. But I did draw a pretty good part in New York, and my friends complimented me by calling me a genuine Smithfield ham."[6]

It was in 1932, twenty-five years before the Wismer controversy, that George Preston Marshall dipped his toe into the world of professional football. Along with three partners Marshall purchased the Pottsville, Pennsylvania, franchise of the NFL. Immediately upon taking possession of the outfit the new proprietors transferred their club, now named the Braves, to Boston.

Why Boston?

"I got talked into it," Marshall explained. "I told them we would lose $25,000 the first year. They mentioned Washington and I said, 'No!' I didn't want to bring a football team to Washington. I got rapped for the free advertising I was getting from my basketball team.

"We decided on Boston. I owned one-fifth. Two dropped out before the season and that left Larry Doyle, Vincent Bendix, and myself. We each owned a third."[7]

After just one season in the business Marshall decided he knew how to make the fairly primitive sport more spectator-friendly. At a league meeting following the 1932 season Marshall rose from his seat and addressed his fellow owners gathered in the room: "Gentlemen, it's about time we realized that we're not only in the football business, we're in the entertainment business."

With that statement Marshall introduced several rule changes, all of which, he believed, would enhance the visual quality of the sport. First he proposed moving the goalposts from the back of the end zone to the goal line, which would increase scoring by relaxing field goal difficulty. Second he called for creating hash marks 15 yards inbounds to allow greater maneuverability for the offense. His last proposal was to legalize the forward pass anywhere behind the line of scrimmage. Previously a pass had to originate at least 5 yards behind the line of scrimmage.[8] This last suggestion was vehemently opposed by a smattering of boisterous opposition, including Marshall's primary antagonist, Chicago Bears owner George Halas, as well as Benny Friedman, a player and coach with the Brooklyn Dodgers football team. "Halas, I could understand opposing me," Marshall acknowledged. "He opposed me because of me. But I could never figure out why Benny Friedman was against it. Benny was one of the great college passers."[9]

Adjusting and refining the game on the field was important for improving the product, but equally vital was the need to provide a bit of theater for spectators.

"For the women, football alone is not enough," Marshall explained, for he did not want an audience consisting solely of men. No, he believed attracting the "fairer sex" to the ballpark was needed to expand the popularity of pro football. "I always try to present halftime entertainment to give them something to look forward to—a little music, dancing, color, something they can understand and enjoy," he said, adding that "the women add class to a sports gathering. They'll discourage a rowdy element."[10]

"If you get women and the kids steamed up over a football game," he said, "you have papa hooked."[11]

On another occasion, Marshall flatly and firmly declared, "Men who don't like football are no good for America."[12]

Marshall was an innovator on the entertainment aspect of the game, including halftime shows featuring marching bands. The beginnings of Marshall's Redskins Marching Band were quite modest. In 1937 Marshall was asked by a small band, a group whose members all worked together at a local milk company, if they could perform at the Redskins' first home game of the coming season. Marshall agreed to the proposal; the game certainly needed more showmanship, more glamour. The band's performance energized Marshall, and the ensemble continued to entertain Washington fans for the remainder of the season. Marshall was captivated. He also had an epiphany: what his Redskins needed was their very own band. The following year he established the Redskins Marching Band, a group consisting of men and women from many walks of life. Law and medical students, mechanics, construction workers, salesmen, and plumbers, and there was even a musician or two in the bunch. The schedule of the band consisted of a Tuesday afternoon meeting, a Thursday rehearsal at Griffith Stadium, and, of course, the Sunday afternoon performance.

"We have spirit in that band," Marshall proudly stated. "When you see one-hundred and ten people stand in ice, snow, or mud, at night for a cup of coffee and a hot dog as they sometimes do at rehearsal, you have a lot of respect for them. That is the Redskins Band."[13]

Marshall was a hands-on owner in every way, and there was no aspect of his team that interested him more than his marching band. He rarely missed a rehearsal, and when practice was held at Griffith Stadium Marshall took a seat in the grandstand and bellowed instructions down to the field. Occasionally rehearsal took place in the lunchroom on the top floor of the Palace Laundry building at Ninth and H Streets. Marshall would sit with John D'Andelet, the first leader of the Redskins Marching Band, planning the upcoming halftime show.

Marshall would stand and begin demonstrating exactly how he wanted the show performed. He marched in steps, making sharp, military-precision turns.

"Now this is the way you do it," Marshall coached. "Oompah, oompah, oompah! Turn Boom. Boom. Boom Turn!

"Football is a game of pageantry," Marshall explained. "It derives historically as a spectacle from the Roman gladiator shows and the Greek wrestling shows. It is strictly amphitheater. It needs that atmosphere. Its great success is due to the color surrounding it. Nothing is duller than two teams scrimmaging without music or bands. I would liken football without a band to a musical show without an orchestra. I think the fact that pro football has not gone farther than it has is due to a weakness in the side show."[14]

Marshall's hands-on approach wasn't limited to the entertainment aspect of his club's operation. In Boston an oft-told story had Marshall instructing his coach, William "Lone Star" Dietz, to kick off if the Redskins won the coin toss. Conventional wisdom held that the winning team would opt to receive the opening kickoff, but Marshall's instructions were to kick off. Marshall then proceeded to his box upstairs. When he reached his seat he noticed the Redskins were in formation to receive a kickoff.

Furious at what he perceived to be insubordination, Marshall reached for the phone with a direct line to the bench.

"I told you to kick off!" he barked into the mouthpiece.

On the other end of the line was Coach Dietz. "We did," he replied. "They ran it back for a touchdown."[15]

The novice owner didn't always watch his team from the owner's box high above the playing field. Occasionally he would take in the game from the sideline, and he was anything but a disinterested observer. Marshall would exhort his team and intermittently second-guess his coach. When a substitute was sent in, Marshall would grab the player and give a few last-minute instructions. Not surprisingly such behavior didn't endear Marshall to his coaches, but this displeasure was kept out of earshot of Marshall. This practice ended when Marshall hired Ray Flaherty in 1936. Flaherty had a special clause inserted into his contract that Marshall had to sit in the stands—and stay there.

Some of Marshall's ideas were archaic, to say the least. Like the time he had his Redskins wear "war paint" on the field. In the midst of one game a rainstorm came and the theatrical makeup ran into the players' eyes. One Redskin suggested that they remove the ridiculous mess from their faces. A teammate nodded toward the sidelines, where Marshall was pacing.

"Not as long as he's watching."[16]

At the close of the '33 season, Marshall approached George Halas and Art Rooney.

Why Halas and Rooney?

Halas, as the titular head of the NFL, held more sway than any other team owner. And Rooney, though he had been a part of the league for only one year, was widely respected and well liked by his peers. Rooney's Pittsburgh Pirates squad had employed a black player, Ray Kemp, for the first three weeks of the '33 season. At that time Kemp and Joe Lillard, of the Chicago Cardinals, were the only black players in the NFL. Kemp was cut by the Pirates' head coach, Forrest "Jap" Douds, following the third game of the year.[17]

The National Football League needed to be an all-white affair, Marshall argued.

Halas, with no particular dog in the fight and having never used a black player previously, went along with Marshall's resolve. Rooney's acquiescence, however, was more interesting. An accomplished semipro football player and professional baseball player in his youth, Rooney had been in countless contests with and against Negro athletes. Rooney had also never displayed any outward prejudice nor did he seem to harbor any racial bias. Still, as the new kid in the league, Rooney opted not to fight Marshall's intolerance.

And so, though the decree was never put on paper or officially acknowledged, the National Football League became an all-white affair.

The city of Boston never did warm up to Marshall's Braves, who after one season were renamed the Redskins. The Hub was a baseball town, and Marshall's football club was producing nothing but red ink. Try as he might Marshall couldn't sway local fans to support his team. The college brand of football was modestly supported, but the pro game was unable to grab the attention of the paying customer or the newspaper writers who reported on sporting exploits.

The final straw wasn't the day the *Boston Globe* gave more ink to the Radcliffe women's hockey team than a Redskins contest, though Marshall chafed with indignation. No, the scales were tipped in November 1936, on a cold, rainy day when Boston played host to Pittsburgh. A victory by the Redskins would place them in the league championship. Despite the import of the contest for the home club only five thousand of Fenway Park's thirty-five thousand seats were occupied that afternoon.

Following the Redskins' victory Marshall had his retribution. The title contest was moved to the neutral site of New York, a decision that burned the last bridge back to Boston.

Five years of apathy in Boston had been enough for Marshall. Following Boston's 21–6 loss to the Packers in the championship game the Redskins packed their belongings and relocated the nation's capital.

"I knew I was in the wrong town when a Harvard-Princeton game drew only 20,000 spectators on the same day that the Narragansett race track drew 40,000," Marshall later remembered. "That's when I was sure that New England had sold its soul to the mutual machines."[18]

Boston was a bust; that much was certain. But Washington would prove to be an entirely different story.

Washington took to Marshall's outsized personality like Boston fans never did. Winning undoubtedly helped, but despite his abrasive nature and blatant self-promotion Marshall was viewed with a bit of bemused fascination after the Redskins had a championship season so soon after moving to the nation's capital.

"George Preston Marshall is the third most interesting sight, preceded only by the Washington Monument and the Lincoln Memorial," Thomas Sugrue remarked. "Any Washingtonian would rather watch Marshall go berserk at a baseball game or football game, especially when his team is losing, than see the best stage or screen show."[19]

Upon arriving in Washington, Marshall made certain the local press understood that his football club was in for the long haul. "[The Redskins] were here to stay," Marshall declared, "not just for 1937."[20]

He set up shop for his team on Ninth Street NW.

A cigar store Indian stood watch in the window of the club's headquarters. Marshall's office in the building was decorated with artwork depicting Native Americans, and the walls were filled with framed copies of old Redskins programs.

Marshall and Halas were the best of friends—friends who were often at one another's throats. At one point in their relationship the two men had completely stopped speaking to each other. All communication between the two clubs was carried on through general managers Dick McCann and Rudy Custer. Eventually the stalemate ended, whatever disagreement that existed having been forgotten because neither man could recall what the quarrel was about.

Marshall was an owner and also a fan; he was watching from a field box in Wrigley Field as his champion Redskins met George Halas's Bears in a November 1938 contest. In the first quarter of the game the Bears manhandled and pummeled Redskins players. Several brawls broke out on the field, and three players were ejected from the game while a number of Washington players went to the sideline with injuries. Ten minutes into the game Marshall vaulted from his seat and jumped the railing to the playing field. In a blind rage Marshall excoriated officials on behalf of his team, demanding justice.

The Bears' coach/owner George Halas came over from Chicago's side of the field.

"Get back in that box," he shouted at Marshall. "Too bad it isn't a cage, you son of a bitch."

Momentarily distracted from his diatribe Marshall turned his fury toward Halas: "Shut that filthy mouth of yours before I punch those gold teeth down that red throat of yours, you miserable SOB."[21]

And then, for a brief moment, two of the NFL's leading citizens engaged in a slight physical confrontation—a couple of shoves back and forth and a few more words before the two were forcibly separated.

Marshall then left the playing field and returned to his seat in the Wrigley Field stands. Waiting for him was his wife.

"How disgraceful," Corinne said, "you fighting with that awful man."

"Be careful what you say," Marshall replied. "George Halas is a good friend of mine."[22]

Marshall and Halas had been squabbling for some time. In fact they had been going at one another since 1925, when they were both instrumental in organizing the American Basketball League (ABL). For several years prior Marshall had fielded a semipro team that played under the name Palace Five. A professional league such as the ABL, Marshall reasoned, was an excellent avenue toward promoting and expanding his laundry business. His team in the ABL featured some legendary names, including Gary Schmelke, John "Red" Conaty, Rod Coones, and George "Horse" Haggarty.

Before venturing into the world of professional sports Marshall was a successful businessman in his hometown of Washington. After his father died in 1918 Marshall's inheritance included a small laundry business. Within a few years he had parlayed that modest legacy into the area's largest chain of cleaners, Palace Laundries. Marshall famously paid for a full-page advertisement in local newspapers with the ad consisting of a page completely blank with the exception of six small script words: "*This space cleaned by Palace Laundry.*"

Marshall vowed to "apply theatrical principles to merchandising," and he most certainly did.

While much of the world was mired in war and America was teetering on the brink, Marshall issued a statement to his Palace employees: "Your Palace organization is 100% American—employs only 100% Americans. Your United States of America is a neutral country . . . therefore the discussion or conversation of the conflict in Europe with customers or with anyone is in strict violation of the rules of this organization—and anyone who violates this rule will be dismissed."[23]

At the company's zenith there were fifty-four Palace Laundry outlets located throughout Washington. Marshall dressed his employees in elegant uniforms of blue and gold. The stores were easily recognizable by the prominent blue-and-gold color scheme, and their window décor was a simple flower appropriate to the current season.

Long before his name became synonymous with the Washington Redskins Marshall was known throughout the city as the owner of Palace Laundries. An unknown writer sarcastically dubbed Marshall "Wet Wash" knowing full well that the designation grated. The nickname was picked up by sports reporters around the country, and its use continued even after Marshall had sold his interest in the laundry business.

"I was never in the wet-wash business," Marshall explained. "This was considered the lowest form of laundry business, and it was used by a lot of writers in derision."[24]

Following the Redskins' 7–3 defeat of the Bears on November 17, 1940, Chicago players were in a dither. A possible game-winning touchdown had been denied by a Washington pass interference, an infraction the officials did not acknowledge. Hearing of the Chicago team's complaints, Marshall ran his mouth to the press.

"Crybabies," Marshall declared. "They're frontrunners. They're not a second-half team. The Bears are quitters."

The Bears are quitters. George Halas couldn't have asked for better bulletin board material. Halas made certain that every member of his squad was aware of Marshall's statement by placing copies throughout the Chicago dressing room.

"This is what the people in Washington have to say about you," Halas said to his team, while displaying a newspaper article containing Marshall's incendiary quote.

"Gentlemen, we've never been crybabies. Here's the headline. Go out and play the best football of your life."[25]

Three weeks later the two clubs met again, and this time the league championship was on the line. It was an afternoon that Marshall would long prefer to forget, but the memory continued to haunt him.

Unfortunately for Marshall and his Redskins, Halas's Bears made history that day when Chicago whitewashed Washington 73–0 in the NFL championship.

"The unluckiest guy in the crowd was the five-buck bettor who took the Redskins and seventy points," Bob Considine quipped in the *Washington Post* the following day.[26]

In the midst of the Redskins' humiliation a fan seated below Marshall's box had seen more than enough.

"Take the Bums back to Boston," the fan bellowed.[27]

Being flogged on the field was bad enough, but Marshall refused to stand by and listen to profane suggestions from the paying customers. Marshall burst from his seat and confronted the heckler. Marshall wisely stopped short of a physical skirmish, but he did assure the press after the altercation that the fan would not be welcomed back next season.

In defeat as well as victory Marshall was equally entertaining.

One evening in 1952 Marshall was nursing a drink at Buffalo's Club 31 with a few writers when he made a prediction: "You'll see the time comes when having good seats to a pro football game becomes a status symbol, when almost every stadium in the land is sold out before the season begins. . . . Going to football games will be the thing to do in the social fabric of the nation. It will be all that because we're going to make fans of the women, and what appeals to women will carry along the men who are national football fans."[28]

It's not as if the Redskins were struggling at the turnstile. In fact Marshall bragged at one point, "For seven years, 1941–1947, we never had to employ a ticket seller the day of a game. We were sold out for forty-two consecutive games."[29]

But such times wouldn't last.

Some said the troubles began in 1952—that's when Sammy Baugh hung up his cleats. A two-time All-American from Texas Christian, Baugh had been selected by Marshall with the sixth pick of the 1937 college draft.

Ever the showman, Marshall had presented his new quarterback to the Washington press in style. Marshall dressed Baugh up in full cowboy regalia, including a checked shirt, wide-brimmed cowboy hat, and western boots. This young Sammy Baugh was a gunslinger. He was also a fine businessman. Baugh rejected Marshall's initial offer of $5,000 and eventually signed for $8,000.

"When I found out what the rest of the players were making, I felt badly about asking for so much money," Sammy had said after learning that he was making roughly double the salary earned by most of his contemporaries.[30]

For Marshall, though, Samuel Adrian Baugh was worth every penny.

His Washington debut, on September 16, 1937, was a rousing success. The Redskins defeated the Giants 13–3, but observers saw even more than a victory on the field; they recognized the birth of a star before them.

"It was a coming out party the Redskins threw last night in the mazda glow of Griffith Stadium," Lewis Atchison wrote, beginning his game account. "Baugh, heretofore just another 42-point Roman head in the *Post's* banner line, wormed his way into the affections of those 24,000 fans who witnessed last night's contest by his arrow-like passes."[31]

Shirley Povich, too, was taken by Sammy Baugh's command on the field.

Baugh put "his college reputation squarely on the spot" and "justif[ied] every advance notice with his magnificent forward-passing barrage against the Giants," Povich wrote. "No touchdown pass sped from the throwing hand of Baugh, but glory fairly dripped from the lean, lank Texas kid."[32]

Although Baugh played quarterback, and he played the position as well as anyone ever had, he also served as the team's punter, place-kicker, and defensive back. And in his first professional season, as well as the Redskins' initial year in Washington, Baugh carried his team to a championship.

Baugh, he of "Slingin' Sammy" fame, was the greatest Redskin who ever put on the burgundy and gold. It is true that all good things will come to pass, and so, too, did Sammy's time in the sun. Behind Baugh the Redskins were a perennial powerhouse. Without Sammy, the son of Sweetwater, Texas, Washington had become an also-ran, something of a laughingstock.

It wasn't just the absence of Baugh that caused the Redskins' decline. Marshall's continual meddling with the teams on field affairs, his stubborn refusal to recruit black players, and the endless parade of coaches all played a part in the Redskins' collapse.

In August 1954 Marshall dismissed the legendary coach Earl "Curly" Lambeau. Lambeau's legend was made in Green Bay, however, not Washington. In his brief two-year stay as head coach of the Redskins, Lambeau compiled ten wins against thirteen losses and a tie. Lambeau was Marshall's eleventh head coach in twenty years, and his firing prompted a column of reminiscence from the *Post*'s Bob Addie.

"I personally have something like nine battle stars for as many campaigns with the Redskins," Addie wrote. "Naturally, in those years, I was subjected to demonstrations of Mount Marshall's volcanic eruptions."

Over the course of his nearly ten years of covering the Redskins Addie was witness to Marshall's trademark outbursts.

"There was one time George made some uncomplimentary reference to the ancestry of Frank Filchock, after the latter, in relieving Sammy Baugh, had tossed a pass, which was intercepted for a game-winning touchdown by the opposition. It is my recollection that Filchock did a swan dive over my head and attached himself to Mr. Marshall's hide like a mustard plaster. It took several grown men to dissuade him from his felonious intent."

Addie's walk down memory lane continued with a remembrance of the many Redskins coaches who had passed through during the previous decade. With his engaging column Addie offered a peek at life working under the impulsive Marshall.

"No Redskins coach worth his salt (George Preston Marshall supplies the pepper) has ever quit. You've got to be fired to belong to the club. Being a Redskins coach is about as permanent as selling American flags in Moscow. A guy sitting in an air tight room holding a stick of dynamite over a blazing fire would have more chance of survival than a Redskin coach."

Unlike the litany of men who followed him, Ray Flaherty was rarely subjected to the wrath of Marshall. Flaherty was given something of a pass only because his teams won. It wasn't all kisses and hugs, though, even during the Redskins' halcyon days.

"I can remember many occasions when Flaherty and Marshall would be glaring at each other like pit bulldogs in the days Ray was holding down the score to something like 50–0," Addie remembered.

"Dutch Bergman was a scrapper who had been a great Notre Dame player when he was a little guy and giants tore you apart. Then he had been a dare devil pilot in the Lafayette Escadrille and wasn't one to back down to Marshall.

"Vice-Admiral John Whelchel was a misfit as a Redskin coach. The admiral had too much class. He was too much the Navy gentleman with honor and clean young men and integrity too firmly ingrained his character. He was too used to being piped aboard and giving orders from the poop deck or the fantail or the bridge and there was nothing in the Navy regs that took care of the hard commercialism of pro ball, and the violence that took care of the hard commercialism of pro ball, and the violent explosion of Boss Marshall."

"[Dudley] DeGroot was a rarity. He was this Beta Kappa—an intellectual—and his trouble was that he reasoned out everything with a disconcerting logic. Logic, of course, is no way to calm a hot-headed man. You've got to be a shouter and drown him out in a storm of your own.

"With [Albert] Turk Edwards, a genial giant, Marshall often assumed the role of Clyde Beatty with a fractious bear. Turk would just about reach the end of his patience and when it would seem he was about to burst his chains, Marshall would soothe him.

"Dick Todd was the Gary Cooper type of Texan. Dick was quiet until roused, and then his anger was of the cold kind. . . . He couldn't take it.

"Herman Ball was another gentleman. He was a kindly, pipe-smoking type who realized that the players were human. He didn't last long."[33]

Lambeau followed Todd into the hot seat. By all appearances he and Marshall got along well. The two men visited each other's homes and shared dinners together. But even for the great founding father of the Green Bay Packers life with the Redskins was brief.

Marshall came close to signing another legendary coach. In the wake of the Turk Edwards firing Marshall had agreed to a deal with Paul Bryant.

"We had a contract all drawn up," Marshall recalled, "and Bryant was set to sign it when Leo De Orsey said, 'Whoa, wait a minute. Until Paul gets his release from Kentucky maybe we just better shake hands on this deal.' We did, but Bryant couldn't get his release."[34]

"You may get the impression from all of this that I dislike Marshall," Addie wrote in the conclusion to his nostalgic column. "I don't. I like him. He's irascible, violent, opinionated, a dictator, and completely uninhibited. He has an almost psychopathic passion for football. But he's colorful and good copy. I like him—but I wouldn't want to work for him."[35]

3

It Takes Ten to Tango

In February 1957 the National Football League was at a crossroad.

The picketers marching in front of the Bellevue-Stratford were nothing more than a minor distraction to the men meeting in the hotel's ballroom. As the Red Roosters marched outside the building, inside the owners of the NFL's twelve franchises were discussing several issues vital to the game's future. The question of whether management should acknowledge the newly founded Players Association sparked a heated debate. Also on the agenda in Philadelphia were items about television. How should the league embrace it? How should the money be divided?

Marshall's difficulties on the issue of hiring black players were little more than a blip on league commissioner Bert Bell's radar when the league's team owners convened in Philadelphia. Television most certainly could change the sporting landscape; at the moment, however, it was but one of many issues challenging Bell.

As usual when team owners gathered, various rule changes were debated and voted on. And, in keeping with habit, nearly every alteration was rejected. The sole exception: beginning with the new season, when a time-out was called, officials would not place the ball in play for sixty seconds. Although it was a minor variance, the modification prevented the offensive team from lining up a few seconds early. This revision, Bell explained, would give television and radio broadcasters an opportunity to sell another commercial.

During the Philadelphia meetings Bell informed the league that several cities were interested in landing an NFL franchise. According to the commissioner Denver, Miami, Minneapolis, and Louisville all wished to bring professional football to their areas. Now was the time to consider expansion, Bell told the gathered owners. Certainly there were other issues on the meeting agenda, such as discussion of the newly organized Players Association, a proposed thirty-five-player limit, and myriad other concerns, including the possibility of expanding the league to fourteen clubs.

The most significant event of the conference was the appearance of Bill MacPhail of CBS. MacPhail had been invited to speak at the owners' annual gathering by Bert Bell. The commissioner was utilizing the meetings as an opportunity to promote an idea he and MacPhail had been trying to formulate: a proposition that would bring the entire league together under one television contract. Bell stepped forward and heartily pitched the plan to the owners.

The plan called for one network contract, with the revenue split equally among all teams; every franchise would be on the same financial footing. The commissioner then introduced MacPhail to the room. The television executive proceeded to lay out all the advantages that came along with an exclusive deal with his network. First and foremost the money would be significantly more than most clubs were receiving. There was also the uniformity that such an arrangement would provide; all National Football League games would be found on the same channel, with each region receiving the contest of most interest to the area.

The proposal was met initially with great skepticism, but Bert Bell had sowed a seed, and a young Los Angeles Rams executive in attendance, Pete Rozelle, listened intently to Bell's novel idea.

Elmer Layden served as NFL commissioner for six years, guiding the circuit through the war.

They were trying years. With many players having been called up to serve their country the quality of play suffered and gate receipts declined significantly. Still, the National Football League survived. Pro football had long taken a backseat to the collegiate brand of ball, not to mention remaining far behind baseball and boxing in popularity. When the hostilities ended, however, professional football was on the verge of breaking through. What the league needed was a new leader, someone with insight and great communication skills.

In June 1944 Chicago sportswriter Arch Ward announced plans to launch a new football league. The new All-American Football Conference (AAFC) would begin play once the war had wound to a close. Layden's lack of tact was on full display when asked for a reaction to the news.

"First get a ball, then make a schedule, then play a game," Layden said dismissively. Sportswriters altered the commissioner's words to "Tell them to get a ball first," and the phrase became a rallying call for the new league.

Following the 1945 season Layden's contract was not renewed, and the league owners looked to one of their own to replace him.

"All I ever wanted to be was a football man," Bert Bell once explained, and a football man he was.[1]

Bert Bell had joined the NFL in 1933 as the owner of the Philadelphia Eagles. Like many clubs in the league Bell's Eagles had struggled to make ends meet throughout that initial decade.

"One day the Eagles were playing the same day the Athletics were," Art Rooney remembered. "It was cloudy, but everybody was going to the baseball game, so Bert gave a guy five dollars and a megaphone and sent him to the ballpark to yell, 'No game today, rain.'"[2]

When the war came things got even tighter. In 1941, following a dizzyingly complicated array of franchise maneuvers, Bell teamed up with Rooney in Pittsburgh. With the Steelers Bell served as co-owner and briefly as coach.

To the minds of many owners Bert Bell was the natural choice to succeed Layden as commissioner.

"He understood our problems, what it was like to run a club," Art Rooney explained of his friend and partner.[3]

"I'm delighted with the job," Bell said upon being named to the position of commissioner. "I expected it, and I'm a strong arm guy."[4]

When Bell's reign began on January 11, 1946, the new commissioner swiftly confronted questions concerning the AAFC. Bell responded with a bit more delicacy than his predecessor, but he could not conceal his disdain for the upstart league.

"The other league," Bell sniffed. "We're not interested in the other league."[5]

When he was two years old young De Benneville "Bert" Bell had a nanny. At six he had his own pony. At the age of twelve Bell owned his own tux and at seventeen, a Marmon roadster. So even at a young age Bert Bell was a bit of a dandy. He was certainly born on the right side of the tracks. But Bell didn't reach the top position in football without hard work. As commissioner he put in sixteen-hour days and ran up nearly $10,000 a year in phone bills. Bell held the inherent belief that the spoken word always trumped the written word. As a registered lobbyist Bell was especially careful to not put too much into the written record. The minutes of league meetings were purposely murky.

"Why write when you can say it?" Bell rhetorically asked. "Besides, the way things are today, if you write 'these' instead of 'those' some lawyer will try to make a federal case out of it. I'm not tryin' to hide anything. I haven't got anything to hide. I'd just rather explain it.

"Sometimes my wife gets sore when the phone at home rings at two or three in the morning," Bell continued. "Those west coast fellas forget there's a difference in time here, but I tell her, anytime a ballplayer or a newspaperman or a radio to TV man calls, he's making a living."[6]

The All-American Football Conference did its best to live up to its name by placing teams across the country—in New York in the East, Los Angeles and San Francisco in the West, and Miami in the South, as well as a healthy representation in the heartland. Bell led his league through that competitive storm as the AAFC went out of business in 1950 and the NFL absorbed its more successful franchises. And it was Bell who reassured an audience whose faith was shaken in the aftermath of a gambling scandal that marred the 1946 league title game when a group of New York plungers tried to fix the point spread of the championship. After the scandal was revealed Bell cracked down on players who were suspected of being in cahoots with a contingent of gamblers. Merle Hapes, a fullback with the Giants, was suspended for the game, while New York quarterback Frank Filchock was suspended when his involvement was later revealed.

After the controversy Bell said that "on any given Sunday, any team can beat any other team." But he did more than offer up empty slogans in the wake of the scandal. Bell brought in former FBI agent Austin Gunsel to prevent a gambling element from infiltrating the game. Gunsel was hired not to track players but to keep a close eye on gamblers who might try to undermine the integrity of the league.

Bell did his own bit to keep the corrupt components away from his league. The new commissioner followed the odds on games very closely, watching for any suspicious activity. He even ventured into known Philadelphia gambling parlors to investigate rumors he had heard.

There was also the commissioner's annual talk with each club. Every year without fail Bell would bring up the evils of gambling and how such an element could subtly infiltrate the game.

"Gamblers bet millions on our games," Bell began. "You boys go around knocking the officials and people get dirty ideas. Watch out for the wise-guys . . . the winkers.

"They're not gamblers or bookies, or even fans," Bell continued. "They are winkers. They come to you in a restaurant and say, 'You're Jimmy Smith,' let me buy you dinner. Then they go back to the bar and say, 'Bet such and such real big. You just saw me talking to Smith, didn't you.' . . . Watch out for the winkers."[7]

When Bell took over as commissioner in 1946 only four of the league's twelve teams were showing a profit. A dozen years later nearly every franchise was making money. During the 1957 season more than 2.8 million fans would attend NFL games. As head of the NFL Bell became the most powerful and influential commissioner of the four major sports leagues.

Occasionally Bell would make autocratic decisions. Whenever an owner affected by one of those decisions demanded, "Who gave you the authority?" Bell had a pat response: "It's all in Article 1, section 14, paragraph (b)."[8]

It became an often repeated refrain: "It's all in Article 1, section 14, paragraph (b)."

An anonymous owner admitted to the journalist Al Hirshberg, "Bert's not a czar. He just does what he jolly well pleases. And we wouldn't have it any other way."[9]

It did indeed please Bell to seek several rule changes. Every year he ardently advocated abolishing the extra point opportunity following a touchdown. Bell argued that the kick had become so undemanding that it was practically automatic. The kick thus did little more than consume time, while holding no measure of tension or excitement for the fans.

Bell's guidance helped increase both the popularity of pro football and in 1950 the number of league teams when the NFL absorbed the most prosperous teams from the AAFC. Despite the increased revenue and wider exposure for the NFL, behind closed doors the league retained much of its innocent charm. Something as vital to league structure as scheduling was done with the unsophisticated simplicity of a blackboard and a roomful of haggling owners.

"The way we used to do it," Art Rooney explained, "we'd have a league meeting and it would last day and night, for maybe a whole week. Everybody tried to get the best schedule. You'd want the teams that drew the biggest crowds. But early in the season you'd want the teams you could beat, so you could start off winning. The owners who had staying power, who were willing to stay in that room day and night arguing, they wound up with the best schedules. The guys who got tired and went home, they got murdered. One time we worked two or three days getting a schedule up there on the blackboard, but when it was just about done, George Marshall got sore. He went up to the board and wiped it all out. We had to go back to work for two more days, because nobody had copied down the schedule."[10]

Marshall was indeed a master at getting his way during league gatherings. If he sensed the room was turning against him Marshall would table the issue at hand. He would then drag out the meeting far into the evening. Marshall would carry on until he sensed the exasperation of his colleagues; the other owners would be itching to get to their rooms or the hotel bar. Just as the banquet hall was about to empty Marshall would speak up.

"Wait a minute. We tabled this motion to be brought up later."[11]

Invariably there would be consensus; everyone would vote whichever way Marshall wished—anything to get out of that room.

"Charlie [Bidwill], Bert and I just used to sit back and watch the two of them [Marshall and George Halas] get redder and redder as they yelled at one each other," Art Rooney remembered. "Maybe it was the schedule or a change in rules. It didn't make no difference. They just naturally liked to fight."[12]

"Art and Bert and the other owners always acted in the best interests of the league," Halas explained, "but [Marshall] had a tendency to act in his own best interests. For example he might try to schedule just those teams he knew would bring in big crowds. The Bears and the Giants were another. The Steelers usually weren't too good a drawing card because of their record.

But we never let him get away with it and one of the best things that ever happened to this league was when we decided to let the commissioner make up the schedule for all of us."[13]

Marshall undeniably stuck his beak into nearly every issue that touched the league. He had an opinion, a stance, an argument on any subject that affected the National Football League. In 1953 Marshall fought hard against the entry of the Baltimore Colts into the NFL. A failed Dallas franchise was invited to move to Baltimore, though not without an array of stipulations set by George Marshall.

For trespassing within a seventy-five-mile territory around Washington that Marshall considered his own, he demanded that the Colts pay the Redskins $150,000, an amount to be paid out over the course of three years. The Baltimore franchise would also be prohibited from televising any of their games into Marshall's vast Dixie television network. Generously, in his view alone, Marshall allowed the Colts the market of Baltimore, as well as that of York and Harrisburg, Pennsylvania.

Marshall also gerrymandered the league divisions to suit himself. The Colts would not be placed in the East but would instead join the San Francisco 49ers and the Los Angeles Rams in the Western Conference. All the while Marshall's Redskins, who played their home games thirty-four miles to the west of the Colts' Memorial Stadium, remained in the Eastern Conference.

George added one other stipulation: since every Eastern Conference team was scheduled to play a Western Conference team each season, Marshall demanded that Baltimore be the Redskins' annual western rival. This stipulation saved the Redskins a substantial amount of cash in transportation.

And then television changed everything.

The emergence of the new medium drastically altered the politics and financial state of the game. Bell did negotiate a deal to have the DuMont Television Network nationally televise the 1951 championship game, but he was slow to fully embrace the medium for regular-season games. One year after inking his deal with DuMont the commissioner instituted the "seventy-five-mile rule," a decree that prohibited the airing of league contests within a seventy-five-mile radius of a game, even if that game was sold out.

"I don't believe there is any honesty in selling a person a ticket and then, after you've taken his dollars, decide to put the game on television where he could have seen it for nothing," Bell rationalized. "As long as I have anything to do with this league, home games won't be televised period."[14]

The NFL commissioner even offered advice to those reporting the play-by-play action.

"Now don't precede the officials on a call," Bell counseled the men who would announce the games on television broadcasts. "Let them call it. That's what they're paid for. When a play doesn't go, don't knock a player. Give credit to the guy who stopped it. . . . Also, don't dwell on injuries. Say, 'So and so was shaken up on that play, but he'll be all right.' And one more thing: People say we pass too much in this league, so stress the running game. Anytime a guy makes a good run, play it up."[15]

"I'm a great believer in TV," Bell admitted. "It creates interest, but it's only as good as long as you can protect your home gate. You can't give it to the public for free on television and expect them to pay to go to the ballpark for the same game."[16]

Undoubtedly, Bell had an intense and unlimited interest in the game's well-being.

He did a little bit of everything; anything needed to make the league run smoothly Bert Bell attended to. The commissioner set schedules, assigned officials, ran the college draft, settled disputes between owners, checked players' contracts, and fined the obstinate. He pushed for a Thursday injury report to thwart gambling interests who could get inside dope on the health of players and bet accordingly. The commissioner received some pushback on the proposal, but like so many of his ideas the suggestion became a fixture of the game. Behind Bell's leadership pro football enjoyed a boom in popularity, yet even with the sport's newfound prominence the league meetings remained relaxed get-togethers.

"He could persuade you," Wellington Mara acknowledged. "Politics is the art of the possible and Bert knew what could be attempted. He passed important pieces of league legislation in four day meetings by holding them until the last two hours because he knew we all wanted to go home."[17]

The commissioner was easily ruffled. He had an even-keel personality. During some of the most boisterous league gatherings Bell maintained his cool. However, there was a sure sign that every official in the room recognized as an indication that Bell was getting angry. When he was pushed to his tipping point Bert would remove his dentures and place them in a glass of water on the table.[18]

From the outside looking in the NFL seemed to possess a sort of "Mom and Pop" quality, but Bell's informal nature served the league well. The stability of team ownership, as well as the camaraderie that had developed among these men through the years, contributed much to the game's progression. As the fifties progressed the issues facing the NFL became more complex and the differences among the game's leaders became more marked. So many of the faces, however, remained the same. Halas, Mara, Bidwill, Bell, Rooney, and Marshall—they were the founding fathers of the NFL and they were the men leading the league into a new period. And whether they were ready or not, television would usher them all into a new and lucrative era.

In 1950 the Redskins, along with the Los Angeles Rams, became the first teams to televise all their home and away games. At the time TV was a fairly new form of entertainment, but as the decade wore on and the popularity of the medium spread NFL teams looked to cash in. There was no cohesion among franchises, as each team looked out for its own self-interest.

The New York Giants, along with several other clubs, were under contract to CBS. The Giants, however, received far more compensation than any of their competitors. The Redskins, too, enjoyed a financially beneficial television network arrangement that covered a large swath of the South. Washington games could be viewed from Virginia to the Carolinas, Georgia, and even Florida. The Cleveland Browns, sponsored by Carling Beer and Standard Oil, also built an impressive network of stations that extended throughout Ohio and several neighboring states.

New York, Washington, Cleveland, and Chicago were the exceptions, however. The disparity between those clubs' broadcasting deals and the television contracts of the rest of the league was glaring. Baltimore and Pittsburgh, for instance, each had an agreement with NBC, which paid a fraction of what the competing networks did. The disparate agreements troubled Bell. The widening gap of revenue between teams needed to be addressed before the NFL ended up a league of "haves" and "have nots."

As the league leaders gathered in Philadelphia in the first week of February 1957, however, this disparity was but one issue Commissioner Bell was juggling. The Supreme Court was due any day to announce its decision as to whether the National Football League would be granted an antitrust exemption. The case came before the court thanks to Bill Radovich, a one-time run-of-the-mill guard with the Detroit Lions.

Upon his return from the war Bill Radovich had requested a trade from the Lions to the West Coast. A native of California, Radovich demanded either a trade to the Los Angeles Rams or a raise in salary to help cover his travel expenses to Detroit. This ultimatum was rejected out of hand by Detroit's front office. Just one year earlier Radovich's options would have been limited to remaining in Detroit or perhaps jumping to Canada to play in the Canadian Football League. In 1946, however, there was a new league starting up, the All-American Football Conference. The new league, propitiously for Radovich, had a team in Los Angeles, the Dons.

The beefy lineman reached out to the LA Dons, and he was tendered a contract that would pay him almost triple his previous salary with the Lions. The Dons may not have been the NFL, but Radovich was heading home.

Following two seasons with the Dons Radovich was offered a position with the San Francisco Clippers, a minor league affiliate of the NFL. The Clippers were a member of the struggling Pacific Coast League, and the team's owner, Frank Ciraolo, had recently bid for a franchise in the NFL. When word reached Philadelphia that Bill Radovich had been offered a job with the San Francisco outfit, Bert Bell placed a phone call to the West Coast.

The message was clear. Do not hire Bill Radovich. And Ciraolo, whose fleeting hopes of joining the NFL were pinned to the whims of Bert Bell, heard the implication of the commissioner's words clearly.

Ciraolo rescinded his offer to Radovich.

The ensuing mess could have been avoided had Bell not used his authority to deny Radovich a player/coach position with a little-known team. The commissioner, however, had seemingly overreached.

Radovich decided to take his grievance to court and sued the National Football League for $105,000 in damages, charging that he was illegally denied employment opportunities. There was a significant difference between football and baseball, Radovich argued. Football teams draft a player directly out of college and then the NFL forces the reserve clause upon him. Baseball teams, on the other hand, didn't draft players, which offered freedom of choice to the athlete before the reserve clause was in effect. Radovich's suit made its way through the court system, and on October 6, 1956, the Supreme Court announced that it would hear the antitrust case.

"I don't know what the law has to do with football, but if it would help the Redskins I'd be glad to have it take over," George Marshall said in reaction to the news that the high court was going to weigh in on football business. "Although I would hate to part with Coach Joe Kuharich," he said, "I will consider one of the Supreme Court justices as coach if he will guarantee us touchdowns."[19]

Turning serious for a moment, Marshall opined that "collusion is impossible," because the NFL was not affiliated with any other football league.

Five months later the case came before the high court.

To the dismay of many owners the league's dirty laundry was publicly aired in court and debated in newspapers across the country. Commissioner Bell went on the offensive, putting forth his argument to the press that the precedent had been set a number of years earlier, back in 1922, when the Supreme Court had bestowed upon Major League Baseball an antitrust exemption ruling that declared baseball was not interstate commerce.

"If any of these should now be held by the courts to be an unreasonable restraint of trade organized professional football, the highly competitive and colorful sport that we know today, would come to an end," Bell explained.[20]

The court telegraphed its predisposition from the bench. Chief Justice Earl Warren asked pointed questions of the NFL's counsel on "your player selection committee." The 6–3 decision was handed down on February 25, 1957, by Justice Tom Clark. The decision ruled that pro football, unlike professional baseball, was subject to the antitrust laws of the United States, and football officials were shocked. The ruling placed the legality of the NFL's draft system in question. Also coming under scrutiny were the reserve clause, the commissioner's powers, and the territorial rights of individual franchises. The decision, in essence, passed the buck back to Congress.

Justice Clark tried to explain the court's seemingly contradictory ruling, which he acknowledged might seem "unrealistic, inconsistent or illogical" when viewed next to baseball's exemption. But, he stated, "were we considering the question of baseball for the first time with a clean slate we would have no doubts."[21]

The news devastated Bell. He recognized the decision for what it was: a direct threat to the makeup of the league. The college draft and the reserve clause were notably in jeopardy.

"I always thought that under the Constitution of the United States all people were regarded as being equal. Evidently, under the Supreme Court decision, baseball, a team sport, is different from football, a team sport.

"I don't know why baseball is any different from football, hockey, basketball or any other professional team sport that conducts itself properly," Bell wondered.[22]

After his football career ended Bill Radovich appeared in a number of movies as an uncredited bit player. He was also a partner in a Sherman Oaks auto dealership.

"I'm not out to wreck football or sports," Radovich explained upon learning of the high court's ruling. "I wouldn't want to do anything like that. I put twenty-two years in the game. But I didn't like to have a man tell me I could play for one club and nobody else."[23]

Marshall predicted the Supreme Court's decision would result "in millionaires taking over professional football to bolster its economic condition, due primarily to the unfair distribution of players."[24]

"How can a layman like myself be able to comment on a decision in which the three most able and experienced jurists decide one way and the six with less judicial experience decide another?" Marshall asked. He went on to describe the college draft as "the greatest thing ever invented by the league."[25]

"It protects the interest of the public," he explained. "It equalizes the strength of the teams. An attempt to destroy the draft system would be harmful to the public." Marshall noted that "the draft was proposed by Bell and seconded by me." Bell had indeed pushed for an orderly system, one in which the last-place team selected first and the champions picked last.

"It was designed to protect the fans by keeping the teams fairly equal," Marshall continued. "In theory it makes it possible for all teams to be treated equally; it gives the have nots a chance to get back into contention. The opponents have been liberal thinkers who contend it is a restraint on the player. I say the measure is liberal in the extreme in its restraint upon capital. Money cannot dominate the player market as it does in baseball."[26]

"The first thing to remember is that football is not a full time occupation," Marshall argued. "This system devised by the NFL, since copied by pro basketball, is the greatest thing that ever has been done to protect the interest of the public. It equalizes the strength of the teams.

"The Department of Justice and the courts are entrusted with the duty of protecting the interest of the public. An attempt to destroy the draft system would be harmful to the public.

"It would create the situation that exists in baseball where one city has dominated the sport for the past fifty years.

"Until we passed the draft in 1936 we weren't getting anywhere. From 1921 until then the league was nearly broke."[27]

While the college draft allowed for more equitable levels of competition, it did restrict the players' freedom. Attorney Creighton Miller had studied the situation and well understood the importance of the draft to the league's well-being.

A graduate of Notre Dame, Miller was drafted by the Brooklyn Tigers in 1944. A high blood pressure problem prevented Miller from pursuing a career as a professional player, but he stayed close to the game by coaching, first at his alma mater and then, in 1946, with the Cleveland Browns under Paul Brown. Miller was a member of the Browns staff for just one season before entering law school. Upon graduation Miller continued to stay close to the game, serving as the Browns' legal counsel for a few years. Miller was in the employ of the Browns when he was approached by Abe Gibron and Dante Lavelli with the idea of forming an association of professional football players. The requests to be presented to the owners were nominal, such as a $5,000 minimum salary (which nearly every player in the league already made). Exhibition conditions were also an issue; for example, there were no salaries paid for training camp or preseason contests. Two years of talk and planning resulted in the founding of the National Football League Players Association in November 1956.

Up until that point the players had had no representation.

The owners' operating principle was, in essence, "If you want to play pro ball, you'll play by our rules."

Bert Bell and Creighton Miller came to an agreement before the owners' meeting in January 1957. Miller and the Players Association would endorse the continuation of the college draft, and Bell would promote the association to the owners. The owners, however, weren't on board with the idea of a players' union. When the vote came back from the Philadelphia meeting unanimously vetoing the acknowledgment of a players' association, Miller felt as if Bell had sold him a bill of goods.

In early March 1957 Marshall penned a letter to William E. Miller, a member of Congress from the state of New York. The Republican representative had recently been quoted as saying the National Football League teams were "making an enormous amount of money."

Marshall believed that such a distortion of the truth demanded a reply. To set the record straight, he sent a missive to Miller. "[Your] statement simply isn't true," Marshall wrote. Despite enjoying the most lucrative season yet, the NFL had earned rather modest proceeds.

"Including television revenue," Marshall continued, "the league's gross receipts for 1956 were less than $9,000,000. For twelve franchises that is not as much gross business as is done by small department stores in any one of the many cities in the United States. The net profits would be less than $500,000 for the twelve clubs."

As for the congressman's suggestion that the NFL should expand into new cities, Marshall argued, "This would increase the economic hazards of which we have many and would also bring about a more competitive situation with college football."[28]

Marshall primarily defended the NFL's draft system, which he proclaimed to be the finest system yet devised to distribute players equally. The players, Marshall noted in his letter, had not offered any complaint about the system. Hell, even the proposed Players Association offered no argument against the draft. "The fact that there are no other leagues in the United States than ours,"

Marshall wrote in conclusion, "has been due to public acceptance, there being no compulsion in the matter of playing football."[29]

Several months later, in July, a congressional subcommittee was convened, and it was headed by Emanuel Celler of New York. With the Supreme Court moving further action on the NFL across First Street to Congress, the Celler subcommittee was considering bills designed to mitigate the effects of the Supreme Court decision. The college draft, television, gambling—these were central issues before the committee.

Celler had been a boisterously liberal voice for his Brooklyn constituents since 1923. In the early 1940s Celler had gone against public sentiment, as well as the Roosevelt administration, and advocated relaxing immigration laws to allow Jews escaping Europe to enter the United States. A decade later Celler unleashed a blistering rebuke of Senator Joseph McCarthy on the floor of the House.

"Deliberately and calculatedly, McCarthyism has set before itself the task of undermining the faith of the people in their government," Celler said from the floor of the House. "It has undertaken to sow suspicion everywhere to set friend against friend and brother against brother. It deals in coercion and in intimidating, tying the hands of citizens and officials with the fear of a smear attack."[30]

The National Football League may not have been threatening the very essence of democracy, but Celler recognized a great opportunity for publicity. The subcommittee's hearing on pro football's antitrust exemption would garner notice and bring the member of Congress cherished headlines.

On Thursday, July 24, Bert Bell climbed the steps to the Old House Office Building. He had been to the Hill countless times to lobby on behalf of his league. This morning, however, would be the most important appearance. The feisty little Bell was the day's leadoff witness at 10:00 a.m. in Room 346. He came to the Capitol ready for battle and persuasion. Bell answered the committee's questions and read from a lengthy, thirty-five-page prepared statement, which included four things vital to the continued viability of professional football:

1. The player selection system
2. The reserve clause
3. The provision of the bylaws, which vest in the commissioner authority to act in matters involving conduct detrimental to pro football
4. The territorial rights of teams

Bell was interrupted frequently as he attempted to read from his statement. Representative William McCulloch of Ohio asked Bell where his loyalties as commissioner lay.

Without blinking Bell answered, "With the public and my conscience I also feel I owe greater loyalty to the players than the owners. They're younger and they don't know all the angles."

But what would happen if the commissioner became an advocate exclusively of the owners?

"The public, players, and writers would get you fired," Bell responded.

Shortly after the war Bell had hired former FBI agents to work in every league city. They were given the dictate to keep pro football free of gamblers and their influence.

"There isn't any such thing as a fix. Each year, I caution our players to beware of strangers," the commissioner explained to his congressional questioner. "Innocently they could sit down and have dinner with a gambler. That's all gamblers want to do anyway, be seen with the players. Then the rumors start."

The commissioner was asked about the college draft. Wasn't the practice simply some sort of feudal system?

"A player who does not desire to play with a particular club is usually not selected by that club," Bell insisted. He then explained the main function of the college draft was not to limit players' options but to bring better balance among the league's teams.

Just look at the dominance the New York Yankees held over baseball, Bell told the committee members. He said that sort of dominance was what the National Football League would have without the "player selection system."

The "bonus pick" system had been a part of the college draft for years. This extra selection granted one fortunate team two picks early in the draft instead of one.

"How do you decide which is the lucky team?" Representative Celler asked.

"We pull its name out of a hat," Bell replied.

"This sounds like a lottery," the congressman stated.

"If you think it's a lottery, we'll eliminate it," Bell said.[31]

Bell's response reflected his favorite phrase: Article 1, section 14, paragraph (b).

His voice had turned hoarse and gravelly from a two-packs-a-day Chesterfields habit, but Bell's testimony continued beyond the scheduled lunch break. Following three hours of testimony by Bell, Celler called a halt to the proceedings. The subcommittee had certainly been edified on the issues, Celler assured Bell. Perhaps the commissioner would consent to come back for further discussion after the subcommittee had spoken with proponents of a players' association.

Without hesitation Bell agreed to return whenever called.

The commissioner immediately boarded a train and returned to Philadelphia. Once at home he met with Hugh Brown of the *Philadelphia Bulletin*.

"I couldn't have been treated better," Bell said of his visit to DC. But Brown, pushing harder in his questioning, followed up with this one: did any of those congressmen understand football's problems?

Shaking his head, Bell answered, "None of them knew anything about the game."[32]

Seven days later Bell was again on his way to the Capitol. During the intervening week the legendary Harold "Red" Grange and the former Bears quarterback Sid Luckman, now contracted to the Eagles, had both appeared before the subcommittee. Neither of the men representing the players' interests had anything disparaging to say about the reserve system or the college draft. However, since Bell was last in Washington the committee had heard from Creighton Miller, who had argued for the necessity of a players association.

In the midst of his testimony Bell dropped a bombshell on the subcommittee.

"Accordingly, in keeping with my assurances that we would do whatever you gentlemen consider to be in the best interest of the public, on behalf of the National Football League I hereby recognize the National Football League's Players Association," he announced.

The commissioner then added that he was "prepared to negotiate immediately with the representatives of that association concerning any difference between the players and the club that may exist."[33]

An obviously pleased and surprised Celler responded to Bell's revelation, commenting that he assumed Bell would not have made such an announcement without prior approval from some of the owners.

Bell leaned forward and admitted, "I did not confer with owners or anybody else."[34]

Conspicuously absent from the hearing was George Marshall.

He had indeed been invited to testify by the House subcommittee, but the commissioner demurred. Bell knew Marshall well, and chances were that Marshall would turn the tables while testifying and tell his inquisitors what was wrong with Congress. The commissioner couldn't take the chance of allowing Marshall and his notoriously loose lips to testify. How about George Halas? Bell asked the subcommittee.

The untamed and uncontrollable Marshall was out, and the more reserved though no less opinionated Halas was in.

Speaking with *Star* columnist Francis Stann from his suite at the Mayflower Hotel, Halas explained his position on the players' "union."

"I'm not against an Association," Papa Bear explained to Stann. "It's just that I have a few qualifications."

At the moment he was speaking with the columnist, Halas's Bears did not have a single player belonging to the Players Association.

"If each of the twelve teams had a representative—and we don't, and now the Redskins don't—I wouldn't mind. But . . . the player representative of the Redskins should plead cases only to the owner of the Redskins. The Bears representative should plead to the Bears' front office, and so on. I don't want my players beholden to any player representative from any other club.

"I think Commissioner Bell should be available for consultation with the twelve representatives and with the twelve owners. I think it shouldn't be compulsory for a player to join the Association or union. The National Labor Relations Board cleared that up for workers in other fields."[35]

The Redskins' owner did not appear on Capitol Hill either as a spectator or a witness, but the press still found Marshall for comment—or he found them and proceeded to vent his spleen.

Moments after Bell's congressional testimony the phone inside Marshall's Ninth Street office was ringing.

"I talked to him [Bell] on Wednesday night," Marshall told Francis Stann of the *Star*. "I told him he didn't have to drop the bomb, but he did it anyway."[36]

Marshall went on to challenge Bell's right to recognize the NFL Players Association because of two articles in the player contract and the NFL constitution.

"Bell's action violates Article 13 of the player contract and also Article 1, Section 19 of the National Football League constitution. Neither of which can be changed without the approval of at least 10 of the 12 club owners," Marshall stated.[37]

Article 13 of the player contract read as follows: "This agreement contains the entire agreement between the parties and there are no oral and written inducements, promises, or agreements except as contained herein. This agreement shall become valid and binding upon each party hereto only. When, and if it shall be approved by the commissioner."

Article 1, section 19: "He [the commissioner] is empowered to negotiate working agreements or contracts on behalf of the league with other leagues, persons, corporations, or partnerships which shall be presented to the National Football League for approval. [A] 10/12 vote of the members shall be required for approval.

"[The commissioner] does not have the authority under the constitution to recognize the NFL Players Association."

"That's my opinion," Marshall added. "I think Mr. Bell exceeded his authority. I agree that the commissioner's door should be open to the players who want to air their grievances but that no collective bargaining should be encouraged.

"The reason I say this is because football is a physical contact sport and the minority should be protected.

"Most of the players I spoke with don't want an association or a union[.]

I think they are afraid that if there is a minimum salary, there will also be a maximum salary."

In conclusion Marshall said, "I am very fond of Mr. Bell, but commissioners sometimes have a habit of talking too much."[38]

In private Marshall was completely dismissive of the mere mention of a players' union.

"Who the hell do they think they are?" he roared. "They play four months a year. Why don't they get an honest job?"[39]

The league owners may have supported their commissioner; there was almost certainly unanimous consensus that Bell was a man of undeniable integrity. Still, with this Players Association business, the leaders of the game questioned Bell's opinion on the subject.

Halas was in firm agreement with Marshall, as was Paul Brown, who also questioned Bell's authority on the matter.

On September 19 Bert Bell was a guest at the annual Welcome Home luncheon for the Redskins. As had been the case for a number of years the event was held at the Hotel Statler. The commissioner rose from his seat on the dais and offered a few words on the topic foremost on his mind: pay television for NFL contests.

"There will be no pay TV of our league games as long as I am commissioner," Bell emphatically stated. "We can't take away television from the kids who might not be able to afford pay-TV.

"How are we going to educate them about football? How are we going to develop fans and players if we don't let the kids see their heroes free on home television?

"That's what they are used to, and there will be no change as long as I'm alive."[40]

Bell's comments were certainly not revelatory; the commissioner's words mirrored almost precisely the sentiments he had expressed when speaking before Congress earlier in the summer. Bell was, however, taking a stand in direct opposition to several owners who believed the future of the league would be tied to pay television.

Following the luncheon the commissioner paid a visit to the Redskins.

To the team's coaching staff and players Bell delivered his message. He cautioned the players against signing endorsement contracts without first "consulting their superiors." Bell also warned players about the need to plan their life beyond football. Beware of associating with an "undesirable" element, he told them.[41]

If Marshall believed the ruckus stirred up by Harry Wismer had faded from memory, he was terribly mistaken. Despite the relative quiet of the preceding six months Marshall's stringent hiring habits had not been forgotten.

Prior to the Redskins' annual exhibition with the Rams, the *Los Angeles Times* was asked by civic leaders in the black community to address Marshall's blatant bigotry. As the sponsor of the yearly event, the newspaper was asked to withdraw its support of the game. The *Times* did not acknowledge the controversy, nor did any member of the newspaper staff meet with leaders of the local black community. The only response by the *Los Angeles Times* was an agreement between the newspaper and the Redskins to renew their contract for the yearly preseason game for five years.

Following the annual training period in California Marshall scheduled a preseason exhibition contest deep in the heart of Dixie, as he was pleased to do every year. Just prior to the start of the 1957 season the Los Angeles Rams traveled to Mobile, Alabama, to face Marshall's Redskins.

"Why in the hell did the Rams agree to this game in the first place?" Brad Pye wrote in the *Los Angeles Sentinel.* Pye believed it was bad enough that the Rams had invited the Redskins to Los Angeles for an annual exhibition game, but agreeing to send the Rams and their five black players to Alabama was beyond the pale in Pye's opinion.

"They bring these Washington Redskins here every year to insult their Negro customers in the first game of the season. Now is it necessary to take [Paul] Younger and company to Alabama to meet the only team in the National Football League which refuses to join the integration movement."[42]

Pete Rozelle, the Rams' general manager, acknowledged that his team's black players would have to be accommodated separately, away from their white teammates, in a private home in Mobile.

The Rams "[were] forced into the game," Rozelle explained to Pye during a telephone interview. "The [Rams'] owners are definitely set against it. We have been trying for four months to get this thing cleared up.

"There is [an] NFL rule," Rozelle explained, "which says a Western team must play five exhibition games against Eastern teams and the Rams needed one more game and the Redskins were the only available opponent."

Pye wasn't buying Rozelle's explanation. "The Rams should be ashamed for going through with such a game," Pye wrote. "Integration is having its problem making the team in Dixie and . . . asking [the black members of the Rams] to stoop to this Dixie treatment is a downright injustice that should have been prevented."[43]

The troubles followed Marshall into the regular season. He did not make the trip to New York for the Redskins' October 27 game against the Giants. Had he boarded the train to New York he would have been confronted by a line of protesters led by the same man who was behind the demonstration in Philadelphia.

As he did the previous February at the owners' meetings, John Young led an assembly of picketers. This time he was heading a group called the Committee against Discrimination in Sports. Twenty-five protesters began marching in front of Yankee Stadium at 9:00 a.m., and they continued until fifteen minutes after the two o'clock kickoff. Included among the picketers was a group from Washington known as the Characters Social Club of DC, which had been picketing the Redskins' home games.

In his October 17, 1957, *Washington Post* column Bob Addie noted, "George Marshall has every right to feel a bit smug these days." Addie wrote that "his Redskins drew the day's second largest crowd Sunday when they played the Giants; over 30,000 people.

"Marshall had always been one of the mavericks of the National Football League, but his pronouncements often make a lot of sense. For instance, he was the one who thought of the idea of televising only road games[,] a plan which gradually is being adopted by the baseball clubs." Furthermore, "Mr. Marshall has been on an Indian kick the past few years. Maybe he always was, but never before did his office contain so many curios of our first citizens as it does now. George is well versed in Indian lore."[44]

Inside the Redskins' Ninth Street headquarters the ornamentation of Marshall's personal office consisted of Native American images and artwork, which mingled with a few photos that documented the Redskins' glory days.

Standing out on the wall, though, was a framed letter from the late chief justice of the United States, Fred Vinson, who had been an avid sports fan. In the inscription, dated 1947, Vinson wrote, "I always enjoy your games, probably because I'm a quarterback on the field and in the stands."[45]

Early in the fall Marshall gave an interview to *Sport Magazine* for a highly publicized profile. The publicity over the previous month had prompted the monthly magazine to give its readers a closer look at the personality behind the story. George Marshall had long possessed a personality that begged careful inspection. Although Marshall's role in professional football had made him prominent in his sport, the national audience at large knew little about the Redskins' outspoken owner. Wismer's accusation early in the year, however, had raised his profile and prompted the magazine's editors to commission a piece on the opinionated Marshall.

Freelance writer Ed Linn tackled every issue head on. The feuds with Wismer and *Washington Post* columnist Shirley Povich, the refusal to sign any black player for the Redskins, Marshall's dogmatic opposition to a players' association—the article was anything but a puff piece. Through it all, however, Marshall stood fast, speaking his mind and standing by his beliefs.

"Wismer was broadcasting for the Detroit Lions when our games went on a national network. I had the choice of naming anyone I wanted and I chose Wismer. Well, I inflicted him upon the public, so I'm probably only getting a just retribution. . . . I made him a big shot and he turned around and bit me. As some consolation, I am not the only one he's bit," Marshall said.

Linn pointed out to readers that when speaking off the record, Marshall "refers to Negro[e]s in a manner which leaves little doubt that his objection to them is based purely on racial lines."

Marshall indeed made no effort to hide his political views, no matter how extreme they may have seemed to some. He was conservative, certainly, and so far to the right, Linn wrote, that "[Marshall is] violently against the income tax—not just on April 15 like the rest of us, but in theory and principle."

"I am a strong believer in local autonomy or states['] rights," Marshall explained. "Every effort to centralize has been a failure in government, and it is no more healthy in sports. The more power the league gives to the original operation, the better off it is going to be. I fought for a written constitution and got it, so that there would be a minimum of ruling from above."

This basic belief carried over to his sport. Few topics raised Marshall's ire more than the incessant talk of a players' association.

"I am not anti-union," he told Linn. "I simply do not think there is a place for a players' union in professional football. There is no commodity involved here, nor do players perform by a script. Football is an emotional contact sport[;] it is not comparable to the ordinary way of earning a living. A players' association can only become feasible if there are complaints under the bylaws[;] a player with [a] grievance can appeal first to the club, and if he gets no satisfaction there, to the commissioner. It is a system that has worked.

"There is no way a union could benefit either the player or the employer. If there were any benefit, it would be to the employer, because under union rules he would certainly be given the right to reduce salaries. Under the present system, that never happens. Winning has become more important than economics in general and social security in particular and that has been the main reason for the success of our league."[46]

Given Marshall's stature in the league, Linn reasoned that the Redskins owner had the clout to prevent the formation of a union.

"If I have any extra influence it's because I've been lucky enough to have been right about a lot of things through the years," Marshall modestly explained. "To get anything passed or revoked, we need ten votes out of twelve. No one can call the tune when it takes ten to tango."

Marshall chose his words very carefully while speaking with Linn about his all-white roster. "There has never been a policy of segregation in the park itself," he said, "even in the days when the Washington theaters were segregated. Anyway, Negroes play against us so what's the difference?"

The obvious question hung in the air, and Linn put it to Marshall. Will a Negro ever play for the Redskins?

"I can't answer that," Marshall replied. "There has been so much pressure placed on us that it would appear as if we were trying to exploit the race angle. I did exploit Indians in Boston. I'll admit that and the same kind of exploitation has taken place with the Negro in baseball. It's wrong.

"It has cost me money in the countless opportunities I've let pass, but I've never found anything I enjoy more. If I get out of football, I'll retire[;] there's nothing else I'd want to do. To do anything well, you have to enjoy it first. And not just for the money either. Anything else is just another form of prostitution."[47]

"Big Noise in Washington" was a fitting title to the profile. *Sport Magazine* had introduced Marshall to the country at large, and what was presented was far from flattering. This was George Preston Marshall, warts and all, and the blemishes far outweighed any admirable qualities. Opinionated and quite uncompromising in his views, Marshall and his essence had been aptly captured by Linn.

Three days before the start of the 1958 season, which would kick off with the Eagles being visited by Marshall's Redskins, Philadelphia's star quarterback Norm Van Brocklin spoke with Dave Brady of the *Washington Post*. Over the previous few years Marshall had engaged in a running feud with Van Brocklin. The origin of the dispute was difficult to discern, but the public verbal sparring only escalated when Van Brocklin became a boisterous supporter of the fledgling Players Association.

Van Brocklin voiced his thoughts on the Redskins releasing four veteran players in favor of four rookies. This move was obviously nothing more than a means to save a few bucks, Van Brocklin told Brady. The dismissal of an old friend, LaVern "Torgy" Torgeson, was particularly galling to Van Brocklin.

"He just unloaded the high salaries of the veterans no matter what the burden it puts on the coach," Van Brocklin said.

Following nine memorable seasons with the Los Angeles Rams Van Brocklin was about to embark on his first year with the Eagles.

"The best thing that could happen to his [Marshall's] players, and the whole National Football League[,] would be for him to step in front of a going cab."[48]

Speaking to the same reporter Marshall wasted little time responding to Van Brocklin's critiques. "I don't wish him the same luck he wished me in traffic," Marshall said the next day. "I just hope the Redskins run over him Sunday but not in an automobile."[49]

Six weeks earlier Marshall and Van Brocklin had found themselves mired in a similar battle in the press. Prior to the Redskins-Eagles exhibition game in Los Angeles Marshall had directed a few barbs toward Van Brocklin, with the Redskins owner stressing the star quarterback's backing of the players' union.

"If Van Brocklin keeps his mind on playing football instead of signing players for his union, we could be in for a tough evening," Marshall said. "But if he goes into the game with a pencil in his hip pocket, he may wind up with lead poisoning."[50]

The Rams quarterback did not let Marshall's verbal sniping go by without a response.

"The Redskins are the worst group of rabble rousers in the league because they're the poorest paid," Van Brocklin said.

To which Marshall had the final say. "Maybe so," he acknowledged. "We just don't give all our money to one player."[51]

Van Brocklin had the final say in the rhetorical tussle when he threw for five touchdowns against the Redskins in the preseason matchup.

While he was criticizing Van Brocklin on one front Marshall found himself engaged once again in a to-and-fro with Sam Lacy. The kickoff of the new season prompted Lacy to once again condemn Marshall in his *Baltimore Afro-American* column.

Marshall responded to Lacy's familiar criticism with his own archetypal defense.

"Your problem seems to be, not that there are no colored football players appearing at Griffith Stadium, but there are none on the Redskins," Marshall wrote in a letter to Lacy. "We have never shown any discrimination against anyone regarding tickets, or who appears there. . . . That attitude, I think, would be satisfactory to most people. Tickets are on sale. If you or any of your friends are interested, we would be glad to accommodate you."[52]

4

There Was Interest

December 28, 1958.

Armed with a camera and not much of a plan to speak of, sixteen-year-old Neil Leifer resourcefully made his way into Yankee Stadium. With imagination and youthful gumption Leifer snuck past security and smartly maneuvered himself behind a goalpost, where he documented the epochal moment of the 1958 championship game.

The Baltimore Colts and New York Giants had found themselves tied 17–17 when the clock ticked to the end of the fourth quarter. An already thrilling contest immediately was transformed into the stuff of legend when it became the first NFL title game to extend into sudden-death overtime. Eight minutes and fifteen seconds into the extra period the Colts had worked their way to the New York 1-yard line thanks to a brilliant drive meticulously orchestrated by Colts quarterback Johnny Unitas. From the New York 1-yard line running back Lino "Alan" Ameche received a handoff from Unitas and dove over the right tackle into the Giants' end zone.

The Colts had won the title, and the play became an image etched in memory, an iconic moment in sport. With one snap of a camera shutter Leifer had captured the scene for posterity. The NFL championship played between the Colts and the Giants that day has been tagged "The Greatest Game Ever Played." Some forty-five million people viewed the epic on television. It was an enthralling spectacle that catapulted professional football into the national consciousness.

The National Football League of 1958 was on the cusp. For years the league had operated like a second-rate organization. The fan base, while hard core, was neither broad nor large. Baseball had long been the national pastime, and both professional boxing and college football elicited far more interest from the paying customer than pro football.

The title game between the Colts and the Giants was a signal moment that foreshadowed a new National Football League.

Art Rooney and Bert Bell had watched the game together in the Polo Grounds stands, and following Ameche's touchdown the two men made their way down to the Colts' locker room to congratulate the newly crowned champions.

Bell came upon Raymond Berry and shook the hand of the Colts' receiver. "It was such a great game," Bell said.

Berry smiled and then noticed the tears in the commissioner's eyes.[1]

Fourteen hundred miles away from Yankee Stadium the scion of an oil tycoon was in his room at Houston's Shamrock Hilton watching the game on television. Lamar Hunt was at something of a crossroad. The twenty-six-year-old graduate of Southern Methodist University would never want for money thanks to the immense fortune he had inherited from his father, H. L. Hunt, an oil mogul. Still, Hunt wanted to make his own mark. As he sat on the edge of his hotel bed Hunt was riveted by the action between the Colts and Giants that was unfolding before him on the television screen.

By the time Ameche landed in the Giants' end zone, Hunt, who was already a sports enthusiast, was determined to get in on the action. The excitement of what he had just witnessed couldn't be matched, and the game played perfectly on television. Professional football was the future, and Lamar Hunt wanted a piece of the action. The Colts' dramatic victory reignited Hunt's passion to own his own professional football club.

He'd tried a year earlier to purchase the second team in the Second City—the Chicago Cardinals—a club that was little more than an afterthought to Halas's Bears in the minds of the media and most fans. In fact the Cardinals had been a postscript on the Chicago sports scene since their inception more than three decades prior. Hunt's proffer was not the first inquiry about purchasing the Cardinals franchise with the intention of relocating the club to another city, one far from George Halas's club. Violet Wolfner, the widow of the Cardinals' founding owner, Charles Bidwill, had inherited the team when her husband died prior to the 1947 season. Upon Charles's death Violet became the first female to be the principal owner of an NFL franchise. She had remarried in 1949, to St. Louis businessman Walter Wolfner. As the Wolfners approached their tenth wedding anniversary they found themselves, as well as their professional football team, the focus of many suitors' attentions. By the time Hunt reached out to them the Wolfners had already turned down overtures from representatives of six different cities, including New Orleans, Minneapolis, Atlanta, and Seattle.

Mrs. Wolfner's response to Hunt was the same she had given to each of the previous propositions: though she was open to selling the team, removing the Cardinals from Chicago was a deal breaker.

Nearly twelve months had passed since Hunt endured Mrs. Wolfner's rejection of his offer to buy her team, but Baltimore's stirring victory in the championship game reignited his passion to possess a football team of his very own.

The indefatigable Hunt decided to make one more stab at purchasing the Cardinals. A face-to-face meeting with the Wolfners again failed to procure the Cardinals for Hunt. However, a passing remark by Mr. Wolfner—that the couple had recently been visited by another young Texas oil man, a fellow by the name of Bud Adams who wanted to buy the Cardinals and relocate them to Houston—resonated with Hunt.

There was interest out there. There was certainly enough capital among the pursuing investors—a helluva lot of money and deep pockets. And there were more than a few cities that would like to play host to a professional football team.

Lamar Hunt began weighing the possibilities.

A new football league? Hunt was ready to travel down that path, but first he wanted to make certain the NFL had closed its doors to him.

Hunt again reached out to Bert Bell and inquired about the possibility of expansion in the NFL. On this occasion the commissioner pointed Hunt toward George Halas, chair of the league's expansion committee. The young Texan reached Halas at the Biltmore Hotel in Phoenix, where the Bears owner wiled away the winter months.

Hunt asked if he could he possibly travel to Arizona and discuss the possibilities of NFL expansion with Halas.

No, Halas answered, such a trip would be a waste of time, both his and Hunt's. The league had no designs to add more teams to the circuit. Furthermore, until Mrs. Wolfner made a decision on what she would do with her Cardinals, the league would not consider expansion.

Expansion, however, was a maneuver that would certainly be an option for staving off the competition. Commissioner Bell gave the notion deep consideration. Bell took the proposal to league owners, and he was met stiff resistance from the owner of the Washington franchise. George Marshall was at the forefront of shooting down the idea of expansion. More teams would mean splitting the revenue pie into more pieces. Diminishing his share of the take was unpalatable to Marshall.

5

Fight for Old Dixie

On the evening of July 21, 1959, the Boston Red Sox and Chicago White Sox met at Comiskey Park.

In the top of the eighth inning Elijah "Pumpsie" Green slipped into the game as a pinch runner for the visiting club. This otherwise nondescript moment was notable because Green's appearance marked the first time a black player took the field for the Boston Red Sox, the last Major League Baseball team to integrate.

That George Marshall's Redskins were now the sole all-white club remaining in the three major professional sports leagues bothered him not one bit. If anything Marshall wore the designation as a badge of honor. More than ever before Marshall marketed his club as the "team of the South." The Redskins' radio network stretched from Louisiana to the Carolinas, Georgia, Alabama, Mississippi, Tennessee, Kentucky, Arkansas, West Virginia, and of course, Virginia, Maryland, and the District of Columbia. Marshall's vast television network covered much of the same ground.

The Redskins were Dixie's team, and, in case that fact wasn't obvious before, Marshall put it in writing in a proclamation of just a single word. It was an alteration that was easy enough to overlook, that's for certain. But that singular word unmistakably transformed the nature of a much beloved refrain.

Hidden in, smack in the middle of the 1959 Washington Redskins media guide, was a slight modification to the lyrics of "Hail to the Redskins." Under the direction of Marshall the catchphrase of the team's fight song was changed from "Fight for Old DC" to "Fight for Old Dixie." One solitary word—that was the single adjustment to the worn tune, but it was also Marshall at his most defiant.

And since it was just one word, the change slipped by many, but Shirley Povich caught the alteration and passed it on to his readers.

"George Marshall has subtly abandoned the Redskins' Washington label for the greener pastures of the whole South, which brings his football TV network a vast profit," he wrote.[1]

"For Redskins Dixie admirers, however, there may be a thread of new stillness at Appomattox," he noted a few weeks later. "The Redskins do not seem to be one of the good football teams in the National Football League."[2]

By 1959 Shirley Povich hadn't set foot in the Redskins' locker room in nearly twenty years. If anything his antagonism toward Marshall had only increased. Povich's literate, finely tuned jabs always found their mark. And when Povich began to focus on Marshall's intransigence the results were often poetic. His overall tone changed markedly, from poking at Marshall's pomposity or his sometimes tight-fisted management of the Redskins to ridiculing the Redskins' owner and his last defiant stand for segregation in professional sports.

Shirley Povich was the emperor of Washington sports.

Although the town had a number of fine writers and more than a few engaging personalities among its sports journalists, Povich stood above them all.

Povich was only eighteen years old in 1923 when he joined the *Washington Post*. Just two years later he became the youngest sports editor in the country. He was low key and unassuming, a homebody who preferred an evening with his wife and kids over a night of carousing with the boys. His two-packs-a-day habit was one of the few blemishes on Povich's character. That is not to say that he was universally loved; to the contrary, some of his colleagues resented Povich. Perhaps Shirley made it all look too easy, or maybe it was because Povich held himself somewhat above the fray. He was urbane, polite, and erudite, but Povich could also be razor sharp when eviscerating a subject in his morning column. This attribute did little to endear Povich to George Preston Marshall, a regular target of the journalist.

"Let him rap me," Marshall said of the *Post* reporter. "The problem is when you're left out. I get more publicity from Povich—even if it's in reverse—than from any other writer in the city."

"That's okay," Povich responded. "He serves my purpose too."[3]

At five feet eight Povich may have been small in stature, but the diminutive writer did not scare easily. With his pen, or rather his typewriter, Povich criticized the powerful, praised the worthy, and censured the deserving. During the war years he was one of the few writers outside the Negro press pushing for the integration of Major League Baseball.

When Branch Rickey and Jackie Robinson finally broke segregation in the national pastime, Povich wrote, "Four hundred and fifty-five years after Columbus eagerly discovered America, major league baseball reluctantly discovered the American Negro."[4]

While Povich celebrated Robinson's arrival and mocked the slowness of baseball's leaders to welcome black players to the game, he was noticeably silent on the subject of his hometown Washington Senators and the slowness of that club to integrate. Professionally, Povich's reputation was nearly beyond reproach. But his relationship with Senators owner Clark Griffith at times brought the reporter's ethics into question. Povich made no secret of his friendship with Griffith, nor did he try to hide his admiration for the old man. But never did Povich criticize Griffith's long refusal to hire any black players for the Senators. It took seven long years after Robinson's debut in Brooklyn before a black man took the field for the Senators.

His column, "This Morning with Shirley Povich," debuted in the *Washington Post* in 1926. Before long Povich became required reading for sports enthusiasts throughout the district. The powerful and influential, such as famed attorney Edward Bennett Williams and Supreme Court justices Tom Clark, Arthur Goldberg, and Earl Warren, all counted themselves as admirers and friends of Povich. Warren sometimes sat with Povich in the press box, where Shirley would provide a commentary on the events taking place down below. Povich's popularity went beyond the judicial branch to the executive. Presidents, from Coolidge to Eisenhower, all set aside time to read Shirley's "This Morning" musings, party affiliation notwithstanding.

Ike, as well as his vice president, had difficulty stomaching the editorial page of the *Post*. Neither Eisenhower nor Dick Nixon had much use for that newspaper. For Povich, however, an exception was made. "Shirley Povich is the only reason I read your paper," Nixon told *Post* publisher Philip Graham at a society gathering.[5]

Povich began each day with two questions: "What day is it?" and "What am I going to write about Marshall?"

In his daily routine Povich would contemplate up to a dozen topics for his next column. He bounced each idea around in his head before rejecting the proposal and moving on to the next. Moments before his four o'clock deadline, the decision would be made and Shirley began transferring his thoughts to his typewriter. The day's indecision behind him, the words came flowing forth in clear, succinct prose. When the piece was finished, Povich was done; he never reread anything.

"I never read a column after I've written it," Povich explained, "and it's a good bet I won't read it the next day either. I instantly despise it. I write in a state of perpetual discontent knowing full well I could have written it better."[6]

His first love was baseball, and Povich's close friendship with the Senators' Clark Griffith could be attributed to that passion. The same couldn't be said about Shirley and George Marshall. At first Povich was genuinely amused by the Redskins' president, but the good feelings didn't last long.

The acrimony began one year into Marshall's Washington residence, following a 1938 Bears-Redskins contest at Wrigley Field. On the train ride home from Chicago Marshall was especially buoyant. His take from the game was the largest ever for a team visiting Chicago, Marshall bragged to Povich. The next day Povich took note that Marshall had his players moved from Pullman cars to coach. After the columnist revealed Marshall's penny-pinching ways in the *Post* the Redskins' owner attempted to bar Povich from his team's dressing room and phoned Casey Jones, the managing editor at the *Post*.

"I don't want Povich covering any more Redskins games," Marshall demanded.

Jones refused to acquiesce. "You run your Goddam Redskins and I'll run the *Washington Post*," Jones said in reply.[7]

Four years later the Redskins participated in an Army relief exhibition game on the West Coast. Money raised from the game was to be directed to a fund that benefited widows and orphans of American servicemen, but before the charity received their cut of the gate Marshall pocketed $13,000 "for expenses." When Povich learned of this incident he wrote an open letter to Secretary of War Henry Stimson.

Stimson had just recently canceled a much ballyhooed rematch between the heavyweight boxing champion, Private Joe Louis, and Private Billy Conn. The proceeds of the match were supposed to go to a U.S. Army relief fund, but after some investigation Stimson learned that the promoter of the fight would be paid off the top before the relief fund received a dime.

"My Dear Mr. Secretary," Povich's piece began in the September 26, 1942, *Post*. "So you were 'shocked,' huh, by what you have learned of the tricky financial arrangements of the Joe Louis–Billy Conn fight. We merely want to observe that this is what usually happens when an amateur outfit like your Army Relief Society starts messing around with professional sports promoters."

Povich then changed the focus of the piece to the Redskins' "benefit" exhibition game.

"Like the Louis-Conn fight, that game was supposed to be played for the widows and orphans and families of our missing and maimed soldiers. Sure enough, when they split up the gate receipts, the widows and orphans came first after the proprietors of the Redskins got their share.

"By what right the Redskins' owners have to $13,000 out of that gate before the Army Relief Society was paid off, we don't know. The game wasn't advertised as for the Redskins' benefit if we remember rightly. But the owners of the Redskins skimmed more dough off the top of that one than they ever got for any other exhibition on the Coast."[8]

Which specific aspect of Povich's open letter most rankled Marshall is difficult to ascertain, but rankle it did. Pro Football, Inc., that is, George Preston Marshall, sued the *Washington Post* and Shirley Povich for $100,000, accusing the reporter of writing a "false, malicious, scandalous, and defamatory article."

The case came to trial a year and a half later, during which time Marshall introduced into evidence a letter from the War Department stating that the Redskins would receive 20 percent of the gate receipts up to a maximum of $20,000. The 20 percent turned out to be $13,608.76.

Under questioning from Milton King, Marshall's attorney, Povich was asked if he had proof that the Redskins were paid before the widows and orphans.

"That game was played eighteen months ago," Povich said from the witness stand. "It was played for the benefit of the widows and orphans of our American servicemen. The Redskins have long since been paid off. This war, however, is still going on, and these widows and orphans might not even become widows and orphans until tomorrow, next week, next month or next year. Consequently they have not been paid off yet."

It took but twenty minutes for the jury to come back with a unanimous verdict in favor of the defendants. The courtroom battle may have been over, but the Marshall versus Povich feud was just coming into bloom. Each man grabbed any opportunity to take a jab at his nemesis. Losing the suit infuriated Marshall, but his options for recourse were limited. He may have lacked the bully pulpit that Povich possessed, but Marshall took retribution wherever and whenever he could. Once again the *Post* columnist found himself banned from the Washington dressing room after his "open letter" column to Secretary Stimson.

"I reserve the right to limit anyone's entrance into our training, dressing room, or hotel," Marshall offered as reasoning for the seemingly arbitrary decision.[9]

Despite his loss of direct access to the Redskins, Povich continued to needle Marshall whenever the opportunity arose. In the winter of 1953 Marshall provided the newspaperman an ideal chance to eviscerate the Redskins' owner in print.

"You could see television on your screen the other night, and also smell it," Povich began his "This Morning" column the day after a show devoted to the hometown team premiered on TV.

"The program that brought the newest dimension into electronics was an insufferable presentation called 'The Redskin Show,' originated by George Preston Marshall, dominated by George P. Marshall, and messed up by George Marshall.

"The Marshall show was a turkey from the opening theme, a recording of 'Hail to the Redskins.' Played in slow, alma-mater style, it served only to emphasize the silly lyrics—'Scalp 'em, swamp 'em. We will take . . .' the pure gibberish with which he is smitten only slightly less than with himself."

Although the bar was set at a lofty height, Povich's piece ranked high among his most devastating critiques of Marshall.

"What started out as an interview of Marshall by his publicist, the emcee of the show, wound up as a monologue by Marshall in front of a camera."

Marshall had much to say to the audience, perhaps too much.

"Men who don't like football are no good for America."

"Communism never affects men who play football."

The February 13 "This Morning" column concluded with, "If 'The Redskins Show' means that Marshall is going to be on camera for the next thirteen weeks, horrors. It is not true that I was prepared to dislike the show even if it was good. I was beginning to get a little bit fond of the man in his proper place, which definitely is not on camera. After all, you had to start feeling a bit more kindly toward a man who hasn't sued you for ten years. Then he had to go and spoil it with this unabashed corn he calls 'The Redskin Show.'"[10]

Occasionally the two men's paths crossed in a social setting. At a party one evening Marshall was seated at a table next to Povich and his wife.

"Isn't it strange how such a charming lady as Ethyl Povich could have married that horrible man," Marshall observed.[11]

On another occasion he remarked, "Povich is one guy, when he was circumcised the wrong piece was thrown away."[12]

Marshall had his wisecracks and sneering asides, but Povich had the forum of Washington's most widely read sports column in which to express his views.

One Sunday afternoon in December 1950, as the Redskins played the Steelers at Forbes Field in Pittsburgh, Marshall marched up and down the Washington sideline exhorting his players and riding his coach. Peering down from his perch high above the playing field, Povich started tapping away on his typewriter.

"If Marshall takes one more step, the Redskins will be penalized for having eleven and a half men on the field," he wrote.[13]

The antagonism ran so deep that Povich even took a few swipes at Marshall's wife. Corinne Marshall was "the veteran star of the silent screen" according to Povich. He bitingly dismissed Corinne's literary effort, *My Life with the Redskins*, saying, "This is the only book I have ever read where the appendix should be kept in and the body removed."[14]

These verbal broadsides entertained readers while enraging their target. Marshall had little recourse, however, other than to ban his nemesis from his weekly bull session.

It was a tradition that had been carried on since the Redskins came to Washington. Every Tuesday during football season Marshall hosted a luncheon for DC sportswriters at Redskins headquarters. In a small room off of Marshall's office a dozen chairs were arranged around an oversized table. The setting was informal, the language coarse and at times offensive. But the focus of the room was always on the head of the table. There Marshall sat, a telephone placed within arm's reach. He'd take calls during the lunch, and if the call came from someone prominent he could impress the room. This weekly affair was simply a platform for Marshall to say provocative things. The writers knew him well, though, and were careful when quoting him. Marshall was an opportunist, no doubt. He was also a bullshitter, and these Tuesday gatherings were the perfect forum for spouting off about whatever topped his agenda that particular week.

"He serves rich dishes accompanied by equally rich reminiscences, making for a delectable potpourri of food for thought," explained Harold Weissman. "One merely has to listen to Mr. Marshall. Has to, indeed. There's little choice. No one else ever gets a word in."[15]

This team has more talent than any Washington squad had ever fielded!
The league bends over backward to give Halas in Chicago whatever he wants.
The National Football League will never acknowledge a players' union!

A few of the regulars enjoyed Marshall's company. A couple came for the gratis food and drink. Others attended purely for professional reasons; their job required their presence. And more than a few came once, never to return. Marshall's bloated "buffoonery" was too much to endure.[16]

In the late fifties and early sixties Washington was a three-newspaper town; the *Daily News* and the *Star* were both afternoon papers, while the *Post* had had a monopoly on mornings since purchasing the *Times-Herald* in 1953. The *News* was the top dog at the start of the 1950s, but the sports department was hardly the newspaper's forte.

Political coverage was the strong suit for the *News*. By the end of the decade, though, the *Daily News* had fallen to third in the pecking order. The *Star* had a strong group of sportswriters, but the newspaper's conservative predisposition influenced its coverage of Marshall's prejudice. Additionally the afternoon newspapers were beginning to feel the effects of the changing habits of the public. They depended on late-breaking news, and the *Star* in particular prided itself on its 5:15 p.m. edition. However, as more and more homes had access to television, the evening news began taking the place of the afternoon newspaper.

Washington's sportswriting fraternity was a close-knit bunch. Even in the competitive world of newspaper reporting the journalists would look out for one another. On occasion the beat writer for the *Daily News* or *Star* might be late arriving to an event, and their counterparts at the *Post* would "lend" their carbon to the tardy competitor. Enough of the wording would be altered to protect all involved parties. There was that one instance, however, when a reporter with the *Star* failed to add his personal touch to the copy, and the next day the *Star* and the *Post* each carried remarkably similar game stories.[17]

The Atlas Club, an after-hours club located on the second and third floors above Bassin's Restaurant at Fourteenth and E Streets, had played host to many early-morning gatherings for local writers. After the 2:00 a.m. legal closing time for taverns the Atlas Club remained open for business. Lawyers, judges, policemen, PR types, and newspapermen filled the modest establishment till the wee hours. Francis Stann and Lew Atchison, reporters for the *Star* and *Post*, respectively, could frequently be seen there nursing a drink. Bob Addie of the *Post* was often front and center, regaling the room with a tale. Mo Siegel might be heard telling an off-color joke that would have the club in stitches.

The Atlas Club was not Siegel's only hangout. Mo also had his own personal table at Duke Zeibert's. Duke's place was a second home to many. Writers were joined at Duke's by politicians, athletes, and celebrities. Duke was a personality in his own right—an oversized, exuberant character that everyone liked. He would greet all his customers democratically, whether a celebrity or someone just off the street. Zeibert's was the place to be and the place to be seen. The tables were situated close together so Duke's patrons could converse back and forth. Often customers would move from table to table, stopping for a few words before moving on to the next booth.

The press box at old Griffith Stadium was filled with a diverse cast: a few bigots, a couple of drunks, and a sprinkling of good guys. They were an eclectic group, certainly.

Of this troupe, though, one reporter stood out from all the others. Not for his writing skills, mind you, but rather for his raffish behavior. An evening spent in the company of Mo Siegel was usually a night to be remembered.

The same could be said of an evening spent in the presence of George Preston Marshall. On the Redskins' very first trip to San Francisco in September 1954 Marshall invited a few writers, including Morris Siegel, out to dinner at Tarantino's. Not seeing a bill of fare on the table, Mo Siegel asked a waiter for a menu.

Marshall waved off the request. "I've already done the ordering," he said.

"How do you know what I want?" Siegel asked.

"I *know*," Marshall responded.

During the course of the meal Marshall was unhappy with the service his table was receiving.

"Where's Mr. Tarantino?" he demanded of the waiter. "I want to talk to him."

"Mr. Marshall," the waiter said, "Mr. Tarantino's been dead three years."

Marshall was not to be deterred. "Well, bring me someone, and do it quickly."[18]

Marshall and Siegel—they were an odd couple who were remarkably alike.

The 1959 edition of the Redskins broke camp in mid-August and began making their way east. The trip home from the West Coast varied little from that of any other year. A brief stopover in Las Vegas, however, did divert Marshall's attention. There, in that glistening desert city, he became enamored with a stunning redheaded showgirl. Marshall had become so entranced with the beauty that he invited the young woman to join the Redskins entourage as they continued their trek toward the nation's capital.

Marshall's companion remained with him throughout the team's run across the South and the Redskins' yearly spate of exhibition games in Dixie. She was still with him when the Touchdown Club held its annual Welcome Home Redskins luncheon. And though the event was typically a stag affair

Marshall insisted that his newfound interest accompany him to the Statler. Despite the best efforts of Touchdown Club officials, they failed to dissuade Marshall. George was adamant; his showgirl would attend, and she would sit next to him at the head table.

Handling the master of ceremonies duties was the irreverent and irascible Mo Siegel.

The festivities began with Siegel presenting the members of the 1959 Washington Redskins. One by one down the line Siegel went, equipped with a wry comment or observation about each player. Mo continued with the introductions until he reached Marshall's date.

"Here's someone who didn't make the team," Siegel cracked, "but the whole team made her."[19]

The ballroom filled with nervous laughter, but Mo's off-color joke fell flat with Marshall. He grabbed his date by the hand and stormed out of the Statler.

Siegel was never one to shy away from poking fun at the humorless Marshall. Their relationship was tempestuous. Mo and George could often be seen around town arm in arm, each sporting a smile as well as a drink in their free hand. But Siegel's sharp-edged humor often cut too close for Marshall's taste. The end result was a scene played out all too often, with Marshall erupting in a fury of anger as Siegel looked on with bemused satisfaction. Over and over Mo would poke Marshall with a pointed barb and Marshall would fume.

For all his faults, however, Marshall did not harbor a grudge.

With his friends at least Marshall could find forgiveness within himself. And several hours after Marshall and his showgirl had made their hasty exit from the '59 Welcome Home luncheon, a few fellows who had attended the event found their way to a drinking establishment on Wisconsin Avenue.

Word of Siegel's crack had already spread across town.

"Well," the bartender said to his new customers, "Marshall and Mo didn't stay mad at each other long."

Having just witnessed Marshall's public tantrum, the men were perplexed. "Why would you say that?" one of them asked.

The bartender nodded out toward the street. "Just look out there," he said. Looking through the front window they were greeted with a view of Mo

Siegel standing side by side with the owner of the Washington Redskins, each man relieving himself on the curb.[20]

Years earlier, in 1952 to be exact, Mo was covering the college draft for the *Post*. Throughout a seemingly endless day Siegel had pleaded with Marshall to let him make a selection for the Redskins. The harangue continued, and the draft had neared its conclusion before finally Marshall relented. As the thirtieth, and final, round approached Marshall leaned over and told Siegel, "Get ready."

Mo was prepared; he'd already done his legwork in the hallway. Siegel had learned from a scout that a six-foot-two tight end from Tennessee Tech would be a steal for Washington. Flavious "Nig" Smith was the player's name, Siegel was informed. But there was a drawback; Smith was black. The possibility brought a mischievous smile to Siegel's face.

And now he had his chance. Flavious Smith it was.

"Congratulations," Marshall told Siegel. "You have just become the first sportswriter to ever draft a player."

Mo returned the praise. "And congratulations to you, George. You have just integrated the Washington Redskins."[21]

Marshall blanched. His rage at Siegel was curtailed only by his eagerness to trade away the rights to Smith. A deal was quickly made with Pittsburgh— Smith for nothing in return. Smith didn't stick with the Steelers, however, nor was he able to catch on with any other team. To make matters worse Marshall made certain that any record of Siegel's draft choice was stricken from the record books.

There was one interesting sidebar to the whole affair. Smith, it turned out, wasn't a black man after all. Other than having a thorough tan, Flavious Smith was as white as Marshall himself.

Mo Siegel was a character. There was no disputing that. But sometimes his gags got him in hot water. One such time was in 1956, when President Eisenhower was set to throw out the first pitch at the All-Star Game, which was held at Griffith Stadium that summer. Ike was readying himself for his moment when Mo rolled a baseball down the screen behind the plate. The ball landed close to the president, a near miss that prompted an official investigation. Within a few moments Secret Service agents found the culprit in the press box and escorted him from the park. Mo was released without being arrested, but he did miss the ball game.

Siegel was a difficult man to dislike, but for all his charm and munificence Mo could also be frustratingly cavalier. He was wonderfully impudent, a rascal, a raconteur. He had a quick wit, always ready with a quip or a jibe that was usually delivered with an edge. Mo loved to play it for laughs. He was a gifted speaker and worked hard at the craft. But, like so many comedians, Mo had some demons and he was quick to anger.

A thick fog of smoke clouded Siegel's desk as he pounded out his column. Three cigarettes smoldered in an ashtray while one burned in his mouth. Discarded copy was never placed in a trash can by Siegel's desk; the floor surrounding his desk was strewn with paper. The resulting prose rarely failed to elicit a smile. Truth be told, though, he wasn't nearly the writer that Povich was. Siegel lacked the fortitude and patience to sweat out a great column, but he was a helluva reporter and always about town breaking stories.

In fact some of the writers in the Griffith Stadium press box were unrepentant racists, and these men never wrote one word criticizing Marshall's bigotry. Siegel wasn't necessarily apolitical, but he also wasn't pushing for change and actively pursuing desegregation. Siegel would rag on the bigots in the press box when they began spewing their nonsense.

"You're a bunch of bastards," Siegel exclaimed, and then he would go about his business. But social criticism remained out of his column, and in glossing over such matters Siegel wasn't alone among Washington sportswriters. In fact the *Daily News* and the *Star* all but ignored the Marshall controversy, leaving Povich at the liberal-leaning *Post* alone in leading the integration crusade. The *Star*'s sports editor, Bill Peeler, looked at the controversy with the thought, "It's Marshall's team, if he wants to be stupid, then it's his decision."[22]

There were other reporters on the Washington football beat. Covering the Redskins for the *Daily News* was Dave Slattery. He was a pleasant fellow, a cheery Irishman who knew football inside out, but what Slattery had in knowledge he lacked in prose. Slattery was a hard-working reporter, but as of late he had become something of an apologist for the Redskins' owner, a stooge for Marshall. It was most apparent back in January 1957, when Wismer shined a light on Marshall's bias.

Francis Stann had been writing sports in DC since the 1930s. In his prime

Stann's "Win, Lose, or Draw" column in the *Star* was must reading. But by the late fifties Stann had seen better days. He smoked too much and drank even more. Far too often Stann missed filing his column due to drink. In every instance, though, one of his colleagues would file for him.

For years Povich had relished taking verbal shots at Marshall. In the fall of 1959, however, the broadsides had increased, both in frequency as well as intensity. Perhaps he was spurred on by Marshall's rebellious change to the lyrics of "Hail to the Redskins." Whatever the motivation, Povich began taking every available opportunity to swipe at Marshall in print.

In early November the Colts came to Washington, and their marching band entertained the Redskins faithful with a tune familiar to their ears.

Povich described the scene for his readers.

"The Baltimore Colts brought their team band, along with their football team and in a pre-game warm-up they rendered Dixie, perhaps as a tribute to the Redskins Southern accent and steadfast color line. Nine Confederate states are learning from Marshall how to make Secession work."[23]

Indeed the Redskins band had longed performed "Dixie" at Griffith Stadium at Marshall's direction. The version they played wasn't mournful or wistful. Marshall preferred his "Dixie" up tempo, celebratory, performed triumphantly. It was "Pomp and Circumstance" with a southern drawl.

The slight change to the lyrics of the team fight song wasn't the only information provided in the Redskins' 1959 media guide. Inside the pamphlet was a listing of the team's extensive radio and television network, a network that encompassed nearly every corner of the former Confederate States of America. Also included was a section titled "Matinee at Mid-Field."

"Days for Dixie" once again this year are important features of halftime show-time at Griffith Stadium.

Each year two states are singled out for special homage. The Redskins and their sponsors—AMOCO and Marlboro, through whose cooperation outstanding high school and college bands are brought to the Nation's Capital to pay tribute to their home state.

Georgia Day is October 18. The famed 130-piece band of the University of Georgia known as the Dixie Red Coats will perform at halftime as the Peach State is honored.

North Carolina Day is observed December 6. The 100-piece Reynolds High School Band from Winston-Salem will represent the Tarheel State.[24]

The 1959 season continued the Redskins' stretch of disappointing campaigns. The club finished the year with a dismal 3-9 record, which included a season-ending string of five consecutive losses. Due to their on-field futility the Redskins would once again be selecting near the top of the college draft. Only three players would be off the board when the Redskins made their first selection.

This scenario was repeated many times through the years. With their pick in the tenth round of the 1960 college draft, the Redskins selected Ernest "Big Ernie" Barnes, an offensive guard. Purportedly within moments Redskins brass realized their gaffe. Barnes hadn't attended North Carolina University, as they believed, but rather North Carolina Central, a historically black school. After realizing their mistake Washington officials quickly traded Barnes to the Baltimore Colts.

That's how the tale was told and repeated so often that even the protagonist came to believe its verity.

The story, however, is apocryphal.

In fact the Redskins traded their tenth-round pick to Baltimore the morning of the draft, and it was the Colts who in fact selected Barnes.

"The Redskins' second choice in the draft was Sam Horner, a back from Virginia Military Institute," Shirley Povich reported the next morning. "He comes highly recommended as one of the finest in college football and his VMI background puts him in solid, man, with George Marshall, who is still trying to restore the Confederacy 94 years after everybody else quit. . . . [D]écor Marshall has chosen for the Redskins . . . is burgundy, gold, and Caucasian."[25]

Povich then acknowledged that perhaps part of Marshall's motivation could be attributed to his vast television and radio network that extended throughout the lands of rebel Dixie.

"But," Povich continued, "for those Redskin fans who are not members of The White Citizens Council it is too bad that too many good football players are ineligible for the Redskins from birth."[26]

6

The Last Word

Griffith Stadium certainly had its charms.

Thanks to its small size there wasn't a bad seat in the house. With a capacity of just twenty-seven thousand, the stadium allowed spectators to sit so close to the action they could practically reach out and touch the participants. In 1957 the forty-six-year-old ballpark had its drawbacks, however. The surrounding neighborhood had deteriorated in recent years. What was once a working-class community was now full of boarded-up buildings and shanty homes beyond the right-field wall. Perhaps the biggest problem with Griffith Stadium was the near complete lack of parking for fans; the few spaces available went to players and club executives. Most fans came to the park on a streetcar. Those who drove themselves parked in the street. Even that didn't come without a price.

Neighborhood kids took advantage of the circumstances. "Watch your car for five bucks, Mister," was a commonly heard refrain.

If the street tax wasn't paid up, fans usually returned to find their vehicles vandalized.

Griffith Stadium was located on Georgia Avenue in Shaw, a neighborhood named for Robert Gould Shaw, the white officer of the Fifty-Fourth Massachusetts Regiment of black soldiers in the Civil War.

The U Street neighborhood in northwest Washington was a bustling community. Art venues, theaters, music, shopping, LeDroit Park, the Shaw district, and Howard University all could be found in the community.

Howard University was founded in 1867 with a mission charter to educate the capital's black citizens. In the years immediately following the Civil War nearly half the residents of Washington were black. Although the city was, relatively speaking, a racially progressive town by the turn of the twentieth century, Washington had evolved into a city distinctly segregated by race.

Under the Woodrow Wilson administration segregation was legally enforced. Black residents were denied employment in the city's number-one industry, the federal government.

When visiting DC in early 1942, the photographer Gordon Parks found a city that "bulged with racism."[1] Conditions improved following the war, but progress came slowly. Fifteen years later the social climate of Washington had improved, but segregation still prevailed throughout the town. At the dawn of the 1960s black residents constituted more than 50 percent of Washington's population, yet they held less than one-eighth of the city's top jobs.

Five years after Parks first visited the capital an editorial writer for the *Washington Star* opined, "The Confederacy, which was never able to capture Washington during the course of that war, now holds it as a helpless pawn."[2]

It was an Easter tradition in Washington.

A large group of children would mobilize on the White House lawn to gather Easter eggs—white children, that is. Black children had their own Easter egg hunt, at the zoo.

On June 30, 1960, several black youths were apprehended at Glen Echo Park, an amusement park located just across the DC line in Maryland. They were arrested for riding the merry-go-round after repeatedly being told by security staff to leave the park.

Over the course of the next eleven weeks a civil rights campaign was organized to protest the privately owned park's admission policy. Like many institutions in the Washington area the amusement park was segregated.

The nation's capital wasn't a city solely divided by politics. It was a town divided between black and white. For all intents and purposes DC was a city of strictly separate entities. Public facilities, schools, and housing were segregated, as were parks and swimming pools. Segregation was so embedded in the nation's capital that even pet cemeteries were affected. A 1948 report on racial segregation in Washington revealed that discrimination had so permeated the district that even a dog cemetery's proprietor refused to inter the pets of black owners. The cemetery's owner "assumed the dogs would not object, but he was afraid his white customers would."[3]

Hecht's department store, a Washington institution, was popular with black residents of DC. Though Hecht's cafeteria was segregated until 1952, black people were welcome as customers. The same could not be said, however, of Hecht's competitor, Garfinkle's. It was understood in the black community that they were not welcome at Garfinkle's flagship store downtown. At other locations black shoppers were unfailingly told, "We don't have that in your size" and denied use of fitting rooms.

Not surprisingly black customers could not eat in Marshall's favorite establishments: Duke Zeibert's, the Statler, and the Touchdown Club. The pat response to a black person's arrival at these locales was, "We can't seat you unless you have a reservation."

And if a reservation had been made by telephone, the excuse not to seat the person became, "We have a dress code."

Mary Church Terrell had been waging battles for women's rights and against institutionalized racism for decades when in 1950 she began a campaign to end discrimination in Washington restaurants. The daughter of former slaves, Terrell was one of the first black women in the country to earn a college degree when she received her master's from Oberlin College in 1888.

Local integration laws that dated to the 1870s required all eating establishment proprietors "to serve any respectable, well-behaved person regardless of color."[4] For failure to comply business owners would face a $1,000 fine and forfeiture of their license. Led by Terrell, protests and pickets organized to end segregation in the city's eateries led the Municipal Court of Appeals to rule on May 24, 1951, that DC restaurants must serve black patrons. This decision was upheld two years later by the Supreme Court, which determined that the "lost" laws of the 1870s banning discrimination remained valid and that racial segregation in Washington restaurants was unconstitutional.

School segregation continued in the capital, however. And the Redskins remained an all-white outfit.

It should come as no surprise that the Redskins, and Marshall in particular, weren't very popular with members of Washington's black community. Indeed "hated" might be a better description of the feeling the district's black residents had toward the Redskins' owner. Truth be told, for the most part the city's black community wanted to root for the home team. They wanted to feel a connection with the local football club. George Preston Marshall, however, made such a prospect nearly impossible. With one look around Griffith Stadium any observer could see that Marshall's prejudice extended far beyond the obvious lack of a black player on the Redskins roster. Not a single black face could be seen hawking souvenirs, taking tickets, or peddling peanuts.

"It seems to me that it is high time for colored fans to stop paying money into the white-Redskins treasury," E. B. Henderson wrote in a letter to the editor published in the *Baltimore Afro-American*. "I realize that many of us like football, and some go to these Redskins home games mainly because they want to see colored boys play on the visiting team.

"To refrain from attending would be a genuine hardship for them. But when we note the thousands of young people throughout the South risking life and limb and going to jail rather than submit to the indignity of racial discrimination, why should we not be able to deny ourselves the luxury of supporting Marshall's racism[?]

"To me it is a tragedy when intelligent people, in this day of moving forward, persist in humiliation with their hard earned dollars."[5]

Edwin Bancroft Henderson was born in 1883 in southwest DC in the home of his grandmother, a former slave.

Henderson's modest beginning belied the pioneering man of influence he would become.

Upon graduating from Harvard, Henderson set out on his primary career—the education of Washington's black youth. Education was Henderson's principal objective, but the promotion of extracurricular sports was a high priority of E.B.'s. He worked as a teacher and volunteered his free time coaching black youths in a variety of sports. Henderson has been credited with bringing the game of basketball to Washington and the town's black youth.

By midcentury Henderson had become one of the city's most prominent voices in the black community. He was a civic leader in the truest sense of the term. Henderson worked tirelessly to better the plight of black Washingtonians.

E. B. Henderson was a frequent writer of letters to the editor, and on Sunday, September 15, 1940, he sat in the stands of Griffith Stadium for the opening day of the NFL season. The Redskins were taking on the Brooklyn

Dodgers. As the national anthem was played Henderson took a look around the ballpark. He marveled at the more than thirty-two thousand spectators standing as one in a salute to their country while overseas much of the world was at war. In a letter to the editor of the *Washington Post* titled "Democracy and Football," Henderson shared a few impressions of the scene at Griffith Stadium:

> Looking up and back into the stern earnest faces of black and white country men, one could not help thinking that every man, woman, and child sensed the oncoming possible destruction of civilization.
>
> In this setting we have democracy at its best. Crowded and packed together. Jew and Gentiles, black and white, thrilled and slumped with the fortunes of Marshall's Indians. That is how it is not in Germany and Italy.
>
> This country must very soon realize that until discriminations based on color, creed, or race in all public relations are abolished, we too, are but a little better off in our practices than those of the condemned totalitarian regime.[6]

The system used by most NFL teams to scout black players during this era was rather rudimentary. It was as simple as opening up a newspaper.

The *Pittsburgh Courier* annually published a roster labeled the Negro All-American team. The *Courier*'s college football reporting was the primary source consulted by coaches for a number of teams working to gather information prior to the college draft. For example, Roosevelt Brown was selected by the New York Giants after team officials read his name in the *Courier*. But no club took greater advantage of the *Courier*'s "scouting report" than the Los Angeles Rams.

The talent of standout players from large eastern or midwestern schools would not likely have been recognized without the help of the *Courier*. Players such as Lenny Moore, Jim Brown, and Jim Parker became professional stars. George Marshall, however, relied almost exclusively on players from southern colleges, that is, all-white southern schools. Critics couldn't help but take note that the Redskins struggled on the field throughout the decade.

"We all try a little harder against the Redskins," Ollie Matson admitted to a reporter.[7] It was a stark admission by the star halfback of the Cardinals. Black players around the NFL were a close-knit community. They compared notes, such as where to eat or where to stay in certain cities. And they also talked among themselves about George Marshall's Redskins.

The black sporting press could boast many great reporters—men who used their forum to promote and advocate for black athletes. Of these respected journalists few wrote with the fervor of the *Afro-American*'s Sam Lacy.

The origins of the *Baltimore Afro-American* may be traced to 1892, when a former slave, John H. Murphy, founded the newspaper with the purpose of reporting the events and distilling the news of Baltimore's black community. In time the *Afro-American* progressed into one of the preeminent voices in the black press. Along with the *Chicago Defender*, the *Pittsburgh Courier*, and the *Amsterdam News*, the *Afro-American* became more than a regional newspaper as it evolved into one of the country's most influential and important media outlets for black America.

The thirty-nine-year-old Sam Lacy was a man with a fair amount of experience when he was hired as the sports editor for the *Baltimore Afro-American* in 1943.

Lacy's career began at the *Washington Tribune*, when he was still in college. Following his graduation from Howard University in 1926, Lacy became a full-time reporter with the *Tribune* before subsequently moving to the *Chicago Defender* and then the *Afro-American*. It was at the *Afro-American* that Lacy established his reputation. Indeed Sam Lacy's name became synonymous with that newspaper. At the *Afro-American* Lacy was at the forefront of black sportswriters promoting the integration of Major League Baseball, among them Wendell Smith, Chet Washington, Joe Bostic, and Frank A. Young. He was an advocate, critic, and reporter. He was opinionated. And Sam Lacy was nothing if not passionate.

He grew up five blocks from Griffith Stadium, and it was at Clark Griffith's park that Sam Lacy held his first job as a youth. Lacy managed to earn a few dollars a day by hustling peanuts and popcorn in the stadium's "colored only" section. When he wasn't working, Lacy took in a number of games as a spectator in the same segregated area, nestled in the right-field stands.

Early in Lacy's career as a sportswriter the press box in most stadiums was closed to him and other members of the black press. Once while covering a game in New Orleans Lacy took a chair and sat atop the press box to ply his trade after being refused entry to the media workplace. A few sympathetic white writers joined the *Afro-American* reporter, and from that vantage point they, too, reported the game's events.

Years before Jackie Robinson joined the Brooklyn Dodgers in 1947 Lacy sought an audience with Kenesaw Mountain Landis, the baseball commissioner. Lacy's agenda for the meeting was to sway the commissioner to permit Negro league players to play in the majors. Although initially agreeing to the summit with Lacy, Landis ultimately refused to give him the time of day and would not even acknowledge that there existed a ban on Negroes in the majors.

In 1948 Lacy became the first black member of the Baseball Writers Association of America (BBWA). Just one year earlier, while covering Robinson's inaugural season, Lacy had been refused entrance to Cincinnati's Crosley Field press box by the chairman of the city's BBWA, Tom Swope.

Lacy was light-skinned, so light in fact that had he chosen to do so Lacy probably could have passed. But the thought of passing never crossed Sam Lacy's mind. No, he was proud of his heritage.

In person Lacy was a soft-spoken, courtly gentleman. In print, however, Lacy pulled no punches, especially when targeting George Marshall. Once, using imagery of the Ku Klux Klan, Lacy referred to "the hooded presence of George Preston Marshall." And on another occasion the reporter's comments were even more inflammatory. "This column has never advocated suicide," he wrote in the *Afro-American*, "but in GPM's case it would be readily forgivable."[8]

On January 26, 1958, Marshall appeared on WTOP-TV's "City Side" program. Serving as the show's moderator was the *Washington Post*'s sports editor, Luther "Bus" Ham. The wide-ranging conversation covered subjects such as the Redskins' prospects for the coming season as well as the newly approved two-point conversion rule for college football.

The primary topic for the evening, however, was the proposed National Guard Armory site for a new sports stadium. Marshall had no problem with the plan, but his current landlord was not pleased with the location.

"We both [the Redskins and Senators] ought to accept it if the Government is willing to build it," Marshall told Ham. "It may be a crooked roulette wheel, but it's the only one in town."[9]

More than a year and half earlier Marshall had begun sowing the seeds for a new, publicly financed stadium that would play host to his beloved Redskins

"I will say the citizens of Washington, if given the opportunity to support an intelligent stadium project, would oversubscribe such a proposition," Marshall explained.

"President Eisenhower indicated private citizens should finance a stadium on land furnished by the Government. No, I don't consider it, 'creeping socialism' to allow the Government to furnish the land. A project like this corresponds to public parks and it should not be strictly in the realm of private enterprise.

"Operation of a baseball or football team is a quasi-civic function. Anyone who doesn't think so ought to try it."[10]

Marshall's campaign intensified in the fall of 1958 as he made numerous appearances on local radio and television promoting the necessity of a new stadium. Without a new building Marshall couldn't promise that he wouldn't move his team to another city. In fact just two years earlier, on October 5, 1956, Marshall warned that Washington could lose not only the Redskins but also the Senators if fans didn't clamor for a new municipal stadium—and take the fight "right up to the White House."

"It is economically impossible to operate a baseball team in Washington with a stadium that has only 18,000 grandstand seats," Marshall said of Griffith Stadium, the use of which he rented from the Senators. "The Nation's Capital needs a new municipal stadium and the fight for one should be carried to the White House immediately."

The Redskins still had four years remaining on their Griffith Stadium lease.

"After the four years are up we would . . . have to sign a new lease if the stadium were sold," Marshall explained. "The ballpark is in a slum area with the highest crime rate in the city and there is no parking space."[11]

And then, just two months later, on January 5, 1957, Representative Oren Harris of Arkansas introduced a bill that provided for the construction of a fifty-thousand-seat stadium in the district. The park would be built on federal land, which was situated north of the National Guard Armory. The news of the bill pleased Marshall, who reiterated early threats that without a new stadium he would seriously consider relocating the Redskins to another locale.

"I'm for any site. With the uncertainty as what the baseball team is going to do and the parking problem, we've either got to have a new stadium or leave town. It seems financially impossible for us to build it ourselves. I've read the Harris bill and I think it's the soundest piece of legislation ever offered on the subject."[12]

Given that Marshall had an opinion on nearly every subject, few were surprised that he considered himself something of an expert on stadiums.

"I don't think anyone in the United States qualifies as more of one," he bragged. "I have twenty-seven years' experience and have visited and studied just about every major stadium in the country.

"I have discussed the mistakes in a lot of them and pointed them out. I'll say flatly that there is not a first-rate stadium in the United States."[13]

On April 22, 1958, the district's Armory Board released plans for a new stadium, which by their timetable would be ready for use in 1960. The edifice would play host not just to the Senators and Redskins but to a wide variety of events, including circuses and pageants.

"It will be an ultra-modern circular structure of steel and reinforced concrete, with a moveable bank of seats allowing ideal spectator and player arrangements for both football and baseball," Marshall explained.[14]

"Bleachers are as old-hat as a hair net," Marshall stated. "Besides, they make for class distinction, and today there is no class distinction."[15]

Calvin Griffith, owner of the Washington Senators, received the news with a detached calm.

"We are not going to give up a ballpark we own with rentals and concessions unless we are given some incentive to move," he said.[16]

For his part Marshall failed to conceal his enthusiasm for the preliminary plans for the new stadium.

"I'm happy with every aspect of the new stadium so far. The stadium site is ideal: there is easy access from Virginia and Maryland. It is favorable to us and similar to what municipal stadiums in other cities are getting from National Football League teams.

"With this stadium both big league baseball and big league football will be guaranteed in the future of Washington.

"It is my hope that we will have a spade in the ground for the new stadium before fall. Those who have criticized the site have done so through lack of study of the situation," he said.[17]

Before construction could begin, however, negotiations with the Interior Department needed to take place. This oddity was necessary because the federal government owned the land at the projected stadium site as well as the adjoining areas intended for parking.

With plans finally in place for the construction of a new stadium, Marshall changed his threatening tune about moving the Redskins if he wasn't provided a new home for the team.

"As long as I am head of the Redskins, the team will remain in Washington," Marshall flatly stated in an interview with the *Washington Post*.

"If the ball club [the Senators] moves, they have to provide for us to play through 1960. In the meantime, I'm hopeful that we'll get a stadium of some sort.

"The only thing that would force us to move would be the lack of a place to play. Of course if they tried to saddle us with some impossible or ridiculous rent or if conditions become unbearable we'd have to move.

"But I like Washington. I want to stay here and you can make that as strong as you like."[18]

From his Baltimore office Sam Lacy was keeping tabs on the stadium negotiations.

"Lately in Wash DC, there has been much discussion about a proposed new stadium," Lacy wrote in the *Afro-American*. "Since plans call for erection of the stadium on federal grounds with federal funds, some are wondering whether a non-discrimination hiring clause in the regulations would pertain to a lessee such as Marshall."[19]

Sam Lacy had educated himself well on the intricacies of federal law.

On the evening of December 22, Marshall, along with his attorney, C. Leo De Orsey, met with city officials in the District Building. At the conclusion of a two-hour, twenty-five-minute summit, the two sides came to an agreement. A $10 million structure would be built at the foot of East Capitol Street. The fifty-thousand-seat stadium would be ready for the 1961 season and have the capability of being enlarged to sixty thousand with use of temporary seating. Thanks to much behind-the-scenes work by De Orsey, the stalemate between the Redskins and the Armory Board was breached and a lease signed committing the club to play home games in the new stadium for thirty years, through 1991.

"The Board of Directors of the Redskins is in complete agreement on the contract," Marshall informed reporters.

His long campaign to bring a modern stadium to the district had finally come to fruition.

"This is the best Christmas present I've ever had," Marshall gushed. "I think it's the best present, too, for the people of the District of Columbia and surrounding areas."[20]

The formal contract signing took place on Christmas Eve in Marshall's Ninth Street office. An agreement was indeed made. However, there was a clause in the contract that caused some consternation in the Redskins camp.

It was the nondiscrimination clause, which had been inserted into all government contracts since being implemented by the Eisenhower administration in 1954. The clause applied to any person or business who entered into contract with the federal government: "In connection with the operations authorized under this contract, the contractor agrees not to discriminate against any employee or applicant for employment because of race, religion, color, or national origin."

A manual published by the President's Committee explained, "Lack of Negroes on the work force may be an indication that the contractor is not in compliance." The ordinance based on the nondiscrimination clause would be enforced only after an investigation and a gathering of evidence.[21]

Marshall was reluctant to place his signature on any such contract.

Through his lawyers Marshall requested the clause be excised from the agreement. After all, he reasoned, he didn't want to be charged with discrimination when he didn't hire a Jew, or a German, a Negro, or a Native American for that matter. He was running a football team, not the damned United Nations.

But try as they might, Marshall, De Orsey, and company couldn't dissuade the government. The nondiscrimination clause was a deal breaker.

Armory Board chairman George Shea, though, attempted to ease Marshall's angst. "That language can't force anybody to hire inferior players simply because of their race or background," Shea insisted.[22]

Could, or would, the government hold a football club to this agreement? Marshall's lawyers wondered. After all, how could the government legislate who was good enough to be placed on a team's roster?

It couldn't, they surmised, and it wouldn't. The federal government wasn't in the sports racket, and the Redskins had no reason to worry about some bureaucrat sticking his nose into their business. With this belief reassuring him Marshall confidently placed his name on the stadium lease.

7

"It's Not That Important"

In late July 1959 Bert Bell had once again traveled to Washington to testify before a Senate subcommittee considering antitrust legislation for pro sports. His objective was to secure the NFL an exemption from the Sherman Act. Two years earlier the commissioner had acknowledged a players' association to aid his cause, and on this occasion Bell came to Washington equipped with evidence that his league was not a monopoly.

Just a few weeks earlier Bell had been visited by the young oil business scion Lamar Hunt. At that time the youthful Hunt had expressed to Bell his intention of forming a new professional football league. The commissioner listened to the Texan, then wished Hunt well on his venture, all the while recognizing that he could use this information to the NFL's advantage.

"I want to tell you about this new league," Bell explained to the congressional subcommittee. "I can't give you any of the details, but they are going to be in eight or nine cities."

Although he wouldn't divulge the source of his information other than to say that the source was "from Texas," those in the know understood the informant to be Lamar Hunt, a figure of some status in the oil industry. Hunt's original intent was to acquire an NFL franchise, but after being denied that particular aspiration he decided to form a league of his own. Hunt's creation was to begin play in 1960 and would field teams in eight cities scattered throughout the country.

To Congress Bert Bell promised cooperation with the new circuit.

"We're in favor of the new league," he insisted. "Not one [NFL] owner is opposed to it."

He even quoted the most obstinate of the brethren, George Marshall, as saying, "If they're great it will be great for us. . . . If not they'll only hurt themselves."[1]

The NFL had consisted of twelve teams since the 1950 merger with the All-American Football Conference, when three AAFC teams—the Cleveland Browns, San Francisco 49ers, and Baltimore Colts—joined the established league. A new league was indeed on the horizon, Bell informed Congress during his testimony, and the commissioner also acknowledged that the NFL was exploring the possibility of expanding into new territories. Discussion of expansion, which began a year earlier, was ratcheted up in the wake of Baltimore's stirring victory over the Giants in the 1958 championship game. In the afterglow of that contest the NFL had reached a new pinnacle of popularity with the American public. Thanks to television the game was being watched in more homes, and although TV coverage of football was still in the primitive stage, viewing a contest from one's living room couch provided an exponential boost to the appeal of the sport.

Not everyone was opting to watch the games from home on Sundays, however, not by a long shot. More than three million tickets to league contests were sold during the 1958 season. Despite the unprecedented attendance and record television ratings, though, one NFL official was steadfast in his opposition to expansion.

"We don't sell out by any means," George Marshall explained to Cooper Rollow of the *Chicago Tribune*. Marshall was in Chicago for a brief stopover while en route to California for the start of training camp. The intrepid Rollow had sought out the loquacious Redskins owner for comment on Bell's announcement of the league's expansion plan when the reporter caught up with him at Chicago's train station.

"There's plenty of room for customer expansion on quite a few of our fronts," Marshall continued. "The Eagles and Steelers are chronically low. The Giants and Browns could improve. Our Redskins attendance leaves a lot to be desired. And, of course, there's the Chicago Cardinals. Chicago has never proved it can support two professional teams."[2]

"We have wrecked Penn, Fordham, and Columbia, and we've knocked the devil out of the west coast colleges. We should do everything in our powers to protect college and high school football, our sources of playing talent.

"We shouldn't let college football stupidity influence our thinking. Regardless of what they do, we should help them."

Marshall certainly anticipated many problems with expansion, but foremost in his mind was the antitrust issue. "No one can give me an intelligent reason for adding a couple more franchises," Marshall said. "The only reason for expansion I've heard from the other owners is that we could destroy the new league. If that is the only reason then we are guilty of monopolistic practices."[3]

On August 29 George Halas, with Art Rooney, the cochairman of the expansion committee, standing by his side, made public the National Football League's intention to add two new clubs in time for the 1961 season.

"The last five years have been a period of consolidation during which every team has been strengthened. Now every team is strong, competition and attendance is at an all-time high, and the time has come to inaugurate a sound expansion program," Halas said from Houston, where his Bears and Rooney's Steelers were meeting for an exhibition game.[4]

The next five years would be a period of expansion starting with the creation of two new franchises, Halas explained, and plans called for the first franchises to be awarded to Houston and Dallas, where interested groups had "virtually unlimited resources."

There were other cities under consideration, Halas added, including Boston, Buffalo, Denver, Minneapolis, Miami, New Orleans, and Louisville.

The Bears' owner also revealed that a plan was in place to stock the rosters of these new clubs with players from the established teams.

"A strong nucleus of experienced players is a must for any franchise," Halas explained. "Our aim is to expand by creating strong teams capable of maintaining the high quality of competition that prevails among all twelve teams in the National Football League."[5]

In addition to selecting players from existing teams, the expansion franchises would be awarded extra selections in the college draft.

When a reporter reached Lamar Hunt for comment, the founding father of the new league was taken aback for a moment. Hunt asked for a moment to gather his thoughts before offering a statement.

"I'd say that Mr. Halas' action is probably unfortunate for the National League," Hunt said. "I think that he must have been poorly advised in making this statement because the Senators or Congressmen from Colorado, the

1. George Marshall (*left*) with Les Arries (*right*) of the Touchdown Club. Reprinted with permission of the DC Public Library, Star Collection, © *Washington Post*.

2. (*Opposite top*) President Harry Truman (*left*) receiving his annual game pass from Bert Bell (*center*) and George Marshall (*right*). Abbie Rowe, National Park Service, Harry S. Truman Library and Museum, Independence MO.

3. (*Opposite bottom*) George Marshall (*left*) with Ray Flaherty (*right*). Reprinted with permission of the DC Public Library, Star Collection, © *Washington Post*.

4. (*Above*) Joe Kuharich (*left*) getting a light from George Marshall (*right*). Reprinted with permission of the DC Public Library, Star Collection, © *Washington Post*.

5. Shirley Povich. Reprinted with permission of the DC Public Library, Star Collection, © *Washington Post*.

6. Mo Siegel. Reprinted with permission of the DC Public Library, Star Collection, © *Washington Post*.

7. (*Above*) George Marshall with a couple of "Redskins girls." Reprinted with permission of the DC Public Library, Star Collection, © *Washington Post*.

8. (*Opposite top*) Bobby Mitchell at the University of Illinois. Cleveland Press Collection, Cleveland State University Library.

9. (*Opposite bottom*) Jim Brown (*left*) and Bobby Mitchell (*right*). Cleveland Press Collection, Cleveland State University Library.

10. Bobby Mitchell practicing with the Cleveland Browns. Cleveland Press Collection, Cleveland State University Library.

11. (*Below*) Pete Rozelle, the so-called boy commissioner. Reprinted with permission of the DC Public Library, Star Collection, © *Washington Post*.

12. The Udall family (*left to right*): Scott, Secretary of the Interior Stewart Udall, Lynn, Tom, Lori, Denis, and Lee. Reprinted with permission of the DC Public Library, Star Collection, © *Washington Post*.

13. Stewart Udall with his wife, Lee. Reprinted with permission of the DC Public Library, Star Collection, © *Washington Post*.

14. President Kennedy (*left*) with Secretary Udall (*far right*) and Dave Powers (*center, in hat*), special assistant to the president, April 10, 1961, opening day at Griffith Stadium. Abbie Rowe, White House Photographs, John F. Kennedy Presidential Library and Museum, Boston.

15. Pete Rozelle (*foreground*). Reprinted with permission of the DC Public Library, Star Collection, © *Washington Post*.

16. Ernie Davis (*left*) meeting President Kennedy (*right*), December 6, 1961. Cecil Stoughton, White House Photographs, John F. Kennedy Presidential Library and Museum, Boston.

17. Ron Hatcher. Reprinted with permission of the DC Public Library, Star Collection, © *Washington Post*.

18. John Nisby. Reprinted with permission of the DC Public Library,
Star Collection, © *Washington Post*.

19. Bobby Mitchell hauling in a pass for the Redskins. Reprinted with permission of the DC Public Library, Star Collection, © *Washington Post*.

20. Bobby Mitchell running free against his old team, the Cleveland Browns. Cleveland Press Collection, Cleveland State University Library.

21. Bobby Mitchell. Cleveland Press Collection, Cleveland State University Library.

22. Secretary of the Interior Stewart Udall, walking the grounds of Mount Vernon. Reprinted with permission of the DC Public Library, Star Collection, © *Washington Post*.

23. (*Above*) George Preston Marshall arriving at Union Station following the Redskins' 1962 training camp, August 16, 1962. Reprinted with permission of the DC Public Library, Star Collection, © *Washington Post*.

24. Bobby Mitchell, out of the shadows for good. Cleveland Press Collection, Cleveland State University Library.

state of Washington, Minnesota, and Florida are not going to be happy at all, as you can imagine.

"They were aware that the National League has been trying to sabotage the formation of this league and I think the reaction is going to be very strong."[6]

Sabotage?

The commissioner of the NFL was likewise taken aback when word of Hunt's charges reached him.

"Any city in the country is fair game for either league," Bert Bell emphatically stated. "Nobody owns any city in this country. Any place is fair territory for our league, the second league, and if there is a third league, for it too. That's what anti-trust laws provide."

Bell added that just several weeks earlier he had advised Hunt "that money is not the most important thing in starting a football team. It's the operation of the sport."

What's more, Bell did not understand Hunt's displeasure with his league's plan of embarking on an expansion into new territories.

"They're going into New York and Los Angeles. We have teams there, too, but we didn't complain."[7]

"Pro football is expanding to all parts of the country," Bell stated, "and there's room for everybody."[8]

October 11, 1959.

It was the third Sunday of the season, and NFL commissioner Bert Bell was seated in the stands at Franklin Field taking in the contest between the Philadelphia Eagles and the Pittsburgh Steelers. It was the same stadium where Bell had played college ball as captain of the University of Pennsylvania football squad and the same park where Bell had watched his Eagles play on countless Sundays. As the clock wound down in the fourth quarter of a 28–24 Philadelphia victory, play was stopped as several police officers ran across the field to retrieve the Steelers' team physician, Dr. John Miller. The officers took Miller to the north end of the stadium, where Bell, seated in his usual box, had gone into cardiac arrest. An ambulance was called, and the commissioner was rushed to University Hospital, located only a couple of blocks away.

Moments after entering the hospital De Benneville Bell was pronounced dead.

Art Rooney rushed from his seat in the Franklin Field stands when he realized that it was his good friend who had been carried from the stadium on a stretcher. The Pittsburgh owner reached the hospital to learn that Bell had passed. The news sent the normally unflappable Rooney into shock. As word spread throughout the country other NFL owners found the words to express the profound loss that a numb Rooney struggled to express.

"Bell was a great leader," George Halas said, "a genius, in fact."[9]

"With no malice meant to any head of any sport dead or alive, Bert Bell was easily the outstanding commissioner of all time in any sport," George Marshall said. "That goes for Judge Landis, too.

"The passing of Bell is obviously a great loss to pro football and let me add, it's a great loss to all of sport. We'll never find a commissioner as good as Bell."[10]

Indeed he was a pal, as well as a benevolent leader, but a replacement was going to be needed.

The NFL constitution called for a meeting of owners within thirty days of the death of a commissioner. With the winter conference already scheduled for early January the decision was made to name fifty-one-year-old Austin Gunsel to serve as interim commissioner until after the first of the year, when the owners would gather together in Miami Beach. Gunsel, a former FBI agent, had been hired by Bell seven years earlier with the directive to protect the league from scandal. He had served as league treasurer since 1956, and by all accounts Gunsel did his job well. Few, though, were willing to commit to Gunsel as anything other than a temporary solution. Finding a permanent successor, however, proved to be an exasperating endeavor.

So many names were tossed about.

How about Paul Brown?

He was a brilliant tactician and an innovative coach, but would Brown's football genius transfer to the commissionership? Perhaps, but Brown withdrew his name from consideration before the debate even began.

Art Rooney's name also was put forth, but the affable Irishman wanted nothing to do with the job.

Marshall and Halas were two names that immediately came up as possible successors to Bell.

"I can't be better than Bell, and I don't want to be second best," an unusually modest George Marshall explained. "Marshall and Halas are too opinionated," he added, referring to himself in the third person. "We'll need someone with more diplomacy."

Marshall advocated for his own his own candidate, Albert "Happy" Chandler, former baseball commissioner and governor of Kentucky, "if he decides not to run for President [of the United States]," Marshall explained. "He did a good job in baseball, better than those who succeeded him."[11]

Chandler as football commissioner, though, was an idea that died on the vine.

League leaders convened in Miami Beach's Kenilworth Hotel on January 20, 1960. They arrived as two distinct factions. One group of owners, which included Marshall, backed Gunsel to be named Bell's permanent successor. Another bloc was equally fervent in their support of Marshall Leahy. Eastern owners had objected to Leahy principally on the grounds that he intended to establish NFL headquarters in San Francisco.

The initial tally was an even 6–6 split between the two candidates. Later that evening another ballot was taken. Leahy garnered eight of the nine votes necessary for election. That would be the closest he would get to the commissionership. On and on it would go. Six days and numerous ballots later the owners were no closer to reaching an accord. The impasse seemed to know no end; writers had even begun checking out of the Kenilworth and heading home. Leahy, too, had left Miami Beach, leaving a forwarding number should he need to be reached.

Finally, on the seventh day, a compromise was reached when thirty-three-year-old Rams executive Pete Rozelle was placed into nomination by Carroll Rosenbloom, the Colts' president. It wasn't an easy job to persuade a room of twelve willful and opinionated men that the relatively unknown and inexperienced Rozelle was up to the job.

Pete Rozelle's original professional goal had been to become the sports editor of the *Los Angeles Times*. The handsome, lanky Californian left the Rams in 1954 to join a San Francisco public relations firm, but he returned to the team as general manager in 1957.

Rozelle may have been a compromise selection for commissioner, but he was ready for the task awaiting. He stepped into his new position with a lot of advantages. It was thirteen months after the epic '58 championship game between the Colts and the Giants, and the sport's popularity had surged. The young commissioner was also confronted with a number of concerns, however. Bert Bell's dream of a unified television contract, which would bring all league teams under the same umbrella, was high on the list of priorities, but expansion was the primary issue before the owners. The matter had been addressed a few weeks earlier in Philadelphia, when the owners had gathered to memorialize and bury their late leader. At that point George Halas had assembled his colleagues and told them that now was the time to expand. There was that new upstart league to deal with, and the NFL needed to strike quickly. Just a few months earlier, while in Houston with Rooney, he had publicly announced the league's intention to expand, but a definite time frame hadn't been chosen nor had the expansion cities been selected.

An informal vote on expansion was held on October 16, 1959, five days after Bell's death. The owners, who had convened in Philadelphia for the late commissioner's funeral, voted 10–2 in favor of expansion. Not surprisingly the dissenting votes belonged to the Wolfners and George Preston Marshall.

"Expansion is impractical, hasty, and definitely would hurt college football," Marshall said, hammering home his oft-used talking points.

Marshall expressed other concerns that would come with expansion. Rearranging schedules would also be an issue. What about conference realignment with the addition of new teams? Marshall insisted that his fellow owners were "giving lip service to expansion without having studied the complex problems."

He continued, laying out his argument against expansion. "Maybe I'm too old for some of these newly found geniuses, the so-called professional sports promoters," he said, "but no matter how little their experience, they should realize such a thing as being so greedy they can kill the calf."[12]

"This whole thing is really disgusting to me," he stated. "We have a wonderful league and we are drawing lots of people. What more do these fellows want? One answer seems to be they want more teams, which will bring more customers."[13]

Marshall seemed to contradict his complaint from just a few months earlier when he decreed that what the league needed "was more customers." Now he apparently was saying that everything was fine, so why mess with a good thing?

Was this the same man who for decades had displayed imagination and foresight that helped the league grow in value and popularity?

What was apparent was that, whether Marshall was on board or not, the league was moving ahead with plans for expansion. Edwin J. Anderson, president and general manager of the Detroit Lions, emerged from the meeting and revealed that the top cities for expansion were Buffalo, Miami, Louisville, Dallas, and Houston.[14]

To expand, Marshall explained, the NFL would be inviting a federal antitrust action because the move would "interfere with the colleges and also bring about suits involving players who sign with teams from both the NFL and AFL." There were at least three such cases brewing.

"The Supreme Court says we cannot use unreasonable restraint in our operations. I would prefer to see the AFL operate for at least three years and see what happens. It would be proof the NFL is not a monopoly."[15]

George Halas turned Marshall's argument on its head. "I think we would violate the anti-trust law by not expanding," Halas argued. "Marshall should realize that it is monopolistic to require a unanimous [vote], or even ten out of twelve. That rule is monopolistic itself."[16]

Even when his colleagues were overwhelmingly in favor of league expansion Marshall remained staunch in his dissent, and if his "monopoly" argument didn't hold water he had a pocketful of other reasons for opposing the idea.

"Right now there is no reason for the NFL to expand. The NFL can't encompass the world. It's not that important. We give football to every city in the United States free of charge. Expansion is bad for the NFL as well as college football," Marshall said. "I don't want to see Saturday television expanded where it encroaches on the colleges.

"And I want to make this prediction. If the Dallas team in either league is a success it will knock the living spots off Southern Methodist, Texas Christian, Baylor, and perhaps the whole Southwest Conference."[17]

No, Marshall did not want league franchises to multiply, and he was especially opposed to having one in the city of Dallas. He disapproved of the location, certainly, but Marshall distinctly disliked the prospective owner of the franchise, Clint Murchison Jr. It seems that Murchison, a Texas oil tycoon, had been, according to Marshall, "personally obnoxious to me."[18]

Murchison badly wanted to place a team in his hometown, and the tactics he used to achieve his goal were ingenious, to say the least. He went after one of Marshall's prized possessions—the Redskins' fight song.

The marriage between George Marshall and Corinne Griffith came to an end in 1960 with a divorce. Corinne explained that she split with Marshall after twenty-two years of wedlock because "he loved football more than me."[19]

"Pro football is a very rugged game," Corinne Griffith had told an interviewer in 1952. "You have to learn to keep in the background and speak when spoken to. Women just aren't necessary to the running of a team."[20]

Part of the divorce settlement between George Marshall and Corinne awarded the rights to "Hail to the Redskins" to its credited composer, the now former Mrs. Marshall.

Clint Murchison then had an epiphany. He approached Corinne with an offer to buy the fight song. Following a modest amount of haggling the song became the property of Murchison, who immediately refused Marshall and the Redskins the right to use the tune.

When Marshall learned of the maneuver, he exploded. Speaking to George Halas on the phone, Marshall made his position clear.

"I'll tell you, no SOB is going to steal *my* song and get into *my* league!"[21]

Every action has an equal and opposite reaction . . . or something like that.

Murchison was a gambling man at heart, and he guessed right on this deal. Marshall wanted his anthem back, and Murchison was willing to deal . . . for a price. If Marshall dropped his opposition to expansion, the Washington faithful could continue singing "Hail to the Redskins."

Marshall seethed and then capitulated.

That's how it all played out, sort of.

Several days before the owners compromised on selecting Pete Rozelle to be the new commissioner, Marshall taped an interview on Jim Gibbons's television show in Chicago. The host asked Marshall if he would be interested in the commissionership. Despite having taken himself out of contention for the position in the immediate aftermath of Bell's death, Marshall altered his tune when Gibbons inquired about the possibility of Marshall being the next commissioner.

"I would take the job in a minute if they offered it to me. . . . And some of the other club owners would be glad to have me in that position because I wouldn't have a vote, or anything to say," Marshall told the television host with a hearty chuckle.[22]

Marshall could have been referring to any number of issues, but at the time of the Gibbons interview he was most assuredly referencing his opposition to league expansion.

One week of politicking and infighting consumed the attention of the writers camped out at the Kenilworth, meeting in the glass-partitioned lobby of the hotel.

Murchison's devilish persuasion had brought Marshall on board to the enlarging of the league. Now only the Wolfners of Chicago stood between a unanimous vote for expansion and the implosion of the whole endeavor.

The marathon Miami Beach meetings were certainly eventful. And, despite being on the losing side of the most prominent matters brought before the league, Marshall put a good spin on events.

"Pete's a good boy with a lot of ability," Marshall said of the new commissioner. "He conducted himself well in the important sessions since he took over. I'd say he has a lot of patience."[23]

Moments after Rozelle was chosen to lead the NFL a motion was put forth that a change in Article 9, section 1, of the league constitution be made. Edwin J. Anderson of the Detroit Lions made the motion, and it was seconded by the Eagles' representative, Joseph A. Donoghue. Such a modification would mean that a unanimous vote of the owners would no longer be necessary to approve expansion. In his first moments on the job Rozelle exerted his strength of leadership and pushed the proposal through. Under the new rule the votes of just ten of twelve clubs could approve the addition of new franchises to the league.

The fix was in. New blood was now inevitable.

The boyish commissioner stepped into the press room at 6:10 p.m., just hours after his appointment to lead the National Football League into a new era. There Rozelle announced to the gathered newsmen that the Dallas Rangers would begin play in 1960. The addition of the Rangers would give the league an odd number of teams, which would complicate scheduling. The Dallas club, Rozelle explained, would be a "swing" team, playing each league club once during the coming season. The following season (1961), the new commissioner explained, a team headed by Max Winter would take the field in Minnesota.

"A strong sentiment was expressed," Rozelle added, "that if the conditions are practical, two more teams would be added within the next three years to give the league two eight-team divisions."[24]

Following Rozelle's brief meeting with the media, George Halas stepped before the press. The sixty-four-year-old founding father of the NFL struggled to suppress a grin from overtaking his face. Speaking before a handful of writers, Halas began by quoting a section of Bert Bell's testimony of July 24, 1957, before the House Judiciary Committee. This appearance by Bell before Congress, Halas pointedly explained, came two years before the American Football League (AFL) was formally organized.

Bell had begun by saying, "I believe we will expand in the next few years. . . . They have talked to us about Houston, Dallas, Fort Worth. They have talked to us about Miami. They have talked about Minneapolis and they talked about Buffalo. . . . These places are crying for football teams."

His point made, Halas relished the part that his antagonist of many years had played in getting the expansion deal done.

"I knew the old pro [Marshall] would come through," Halas chuckled, shaking his head in amusement. "If you can figure out that Marshall . . ."[25]

Simultaneously the owners and executives of the American Football League were holding a meeting of their own at the Statler Hilton in downtown Dallas. Fifteen minutes after Rozelle announced the NFL's intention to expand into Dallas, Joe Foss met with journalists covering a gathering of AFL officials.

"It's an act of war and designed to wreck the infant American Football League," Foss said.

Foss, the man selected as commissioner of the fledgling AFL, had no pro football experience on his résumé. Knowledge and comprehensive understanding of the game may not have been his forte, but Foss had been a two-term governor of South Dakota and possessed contacts in government—an important asset to the new league.

"The National Football League's move into Dallas is an all-out attempt to put our league out of business," the AFL commissioner stated.

Foss, who had served his country as a Marine Corps fighter pilot during World War II, continued his statement with a sense of foreboding.

"We are not tipping our hand as to our course of action, but we are looking into all phases of the matter. The National Football League is striking at the heart of the American League with the idea of folding it. The NFL is out to continue its monopoly on professional football. We will go to court or Congress to prevent them from killing off the Dallas team."

With an ominous tone, the AFL's commissioner then pointed out what seemed obvious to him and the many other observers: the NFL's move into Dallas was calculated.

"There are anti-trust laws to take care of such things. This is like using a Christmas tree for a candle on a small cake."[26]

Shortly after the AFL's commissioner spoke Lamar Hunt echoed the thoughts of Foss.

"Anti-trust laws are designed to foster competition—not to kill off competition, and the National Football League has the monopoly," Hunt said.

Upon hearing the thoughts, as well as the interpreted threats, of the American Football League's leaders, Pete Rozelle again spoke with the press.

"It's a shame to hear the commissioner of the AFL resort to issuing threats when all we are trying to do is establish a harmonious relationship with the new league," he said.

Besides, Rozelle added, "while he [Foss] states that Dallas is a one-team market it might be pointed out that New York and Los Angeles were NFL cities until joined by AFL clubs for the next season.

"We welcome competition and earnestly hope that it will bring about [a] more highly skilled and entertaining brand of football for the fans' enjoyment."[27]

The selection of Pete Rozelle was heartening to some observers and commentators. The hopeful anticipation went beyond Rozelle's business acumen and what the new commissioner would mean to the league's coffers; it extended to the former team executive's open-minded way of building the Rams' roster. It was Rozelle, Brad Pye wrote in the *Los Angeles Sentinel*, who brought Ollie Matson to the Rams.

"I do know what Rozelle can do, but if he could shake Marshall loose from his pre–Civil War beliefs," Pye mused, "he will be accomplishing something that many strong men have failed to do."[28]

A couple of questions facing league officials during the off-season included the matter of expanding the schedule from twelve to fourteen games and how the divisions would be aligned for the 1961 season with the addition of the new Minnesota team.

"I'm for whatever Dallas and Minnesota want," an agreeable Marshall told Lewis Atchison. "If they want to play round robin schedules I'll still vote for it. It takes only three votes to kill that. I'd like to see Dallas in the Eastern Division, but I'm not going to worry about it. I'm tired of solving other people's problem[s].

"My job," he continued, "is to get a winner for the Redskins. I'm going to concentrate on the team, the stadium, the band, and the glee club."[29]

Ultimately, the league owners decided to expand the regular season schedule from twelve to fourteen games, beginning with the 1961 season. Discussion of a commensurate increase in player salaries to compensate for the additional games understandably made the rounds. As could be expected, George Marshall shot down any such proposal.

"Why, teams couldn't afford to give players an extra two game raise," Marshall said. "The way salaries have grown in our league, fourteen games will be needed to maintain the present standard.

"Don't forget we'll be playing fewer exhibitions. Anyway, my experience has been that money is what the player is interested in, not the number of games. Do you realize not one rookie we signed ever asked how many games we play?"[30]

8

The Last Citadel of Segregation

Five days after the Redskins opened their 1960 season with a 20–0 loss at Baltimore on September 25, the Touchdown Club held its annual Welcome Home luncheon for the team. More than five hundred guests filled the Presidential Room at the Hotel Statler, each of them paying $6.50 for the privilege of greeting the 1960 Washington Redskins.

Henry "Red" Krause, the Touchdown Club president and member of the '37 championship club, issued his annual pep talk to his old team. That the Redskins had lost the last five games of the '59 campaign, as well as all six exhibition contests, didn't dampen Krause's enthusiasm. He implored the current group of Redskins to perform well and to appreciate the team's fans—the country's best, Krause insisted.

"Just give 'em all you've got every minute and win or lose you'll find they'll be for you."

The "lose" aspect of "win or lose" had come into play a lot in recent memory for Redskins players and fans, but this history didn't curtail cheerleading for the hometown team. Coach Mike Nixon praised the merits of his squad before those gathered at the Touchdown Club.

"This football team you see in front of you is a damned good one," Nixon proclaimed. "We've lost some battles, in fact we lost them all. . . . But I know the Redskins will be a good team."

Nixon may have been viewing his team through burgundy-colored glasses, but he wasn't alone in his delusion.

George Marshall rose from the head table and addressed the gathering. His brief talk failed to acknowledge the team's many shortcomings.

"I have confidence in this squad and have expressed it publicly," Marshall declared. "I think we're all in one piece. For us, excuses and alibis are gone. There's only action ahead.

"As Amon Carter used to say, the preaching's not over until the singing's finished."

Fittingly Marshall concluded his short speech by leading the ballroom in a boisterous rendition of "Hail to the Redskins."[1]

The following Sunday the Redskins took to the field stirred by the faith their coach and owner had demonstrated in the team. Perhaps a more likely scenario is that the inspiration came from playing an expansion outfit. Whatever the reason, Washington defeated the first-year Dallas Cowboys 26–14 at Griffith Stadium, and Marshall was exultant.

"Now we can walk around town this week for a change," he gushed to reporters. "We won't have to duck into alleys. This one was it, great for the team, the town, for everybody."[2]

Unfortunately the victory over Dallas would prove to be the high point of the season. The Redskins didn't completely fall apart, at least not immediately. They followed up the defeat of the Cowboys with ties in consecutive games with the Giants and the Steelers. Washington's record stood at 1-1-2 when the Cleveland Browns came to town on October 30. Paul Brown's team took apart the Redskins, 31–10.

Marshall was wont to wear his emotions on his sleeve, and being embarrassed on his home field never brought out the best in him. At the weekly Tuesday luncheon Marshall began offering excuses for his team's poor showing, which offended his coach.

"I don't need anyone to alibi for me," Mike Nixon snapped.

Marshall was taken aback by his coach's impudence. "Well I do," Marshall snapped back. "I'm in the ticket-selling business and after you get beat 31–10, you need an alibi."[3]

The morning after the Redskins' embarrassing defeat at the hands of the Browns, Shirley Povich wrote in his column, "From 25 yards out, [Jim] Brown was served the football by Milt Plum on a pitch-out and he integrated the Redskins goal-line with more than deliberate speed[;] perhaps exceeding the famous Supreme Court decree, Brown fled the 25 yards, like a man in an uncommon hurry and the Redskins goal line, at least, became integrated."[4]

In one brilliantly constructed sentence Povich's prose laid bare the folly of Marshall's bigoted philosophy.

Following the loss to Cleveland, the Redskins' dismal season continued in a downward spiral, finishing with eight consecutive defeats and a record of 1-9-2.

Two days after Christmas the representatives of each NFL team assembled in Philadelphia's Warwick Hotel. The gathering was the league's annual ritual of selecting the next class of college players who would graduate to the professional ranks. The draft came several weeks later in the season than past gatherings, which was a Pete Rozelle idea to combat the bidding wars that had occurred a year earlier with the American Football League. The impetuous AFL had instigated the chaos with a rash of premature signings and lawsuits. The upstart league, however, didn't join the NFL in postponing its draft. In fact the AFL held the selection conference more than a month before the National Football League did, gathering in Dallas on November 23.

Whenever and wherever made no difference nor did it alter the edict to the man selecting future Washington Redskins. Dick McCann remained bound by Marshall's directive to select only white players for his squad. Much thought and preparation went into the college draft. A total of five hours was needed to complete the initial round, and with their first choice based on Coach Bill McPeak's strong recommendation the Washington Redskins used their first pick to select Norm Snead, a "tall, Bible-reading" quarterback from Wake Forest.

"To me a quarterback must have three basic things," McPeak explained. "He's got to be able to pass well, and Norman can. He's got to have heart and a good football mind. Norman impressed me as a fellow who had 'em all.

"They say he isn't a good runner. Well he isn't. It helps for a quarterback to be able to run. Often he can't run out of a jam, but Van Brocklin wasn't much of a runner either, and nobody called him a bad quarterback."[5]

Snead had one other trait that McPeak failed to list. Like the other nineteen men selected by the Redskins, Snead was white.

"The Redskins had twenty choices in the draft this week," Shirley Povich wrote the day after the draft. "They didn't choose a single Negro player. This is because the Redskins are playing States Rights football.

"Every other team, with the exception of the Redskins, is happy to have Negro players aboard. Dallas, a more Southern city than George Marshall's

Washington[,] is among them. The referees don't blow the whistle on touchdowns scored by Negro backs. When Ted Don scored the winning touchdown for the Eagles last Sunday, it went up on the board promptly. Nobody asked to look at his birth certificate."[6]

Povich continued his characterization: "In modern era pro football, Marshall is an anachronism as out of date as the drop kick. The other club owners have passed him by. Marshall with his dedication to white supremacy on the football field is still hearing a cry that doesn't exist. The Redskins haven't won any kind of title in 16 years.

"Marshall's rejection of Negro players has been ascribed to his concern for his profitable TV-radio network that takes the Redskins games into Southern states. This would be an over-tender regard for his nonpaying Dixie viewers."[7]

As he had done for years, Marshall spent the winter months in the more inviting climes of Florida. Still, by making frequent calls to subordinates in search of answers to whatever question he might have, Marshall remained in close contact with the Redskins' hierarchy.

"How many tickets did you sell today?" Marshall demanded of Dick McCann. "Doesn't anyone but me care how many tickets are sold?"

Finished with McCann, Marshall moved on.

"Let me speak with Bill," he said, referencing Bill Lally, the club's business manager, who was chased down in the ticket office.

When he had had his say with Lally, Marshall was ready to push ahead.

"I want to speak with Bill McPeak," was the next command, but his head coach was in Pittsburgh, so Marshall settled for Chester Minter. Minter, who served as something of a gofer for Marshall, had just departed the Ninth Street office for a brief visit to a local bank.

"Well then, how about Torgy Torgeson?" Torgeson, who served as an assistant coach with the Redskins, was in the building and available to speak. A brief conversation ensued. At its conclusion Marshall implored of Torgeson, "Now switch me and see if Chester is in now."[8]

An expert telephone operator Torgy was not. As ordered, Torgeson pushed a button, but not the correct button, which resulted in Marshall being disconnected.

On March 16 Marshall received a telephone call. On the other end of the receiver was Thomas McCloskey, the vice president of the company constructing the new DC Stadium. McCloskey assured Marshall that, though the landscaping around the park might not be ready, the field and the stadium itself would be prepped and ready by October 1. This date was two weeks earlier than the estimate being bandied about town by those "in the know." The first of October would be the third week of the NFL season, a perfectly acceptable date for a home opener.

A very pleased Marshall immediately grabbed his office phone and placed a call to Pete Rozelle. The entire league schedule for the upcoming season had been placed on hold pending word on the construction of the new stadium in Washington.

Playing out in the midst of the Redskins' miserable season was the 1960 presidential race between Massachusetts senator John Kennedy and Vice President Richard Nixon, a campaign that had captivated much of the nation. Marshall, once described as being to the right of Attila the Hun, put his full support behind Nixon, a frequent visitor to the owner's box at Redskins games. When his man lost the extremely close election, Marshall was disappointed and more than a little bemused that Joe Kennedy's "boy" was now the leader of the free world.

Marshall went back a ways with the elder Kennedy. In fact Joe had made an attempt to buy the Redskins just a couple of years earlier. That Joe's son would reside in the White House held little interest to Marshall beyond the novelty of the situation. And in the first weeks of Kennedy's presidency, as the power brokers in Washington tried to gain favor with the new administration, Marshall was busying himself by preparing for the opening of his new stadium.

A fierce nor'easter swept across the Eastern seaboard the day before Kennedy's January 20 inauguration. The next morning the city was draped in a blanket of snow, and temperatures hovered in the low twenties when John Fitzgerald Kennedy stood on the steps of the Capitol and took the oath of office, becoming the thirty-fifth president of the United States.

A noticeable transformation came over Washington with the arrival of the new administration, a shift that went beyond the change at the top of the political structure. The youth and vitality of the new administration brought a sense of style and an ethos that had previously been absent in the capital. What had been a quiet southern town nearly devoid of culture was slowly evolving into a cosmopolitan city.

It was a "New Frontier"—a new frontier in education, art, housing, and race relations.

Four days after President Kennedy took the oath of office Martin Luther King Jr. was in Chattanooga, Tennessee, where he took part in the local Emancipation Day celebration.

The thirty-one-year-old civil rights leader publicly asserted that much was expected from the new president.

"We must remind Mr. Kennedy we [black citizens] helped him get into the White House, and that we expect him to use the full weight of his office to remove the burden of segregation from our shoulders," King said.

"We must remind Kennedy that when he gets the pen in his hand, we expect him to write a little with it."[9]

A month and a half after his inauguration, on the morning of March 6, 1961, the White House press office released a statement from President Kennedy, the significance of which was completely lost on Marshall. This pronouncement, Executive Order No. 10925, established the Presidential Committee on Equal Opportunity. The order expanded on rules established under the Eisenhower administration six years earlier.

"Through this vastly strengthened machinery," the president stated, "I intend to ensure that Americans of all colors and beliefs will have equal access to employment within the Government and with those who do business with the Government."

The order directed that government contractors "not discriminate against any employee or applicant in employment because of race, creed, color, or national origin."[10]

During his brief time in the White House, JFK took limited steps to eliminate racial bias. In his first weeks in office President Kennedy had been preoccupied with Laos, a tiny kingdom half a world away. Civil rights actually held little interest for Kennedy. As a candidate, and now as president,

Kennedy needed to be pushed and cajoled into acting on issues of racial inequity and discrimination. There were some symbolic gestures, such as inviting Marian Anderson to sing at the inauguration, and Kennedy had also asked members of his Cabinet to not speak at segregated affairs. The young president did, however, surround himself with people who cared passionately about the issue.

Before joining the Kennedy administration in January 1961 Stewart Udall had served four terms in Congress representing the second district of Arizona. He had used his influence in the state to galvanize Arizona Democrats in support of Senator Kennedy's campaign. After being pegged to head Interior, Udall's contribution to the new president's Cabinet was immediate. His impact was already apparent at the inauguration; it was at Udall's suggestion that his friend, the poet Robert Frost, read at the swearing-in ceremonies.

The forty-one-year-old Udall had taken to his position quickly. In his brief time as the head of Interior Udall had been earnestly preaching the importance of saving America's natural resources and potential park land.

And then he ventured beyond conservationism and quickly found himself embroiled in a national debate.

On March 21 Udall sent a memo to the president. It highlighted several immediate objectives of the Interior Department, including:

1. National Fuels Policy Legislation
2. Economic Development on Indian Reservations
3. International Cooperation—Migratory Waterfowl

A fourth item on Udall's list seemed on the surface to stray from his jurisdiction, but it was this fourth point that would eventually alter the course of the National Football League:

4. Anti-Discrimination—Washington Redskins

"We are prepared to take action against the owner of the Washington Redskins—the last citadel of segregation in professional sports," Udall noted in his memo. "Fred Dutton has been advised of our proposed course of action. This is a priority [northern] area to attack discrimination, and we believe our move will be met with wide applause."[11]

It would be a bold step—issuing a government edict to a private citizen, in essence dictating to that citizen how to operate his business. Never one to act brashly, Udall exhibited acute diligence before proceeding. Did he have the legal standing to force Marshall's hand? This question was foremost in Udall's mind.

When he accepted the Cabinet position Udall was advised that the most important decision he'd make would be the selection of the department's lawyer. To fill that vital role Udall had one man in mind: Frank Gates. Udall had known Gates since the two men were in law school following World War II. Over the ensuing years Gates and Udall grew extraordinarily close, and the new secretary intrinsically trusted Gates's interpretation of the law. Even more important, Udall had complete faith in his friend's honesty.

"I practiced law with Frank," Udall explained, "and I know Frank."[12]

Frank Gates would be sure to shoot straight. Udall did not think twice before asking Gates for advice.

When Udall presented to Gates the Redskins' argument and the contract for the newly constructed DC Stadium, the recently appointed solicitor quickly analyzed the situation before offering his advice.

"You are the landlord," Gates explained. "You, as the representative of the Government, signed the lease, you can tell him that he has to integrate the team."[13]

Emboldened with this advice, Udall now only needed the assurance of the administration before proceeding. George Preston Marshall, with his numerous Washington connections, would surely go over Udall's head if the secretary pushed ahead with his effort to force Marshall's hand. Udall's next move was to notify the attorney general, Robert Kennedy, as well as the White House lawyers, of his intentions. If the Department of Justice or

White House was going to reverse his order, Udall needed to know before issuing his edict.

Both Bobby Kennedy and the White House gave the go ahead, with one caveat: this would be Udall's fight. The Interior Department would be on the front lines of this battle all alone.[14]

9

States' Rights Football

Spring had come early.

Hell, summer had seemingly arrived well before the calendar deemed practical. The first week of March had seen temperatures reach 81 degrees, something the city of Washington had never before recorded for that time of year. However, Friday, March 24, 1961, was overcast and mild.

At three o'clock that afternoon a letter was hand delivered to George Marshall at his Ninth Street office. The letterhead bore the insignia of the Department of the Interior:

Dear Mr. Marshall:

To harmonize our contract policies with the general antidiscrimination policy enunciated by the President a few days ago, we have recently promulgated an amendment to the regulations which govern the use of areas under the jurisdiction of National Capital Parks. This amended regulation prohibits discrimination in employment practices with respect to any activity provided for by a contract, lease or permit with an operator or sub-lessee of any public facility in a park area. I am enclosing a copy of the new regulation for your information.

Your company, Pro Football, Inc., through a lease executed on December 24, 1959, has contracted with the District of Columbia Armory Board to use the new District of Columbia Stadium in Anacostia Park for a series of professional games. Under its terms, the new regulation mentioned above is incorporated into this lease.

I am cognizant of the fact that there have been persistent allegations that your company practices discrimination in the hiring of its players. We are not, at this time, passing judgment on this issue—indeed we assume that your company will fully adhere to its contractual obligations. However, candor compels me to advise you of the implications of this new regulation—and our view of its import.

Signed
Stewart L. Udall
Secretary of the Interior

In other words, integrate the Washington Redskins or else.

Udall's shot across the bow was unexpected. For the better part of three decades Marshall had run his team unfettered by any outside constraints. It was, after all, *his* business, and it was his business to operate however he saw fit. League commissioners and his fellow owners kept their noses out of Redskins affairs, so who was this Kennedy crony to tell him how to run his club?

True to his nature, Marshall's initial response was forthright: "I don't know what the hell it's all about."[1]

Across town, timed to coincide with the delivery of his letter to Marshall, Udall held a press conference at the Department of the Interior. Before a modest gathering of reporters Udall sat behind a desk strewn with papers and fielded a handful of questions.

When asked what the government might do to enforce the hiring of black players, Udall explained that failure to comply with the regulations could bring a misdemeanor charge against club officials. Action could also be taken against the Redskins' right to use the new municipal stadium. But Udall stopped there—he would not speculate as to what specific action his department would choose. The secretary told reporters that "the White House has been consulted in the matter," and he then added, "I intend to handle this matter myself."[2]

However, the secretary noted, if Marshall "wants any argument, which I hope he doesn't, he's going to have one with the President and the Administration."[3] Udall mused that he hoped a confrontation wouldn't be necessary and that Marshall would be "sensible enough to adjust himself."[4]

Stewart Udall, however, did not know George Preston Marshall very well. After taking a few moments to digest the contents of Udall's letter, Marshall sent a copy to his lawyers. His next move was to quickly dictate a response in which he gave no ground:

> I think the matter is thoroughly covered in our lease and it was discussed at length.
>
> All attractions at the new stadium will be those presented by the National Football League. The National Football League has no restrictions I know of, neither do the Redskins.
>
> Naturally, I have turned your letter over to our lawyers, King & Nordlinger.
>
> As to our position at the present moment, we violate no laws of the United States and this lease was made on that basis.
>
> Would be glad to discuss this matter with you at any time.[5]

Marshall dispatched his reply to Udall's office by special messenger and then held court in his office, pleading his case to a large group of journalists.

Marshall's Ninth Street office was jammed with reporters; the non-sports writers easily outnumbered the men who regularly covered the Redskins. The venue, with all attention focused on him, was perfectly suited to Marshall, who could have made a healthy living on stage performing for the masses if only his talents had allowed.

Making certain that all attention, television cameras, and microphones were fully focused on him, Marshall began the press conference he had called by summoning an assistant.

"Get me Ambassador Kennedy in Boston," Marshall bellowed.

Following a brief pause, a writer piped up, "Why do you want to talk to Ambassador Kennedy?"

"I want to tell my old pal what a creep I think his son is."[6]

And so the show began.

Local journalists representing the Washington dailies were on hand, and a number of out-of-town writers were connected to the discussion via telephone. Into their ready notebooks they furiously scribbled the torrent of words that flowed from Marshall. Dealing with this loose cannon made their jobs a breeze. And, as usual, Marshall started rambling without any prompting.

"I obey all laws. If they change them, I'll abide by them," Marshall said. "I didn't know the government had the right to tell the showman how to cast the play.

"No," Marshall acknowledged, "we don't have any Negroes on the team, but we have had a Samoan, a Hawaiian, [an] Indian, and a Cuban in the past."

Besides, Marshall reasoned, "all the other teams we play have Negroes[;] does it matter which team has the Negroes?"

With his feet comfortably propped up on his desk and his debonair fedora tilted at a jaunty angle on his head, Marshall was a model of composure throughout the impromptu conference. He could not disguise his disdain for government interference in his business, however.

"We have been drafting our players primarily from colleges in the South and they don't have Negroes," he said. Besides, Marshall added, "we have made an effort to appeal for Southern business. We have had some success and some failure. All we're interested in is winning games.

"I would consider it a great honor to meet with the President of the United States and would be very appreciative if Mr. Udall would arrange such a meeting."

Marshall indeed relished the possibility of debating President Kennedy. "I could handle him with words," he assured his audience. "I used to be able to handle his old man."[7]

To New York Times reporter David Halberstam, who was reporting on the conference via the telephone, Marshall's behavior was incredible.

The gall. The impudence. When would such government interference end?

"I don't know what this is all about," Marshall cried out to the Times journalist. "Are they going to demand that the National Symphony Orchestra have Negroes? The Army and Navy football teams don't have colored players, will they be barred from playing at the stadium?"

"How many of your top reporters are Negroes?" Marshall asked the Times reporter rhetorically. "Are you going to replace [James] Reston with a Negro?"[8]

To those gathered before him, Marshall (half) facetiously added, "What we want is to get the Negroes off the teams we play . . . guys like Jimmy Brown and Lenny Moore who have been helping to beat us.

"The only question seems to be whether you have to use players from a certain segment of the population.

"I don't want to be in the middle of a political battle. I'm not behind either political party. All I want is a better football team . . . to win a few more games."[9]

"I must be pretty important when the Secretary of the, what is it, Interior, is interested in me. I am surprised that with the world on the brink of war they are worried about whether or not a Negro is going to play for the Redskins. I would think they had more important problems," he fumed.[10]

As Udall expected, there was blowback from his edict. The secretary's decree was questioned by some members of the media, and his office was flooded with letters, a few in support of the action, while other missives questioned Udall's loyalty to all things that made America great. For example,

Dear Sir,

Just what is this United States coming to—when a football owner is forced to put a nigger on his team—just to please the minority that has now taken over our way of life.

This is causing people to lose respect for our form of Government. We fought in the last war for freedom from fear, and freedom of religion and to be able to choose our way of life.

I have been a Democrat all my life, but I'm deserting it now. This has gone too far. Let Mr. Marshall and the public decide what is best for his team.

Very truly yours,
Curtis Williams[11]

Fifteen days later Mr. Williams received a response from Secretary Udall. Enclosed with the letter was a copy of a press release from the Department of the Interior.

It is my hope that when you have an opportunity to review the facts of this situation, you will agree the steps I have taken are in full accord with principles of fair play and non-discrimination, as enunciated by the President a few days earlier, which are a vital part of our American traditions and ideals.

Stewart Udall[12]

On March 28, before a modest gathering of writers, Udall was asked if his office would keep the public updated as to the progress he was, or wasn't, making with Marshall. No, he hadn't been contacted by either Marshall or the team's lawyers, but that fact changed nothing.

The department, Udall explained, had no plans at the moment to implement the agreement. Still, the secretary wanted to make clear that Interior had made its position "on the record."[13] "We are trying to get into strong enough position to make it plain to George that it will be better to cooperate with us and not fight against the department. I am not at this stage taking any steps whatsoever. But I don't want Mr. Marshall to think we've misled him."

The hope was that Pro Football, Inc., would not "engage in any dispute."[14]

"If he [Marshall] talks to his lawyers, he will see what the legal situation is, and we will be bound by our regulations. We want him to get our position on the record," Udall stated.

There was a deadline, Udall explained. The Redskins must comply with the nondiscrimination policy by the start of the 1961 NFL campaign.

"Naturally, we do not intend to take any action other than perhaps to study any facts that may be submitted by him or others prior to that time, because he cannot breach the contract, he cannot be in default, he cannot get in trouble with us until Oct. 1.

"All I'm interested in and all I have a right to be interested in is that Mr. Marshall not discriminate in hiring. This is a very subtle question, I know, but I think if one studies hard enough, that one can reach some conclusions on this matter.

"We are not interested in anything other than the fact that under our contract, we will not permit discrimination in hiring and we do everything we can at the proper time to ascertain 'the facts.'"[15]

Udall was asked what Marshall needed to do in order to be in compliance with the government's regulation.

"I think that the question on October 1, when his performance begins is—does he have a policy of discrimination in the hiring of his players. We may have to pass judgment on that question at that time. I do not think we have to pass judgment on it at this time."

A tenacious journalist wanted a more specific explanation. Exactly how could Marshall prove that he did not discriminate? Would he have to trade for a colored player? Is the administration forcing the Washington Redskins to draft a Negro?

A very composed Udall would neither take the bait nor would he touch on such specifics lest it appear he was trying to commandeer Marshall's club.

The Interior Department had issued numerous regulations directed at businesses and persons with contracts to use the new stadium, Udall explained. The new rule didn't apply solely to the Washington Redskins.

"These are, as you know, as anyone knows who has had anything to do with fair employment practice commissions, very nice questions. But I think we can make judgments if it gets down to that."[16]

The Redskins had two attorneys on the payroll: Bernard I. Nordlinger and Milton King. Both men were out of pocket the day Udall's letter arrived, and neither had the opportunity to confer with Marshall before the Redskins' owner began popping off to the press. As could be expected, the following morning newspapers across the country carried significant portions of Marshall's improvised press conference. While his strident defiance appealed to a portion of the populace, his words appalled more than a few. In an attempt to soften the impact of Marshall's statements, King and Nordlinger both met with the press.

"We'll live up to anything that's in the lease we signed. I haven't even thought about it going to court," King explained.[17] He then added, "Football is a game of skill, and it's up to the team to employ those it feels it needs." However, King admitted, "we may not always be right."[18]

Nordlinger chimed in. "I'm sure the Redskins will conform to all applicable statutes and regulations," he said, "and also do their best to comply with any requests of any Government official, whether based on statute, regulation or not."

Nordlinger also reiterated King's insistence that "the Redskins do not intend to defy any Government authorities. The Redskins are going to study this thing and certainly will do what is required. The last thing we want to become involved in is any contest with Government officials."[19]

But, the attorney added, "on the other hand, it must be remembered that to engage the services of a Negro player simply because he is a Negro is as much discrimination against white players as would be the refusal to hire him because he is colored.

"The history of the Redskins shows tickets have been sold indiscriminately to white and colored."[20]

Jack Walsh of the *Washington Post* contacted Secretary Udall, who was in Williamsburg. Udall, having read the morning papers, was apprised of the Redskins' official, lawyerly response. "If they want a legal battle," Udall said, "we're certainly going to stand our ground. But I would be disappointed if Mr. Marshall should show such bad judgment. We don't want any argument . . . we just want to get on down the road with this thing."

Each side of the dispute continued to put forth its argument. As both the antagonist and protagonist did on the first day of the controversy, Marshall spoke with journalists in his office while Udall made his weekly date with reporters at the Department of the Interior four days after the controversy began.

King and Nordlinger issued statements and made their lawyerly declarations, but Marshall continued his obstinacy.

"I'm bewildered by this," Marshall said. "It sounds personal to me. I didn't realize I was that important, but I guess Udall wants to make a famous man out of me. It's as puzzling to me as it is to a lot of people. What does it mean? Are we expected to have a Negro on our team regardless of anything? Football is a skill. How can you face a skill on other grounds than skill itself? If Abe Saperstein's Harlem Globetrotters played in a civic stadium, would Abe be accused of being anti-white? Should every musical comedy have to have a Chinese in it?"[21]

"I know one thing," the Redskins owner said. "I've been receiving the most mail I've gotten in years.

"I'm not trying to beat city hall or run the world. I intend to keep my lease and I expect the Government to keep its."[22]

After the controversy began, one DC newspaper printed this letter to the editor:

I have read with amazing interest Interior Secretary Udall's threat against the Washington Redskins that they hire a Negro player or else risk President Kennedy's wrath.

The man who is most guilty of discrimination is not George Preston Marshall, but Mr. Udall. I understand that there are no Indians on the Redskins team, paradoxical oversight, I guess.

The Administration must use its "moral power" to assure that each of these minority groups has a berth on the Redskins roster. . . . On the New Frontier, it matters not whether you win or lose, it's who plays the game that counts.[23]

Four days later, the same newspaper printed another letter to the editor on the highly publicized dispute:

No matter how much some of JFK's supporters may agree with the ultra-liberal viewpoint of this administration[,] I'm sure even they must have flinched at the Secretary of Interior's statement about George Marshall and the Redskins.

Reducing prejudice is one thing, but Secretary Udall's statement was a grim warning to us all if he was expressing the feelings of this administration when he said it was up to Marshall to prove he has not been biased. In other words, Marshall is guilty until he can prove himself innocent.

This may be the America of JFK and his political appointees, but I doubt if the rest of us will be willing to go along with it beyond 1964—if that long.[24]

10

"This Isn't a League Affair"

Two weeks after receiving Udall's letter, Marshall seemed to tire of the swirling controversy.

"The less said about the whole thing the better," he told Mo Siegel of the *Daily News*. "I can see no purpose in dragging it out, nothing will be gained by anybody."[1]

The coverage this debate had received in newspapers around the country astounded Marshall, as did the number of letters about it delivered to the Redskins' offices. ("I never realized so many fans were interested in a football team that won only one game.") Much of the mail he'd received expressed support for the Redskins. One note chastised Marshall for never having employed a female on his football team.

"She's right," he said in agreement. "Of course we have had players who played like girls, but never an actual girl player."[2]

Such letters only reinforced Marshall's long-held beliefs, as did the number of newspaper editorials that came to his defense. Much of Marshall's support, not surprisingly, came from below the Mason-Dixon line.

He [Udall] didn't specify the number of Negroes that are to replace white members of the team, but maybe the administration can get Congress to pass a law establishing a proper racial ratio to be maintained and to heck with football ability.

There should, for example, be some definite assurance that Negroes will be proportionately represented among the spectators as well as the participants. If tickets sales don't work out that way, maybe a federal grant can be applied to purchase seats for members of one race or another.

And the "anti-discrimination" on the field shouldn't be limited to players. Let's require the Washington team to hire some Negro coaches, and perhaps it should alternate the head coaching job among representatives of different races.[3]

According to an editorial printed in the *Tulsa World*, Udall was "our unctuous Secretary of Interior" and he was a "first stringer" on the Kennedy squad "for all of three months."[4]

On April 24 league owners gathered in San Francisco for their spring meeting. A number of items were on the agenda, including a "disaster plan" by which each team would replenish a catastrophe-stricken club. Also up for discussion was the players' benefit plan and proposed amendments to the league's constitution.

Yes, these issues would be discussed, but something else was first on the agenda.

To a man, from Commissioner Rozelle to each of the league's fourteen owners, not a single individual wanted anything to do with the growing controversy in Washington. The league was at the threshold of breaking through, of actually competing with baseball as the national pastime, and no one wanted to be distracted by the controversial topic. Besides, many of Marshall's fellow owners thought that, if they put their nose in the Redskins owner's business, who was to say he wouldn't start spouting off about how they went about their own affairs?

Not spoken among the league's leaders was the ongoing negotiation with CBS. Marshall's troubles could only hurt the league and any prospective deal with the network.

The dispute between the federal government and the Redskins came at a difficult time for Rozelle. The commissioner had been heavily involved in discussions for a groundbreaking television contract while the dispute between Marshall and the federal government swirled about in newspaper headlines. The Washington franchise was a significant part of the proposed package, and the controversy and the obstinate bigotry of the team's owner did not play well with a significant portion of the country.

Before a broadcast agreement could be reached television executives needed to know how the league would address the Marshall situation. They asked Rozelle, and behind closed doors the league commissioner assured the CBS officials that Marshall would be dealt with, but delicately and with diplomacy. With such assurance the Columbia Broadcasting System came to an agreement with the NFL on April 26. The deal provided CBS with the exclusive rights to televise all regular-season National Football League games for the 1961 and 1962 seasons.

The agreement was jointly announced in San Francisco by Rozelle and CBS vice president Bill MacPhail before a phalanx of reporters.

"It will be one of the most involved television set-ups in history," MacPhail explained. "We'll be televising as many as seven games at one time—each involving two different clubs, different announcers, technical crews, and so forth."

Rozelle conceded that the television income of a couple of teams would be less with the new agreement, but "the majority will receive more."

The deal packaged all teams together equally, Rozelle explained, to "protect the poor teams."[5]

"This will help us keep our equality of competition," the commissioner said. "A Game of the Day plan destroys balance. Teams that had been making more realize that this will be in the interest of the league."

Rozelle was questioned about the possibility that the contract was in violation of antitrust laws.

That would not be an issue, Rozelle assured the gathered journalists. The league counsel had closely scrutinized the contract, he said, adding, "We were advised that this plan had been used frequently by many other sports and is not in violation of any anti-trust law."[6]

Would the commissioner's office step in and direct George Marshall to integrate the Redskins?

"This is not a league affair," Rozelle firmly stated. "That's strictly a club problem and the league office is not concerned with it," he said.[7] "It is a matter between Marshall and Secretary Udall."[8]

Silence means approval, it's been said. And though he needed little fortification Marshall was emboldened by the implicit backing of his brethren.

Although he was reportedly in favor of the television proposal, Marshall was noticeably absent from the meetings. Providing comment for the Redskins was an unnamed team official who spoke with Steve Guback of the *Star*.

"We get an equal chance in the player draft, the same forty percent of the gate on the road, and now the same share of TV receipts. It's going to keep the strong from getting stronger and the weak from getting weaker," the anonymous representative explained.[9]

Though Marshall did not attend the meetings, a resourceful Jack Walsh of the *Post* reached the Redskins owner in New York for comment via telephone.

"This is a great thing," Marshall gushed. "I'm all for it. In fact, I offered the original resolution at the Philadelphia meeting.

"The beauty of it is that each team gets the same amount. Green Bay will collect as much as New York. I've always been for equal distribution of receipts in every manner possible. It's good for the league. It's fair to the fans and cities all over the league."

Marshall then bragged about the NFL having the most equitable arrangement of any sports league.

Walsh reminded Marshall that the new AFL had signed a similar package deal, with each team receiving $185,000 annually.

"We had tried for one before," Marshall acknowledged, "but the Justice Department told us we couldn't do it.

"I hope there's no hitch in this," he continued. "Certainly, the Government shouldn't object to it. It's sound and others are permitted to do it. In fact, this helps the American Football League because we'll be only on one network where before we were on two."[10]

"I have no racial policy," George Preston Marshall claimed with great authority. "I hire Negroes in many capacities."

On the surface Marshall's claim seemed ridiculous. His entire professional football team, the Washington Redskins, was notoriously "lily-white." And never before had Marshall's hiring practices been under more scrutiny. A month earlier Marshall had been issued a very public warning from the secretary of the interior to either desegregate his football team or not be allowed the use of the brand-new, government-owned DC Stadium. Upon receiving Stewart L. Udall's letter of March 24, Marshall's immediate instinct was to cede the chore of responding to his lawyers. However, before twenty-four hours had passed, Marshall had begun a campaign to state his case. A phone call with Wendell Smith was only the latest attempt by Marshall.

Smith was a veteran reporter with the *Pittsburgh Courier* and one of the foremost black sportswriters in the country. He had been around men like Marshall his entire career. Smith had a long and storied history of fighting existing prejudice throughout the sports world. Prior to the integration of Major League Baseball, Smith had advised Brooklyn Dodgers general manager Branch Rickey, and later he had befriended Jackie Robinson, helping ease the player's acclimation to the big leagues. From his pen came some of the most eloquent pleas for fairness and justice, but this particular issue made Smith wary. Certainly he understood that in Marshall he had a protagonist who was no innocent. But Smith couldn't help but question the government's position and its right to dictate how a private business should function.

To Smith, Marshall may not have been singing to the choir, but neither was he preaching to the converted.

You hire Negroes? Smith asked. For what type of jobs?

"Oh, janitors and things like that," Marshall replied.

Well, then why haven't you ever signed a black player?

That's simple, Marshall explained. "I just haven't come across any that I thought could make my club. I'm not prejudiced, really."

He remained unrepentant.

Marshall was a reporter's dream. Ask a question and you'd get an answer. Sometimes a question wasn't even necessary for Marshall to provide his response.

"I don't see why they are pushing me. After all, since when do you have to hire a certain race of people?"

Realizing that Marshall implicitly acknowledged bias in his hiring, Smith became more aggressive in his questioning. How can you ignore an entire race of people, on purpose, and then expect to play in a stadium paid for by tax dollars?

"That's like asking me when I stopped beating my wife," an irritated Marshall shot back. "Why do you ask me such a question?"

"Because," Smith said, "we want to know."

"Well, I've told you, because I haven't seen any I thought were good enough. Does that satisfy your question?"

Smith explained it wasn't he who needed to be persuaded but rather the government.

"I don't know," Marshall said, "and frankly I'm not overly concerned. I don't see how anyone can tell me who to hire, or what to hire."

"Well," Smith replied, "it looks like you might run into trouble. Secretary Udall says he has some very sound evidence that you have been biased."

"Let him bring up your evidence," Marshall bellowed. "If they can prove that then there is nothing I can do about it, is there?"

But the government can keep the Redskins from playing in a municipal park, Smith reminded Marshall.

"We'll have to see about that," a confident Marshall said, closing out the conversation. "We'll have to see about that."[11]

Some months earlier, in August 1960, Commissioner Rozelle had ordered Harry Wismer to dispose of his Redskins stock. It seemed only prudent; after all Harry was now the majority owner of the AFL's New York Titans. Wismer was agreeable to the commissioner's directive, but he wouldn't be rushed into anything. He would get a fair value for his piece of the Redskins, and he would take his time getting that price.

Ed Williams fit in comfortably in a city chock-full of outsized personalities. He was a prominent DC trial lawyer with a wide array of clients, including Teamsters union boss Jimmy Hoffa, Senator Joseph McCarthy, Representative Adam Clayton Powell, and mobster Frank Costello. Securing a piece of the Washington Redskins appealed to the lawyer's sense of ego. He already knew Marshall socially, but Williams was unfamiliar with Wismer.

Throughout the fall of 1960 Williams wooed Wismer. This task was far more difficult than Williams had anticipated, for he found Wismer to be an overbearing bore. Williams endured weeks of Wismer's bombastic personality before the two men came to an agreement. Wismer would part with his share of the Redskins; $250,000 was the number Wismer took to Marshall. He was willing to pay this price, Williams explained, but first he wanted a tax lawyer to examine the team's books. Marshall blanched at the request, but after some consideration he reluctantly relented. Word was, Marshall had been living very comfortably off the Redskins, and after studying the books Williams's tax lawyer, Coleman Stein, discovered that these rumors were well founded.

Even armed with this knowledge, Williams wanted in. He and Stein paid a visit to Marshall's office.

"I'm willing to meet Wismer's price," Williams said. But there was one caveat. "We can't stay lily-white at this stage. We need Negroes if we are going to win."

Marshall may have opened his books, but there were some things he refused to concede. "No nigger's ever going to play for me," Marshall replied to Williams. "Ed, I don't want to change the world, I just want to have some fun."

That was all Williams needed to hear. He and Stein thanked Marshall and left without buying into the Redskins.[12]

The drawn-out search for someone to buy out Wismer continued. With Williams out of the picture there was no one else on the horizon. People weren't exactly beating down the door on Ninth Street pleading for the opportunity to become a minor shareholder in a business predominantly owned by the dictatorial George Preston Marshall. Still, it wasn't just the commissioner who wanted Wismer out; Marshall desperately wanted to be rid of his nemesis.

As a favor to Marshall, Milton King stepped forward in mid-December and purchased the Wismer shares of the club for $350,000. One of the most familiar characters in Redskins history was now gone, but Wismer didn't go without a making another jab at his old boss. In an open letter to Bus Ham, sports editor of the *Post*, Wismer challenged the Redskins to play his Titans in a postseason bowl game.

"From now on, and I hope forever," Marshall said in response to the challenge, "Harry Wismer will have to get publicity on his own for he no longer has any connection with the National Football League or the Washington Redskins and I wish him well."[13]

King held the stock for only three months. The attorney then unloaded the stock for the same price he'd paid. The buyers were two men, Bill Shea and Jack Kent Cooke.

Cooke had been the owner of the Toronto Maple Leafs baseball club in the International League since 1951. More recently Shea had teamed with Branch Rickey in trying to create a third major league, the Continental League.

The new Redskins shareholders were put before the Washington media on April 23, 1961. Following the introduction of the new minority owners of the Redskins, Shea and Cooke were presented to the press. The issue of discrimination was foremost in the minds of the reporters interviewing Shea.

"There's nothing that can be done about this draft," Shea explained. "We'll have to wait for the next player draft."

Shea then explained that his minor league football team, the Long Island Indians, had begun fielding Negroes in the early 1940s.[14] And he, along with Cooke, was all in favor of the Redskins hiring black players.

"I admit that what Marshall is doing doesn't make common sense," Shea said. "I just can't get in there and fight with him out of nowhere, though, [and] neither can Cooke." Whatever he and Cooke thought mattered not one bit; they were after all just minority stockholders, and Marshall held all the power.

"If you know Marshall you don't do anything frontally," Shea explained. "He's not against colored people. He just doesn't give a damn."[15]

"We can do a real job there but not with speeches, ranting or raving. Making headlines in the papers might get some people saying we're great guys but it will get nothing done. Not with somebody like Marshall anyway. Right now he thinks he's doing right."[16]

"Of all the political appointees who have graced the Washington scene in the last few years," Marshall opined, "our new Secretary of Interior qualifies as King of Buffoonery. First, he chose to intervene in the operation of a private sports enterprise. . . . Of all the Secretary's sage comments, I am most perplexed at the slights and oversights inherent in his proposal to integrate the Redskins' football club. How can he conscientiously do this without insisting on the integration of the Harlem Globetrotters, Lawrence Welk's band, Khrushchev's Olympic team, and the Kennedy football teams?"[17]

On May 1 Marshall spoke at a Redskins luncheon. The primary topic of the day was the Pro Football Hall of Fame, which was currently under construction in Canton, Ohio. Marshall pleaded the case for the induction of Dr. John Brallier, who claimed to be the first professional football player, having been paid ten dollars per game played.

Marshall also acknowledged that perhaps he himself would someday be eligible for induction into the newly established Hall of Fame. Still, what Marshall wished to be his epitaph was his push for a new stadium in the District of Columbia.

"For $10,000 I could have kept it from being built, but I wanted a stadium and I signed a lease that will make the Redskins pay about $20,000 more than they should have paid. Only half of it will be taxable, however, so for $10,000 the city got its stadium."[18]

Days later at a Georgetown cocktail soirée partygoers were disappointed when Marshall didn't take the bait and refused to verbally upbraid Udall for their pleasure.

"We're both in the same business," Marshall explained, "selling tickets. The Secretary and I have nothing to do with one another at all. My lease is with the Armory board, not with Interior."

One attendee told Marshall he was from Northern California and that, while one San Francisco newspaper played up the controversy, the city's other daily completely ignored the issue.

Upon hearing this information Marshall exploded. "This story made page 1 of the *New York Times*! Is that good enough for you? Page 1 of the *New York Times*, do you know what that means?"

The Californian listened politely and then added that Udall seemed to be getting more support out west. It was news that set Marshall off again.

"Listen," he reiterated. "I said it was page 1 in the *New York Times*. That's important to me."[19]

11

In Good Faith

Since issuing his ultimatum in March 1961 to integrate the Redskins, Secretary of the Interior Stewart Udall had been laying the groundwork that he hoped would protect his department from legal action. There was a real possibility that Marshall would take the issue to court. The department's solicitor general, Frank Gates, began an in-depth investigation, the premise of which was to prove that the Redskins practiced discrimination. Gates spoke with newspaper reporters and editors, interviewed college publicists, and talked to coaches at both the collegiate and professional level. The solicitor general even tracked down a number of former Redskins players.

Was there a pattern of discrimination?

Gates's legwork paid dividends. There was a pattern, certainly, but was it enough to make the government's case in court? While scouts for other teams spoke with college coaches at historically black schools, representatives of Howard University, for instance, explained that every team in the NFL had requested information on their football team with the exception of Washington. Not a single historically black school questioned had ever heard from Redskins personnel, nor had Washington scouts ever queried any of the black writers who compiled All-Star rosters of players from these schools about the players they had selected for these honorary teams. In fact there was no evidence that the Redskins had ever expressed any interest in gathering information on Negro players.

While Gates was working behind the scenes there had been no movement between the two antagonists, and few words had been spoken for public consumption about the whole affair for the better part of two months. But here it was the heart of summer, the Redskins were opening training camp in a week, and the inaugural game at DC Stadium was just around the corner. Still the two sides remained at what seemed to be an unbreakable impasse.

In mid-July the writer on the Redskins beat for the *Post*, Jack Walsh, went to Udall for an update.

"They'll have a place to play in the new stadium, on which they have a 30-year lease," Udall explained during the exclusive interview. "As I view it as a lawyer, they hardly can be in violation of any agreement unless they exercise the lease and commit one."

Walsh pushed Udall for a definition of the "discrimination" that the government accused the Redskins of practicing.

"I'd say it's something subjective in someone's mind, exemplified by a pattern of conduct," Udall responded. "One has to pile up evidence to prove a pattern, compare it with that of other people in the same business."

Intrigued, Walsh pressed for an explanation.

"People are working on it," was all Udall would say.

The secretary shook his head. In all his travels he had never run into a character quite like George Preston Marshall.

"Marshall thinks we don't mean business, but we do," Udall continued. "This guy's making a big mistake if he thinks our department merely is trying to get some publicity out of this thing. We're quite serious."

A sense of exasperation overcame the secretary.

"I can't understand this man," Udall said. "I, and I'm sure other members of the Cabinet, are all for giving his team a big push forward in this fine new stadium.

"If he continues to maintain his present attitude, we jolly well aren't."[1]

An enterprising reporter, Walsh made a cross-country phone call to Marshall at the Los Angeles hotel where he was staying. The writer enlightened the Redskins' owner as to Udall's latest comments.

"They seem rather vague to me. If Mr. Udall has any complaints about what we're doing I would think he would direct them to me, not the press," Marshall said.

"We feel we're following the law. If he feels we're in violation of any law, he should state it.

"I've never made any statement as to his seriousness or lack of it in this matter. All I can say is what I've said numerous times; whatever the law is we'll comply."[2]

Robert J. Donovan, Washington correspondent for the *New York Herald Tribune*, reached Marshall in California on the eve of training camp. Marshall had been fairly quiet for the past couple of months, but he remained unrepentant, if not repetitive in his analogies.

"We are obeying the law," he told Donovan. "If the law forces us to hire Eskimos or Chinese or Mongolians or white people we will hire them. Why Negroes in particular? Why not make us hire a player from any other race? There are lots of races in the United States aren't there? Aren't they entitled to the same consideration?"

Donovan politely listened as Marshall railed against Udall, who he said "has absolutely no jurisdiction over the stadium." The reporter interrupted, asking Marshall if he would hire Jim Brown or Lenny Moore.

"I've never been confronted with the problem. That would be a nice problem to be confronted with," Marshall replied. He then flippantly added, "You can't tell what will happen under the guise of liberalism."[3]

Marshall wasn't ready to wave the white flag, but he wanted to know his options. Training camp was just under way, and the regular season was just around the corner.

Would his team even have a place to play in Washington?

Marshall needed a resolution of some sort, and he reached out to Commissioner Rozelle.

Marshall being Marshall, he didn't exactly plead, "Get me out of this." But he did ask the commissioner for some guidance.

Until this point in time Rozelle had successfully avoided injecting himself into the controversy. Privately, however, the commissioner was pleased that Marshall had called. The league did not need the bad press that the issue was stirring. Without any fanfare Rozelle set up a meeting with Udall, and on August 9 he traveled to Washington. The two men, along with several of Udall's Interior assistants, discussed the issue over lunch. There was one thing everyone wanted, including the absent Marshall: to find a compromise upon which all sides could agree.

Udall said he had a "very useful discussion" with the commissioner, but he declined further comment on the meeting.

The culmination of the lunchtime discussion came less than a week later when on August 14 Rozelle released to the media a letter he had received from Marshall.

Marshall's stubborn position had found supporters, but still he recognized that public sentiment had turned against him. With that in mind he made certain that the press received a copy of his letter to the commissioner:

It had been stated that the Washington Redskins discriminate against the hiring of Negro football players. This is not so. The sole aim of this Club has been, is, and will continue to be to field the team that will best represent Washington DC in the National Football League. The Redskins have no policy against the hiring of football players because of their race. You know that the Redskins have employed Negroes for many years. My reputation in this regard is well known in Washington.

I have already informed you that in our scout's report several Negroes rate highly for this year's League selection meeting. Among those players whom we feel can help the Redskins and whom we intend to select are: Ernie Davis, half back at Syracuse[,] and Bob Ferguson, half back at Ohio State, we consider them number one and two picks, respectively.

There it was in black and white—the Washington club did not discriminate against hiring Negro players, including Ferguson and Davis, Marshall insisted, and he hoped to sign a number of Negro stars at the player draft session.

"There are other fine football players," the letter continued, "who would be subsequent choices to the aforementioned. They are Wilburn Hollis, defensive back from Iowa; Felton Rogers[,] defensive end from the same college[,] and Ron Hatcher, fullback from Michigan State.

"I can assure you that if any of these names are still on the [draft] board, I shall be glad to select them."[4]

Marshall had finally capitulated!
That was the overwhelming reaction to Marshall's letter, and that was certainly how Udall read the missive. The secretary of the interior released his own statement:

We are willing to proceed on the assumption that this offer has been made in good faith. If the Washington Redskins management follows through in implementing this policy this should resolve the issue. . . .

I should like to commend Commissioner Rozelle for his constructive action in this matter. He has performed a distinct service to American sports in his attempt to mediate the dispute which has existed between this department and the management of the Washington Redskins.

The Kennedy Administration is determined that every American should have a full and equal opportunity to utilize his or her talents in the classroom, in industry, on the playing field and in all areas of our national life.

If a new spirit is foreshadowed by Mr. Marshall's letter, which indicated clearly that individual merit will be the sole criterion in the future selection of talent, we of course welcome this development.[5]

Everyone saved face for the moment. Udall's resolve wouldn't be tested. Marshall didn't fully commit, and Rozelle could now concentrate on other matters, those that potentially could transform the National Football League into the foremost professional sports league in the country.

Predictably Marshall's letter made headlines. Udall had his say, and Marshall had his letter; however, the voice of the commissioner was missing from the story. The *Star*'s Lewis Atchison reached out to Pete Rozelle for comment on the recent turn of events.

In speaking with Atchison, Rozelle was emphatic in his denial that Marshall's letter was a dodge to keep Udall off his back.

Would the league insist that the Redskins draft a black player?

"The league is not going to insist on anything," Rozelle asserted.[6]

A couple of days after Rozelle spoke with Atchison the *Evening Star* published an editorial stating that "while it may not be crystal clear as to who got whom off the hook, both Secretary of Interior Udall and George Preston Marshall of the Redskins have reason for gratification over a settlement of differences which, though it may be temporary, should become permanent."[7]

Marshall arrived back in Washington from California early on August 15. As he disembarked from the train he was greeted by a couple of reporters. The news of his letter to Rozelle was out, but Marshall had nothing to add to what was printed in the newspapers.

"The commissioner's statement speaks for itself," was all he told writers.[8]

Other than that comment, Marshall offered nothing except a slight chuckle, elicited when one reporter suggested that he had lost the battle to Udall.

Following two seasons and a dismal cumulative record of 4-18-2, Mike Nixon had been sacked as the Redskins' coach at the conclusion of the 1960 campaign.

But that was then. Today was a new day, and Nixon's replacement, Bill McPeak, was bringing his own thoughts and ideas to the team.

A former defensive end with the Steelers, McPeak had served on Nixon's staff during the previous season. The newest in the seemingly neve-rending line of Redskins coaches was working without a written contract. McPeak had taken the position without even a handshake deal with Marshall in place. McPeak and Marshall simply had a gentleman's agreement.

At the beginning of the Redskins' three-week training camp at Occidental College, Lewis Atchison reported that there were marked changes in even the most routine activities.

"McPeak has dotted every *i* and crossed every *t* in his preparation to squeeze the most out of these three weeks," Atchison reported. "Nothing has been left to chance from a planning viewpoint."

Even the most rudimentary practice of running onto the field was altered. No longer would players venture out in groups of twos and threes. Rather, the entire squad would hit the field at the same time. McPeak's first adjustment to the team's daily training schedule was the elimination of early-morning classroom sessions. He then instituted increased study of the on-field tutorials.

"I want to give the time we used to spend in morning meetings to the boys for their personal chores," McPeak explained to the press. "They can write letters, get their hair cut, or whatever they have to do. We may have a meeting with one or two of them like the quarterbacks or a lineman who isn't up on his assignments, but not the entire squad. Going to meetings got to be drudgery and sometimes defeats the purpose."[9]

"The minute you meet this boy you are impressed by his determination and his courage. You know he is going somewhere," Marshall said, speaking of new coach Bill McPeak.

Haven't we been down this road before? Intrepid reporters questioned Marshal about the coaching turnover with the Redskins.

"To make a mistake and pick the wrong man is one thing," Marshall said. "To keep him is compounding the stupidity. I take pride in only one fact, I have never let go a genius, proof of which is that no guy who has ever left me has gone on to conquer the world.

"Actually, all of them have gone from me to obscurity, with the possible exception of Joe Kuharich, who is doing a fair job at Notre Dame."

Kuharich's exit from the Redskins hadn't exactly been free of turmoil. At one point during Kuharich's tenure the then Redskins coach was contacted by the University of Washington and offered the job as the head coach of the Huskies. When Marshall learned of this infiltration he threatened to take the State of Washington to court.

"In professional football we honor a document called a legal contract," Marshall righteously declared. "Our educational leaders will have to learn that people bound to such documents can't be tampered with."

Eventually Kuharich left the Redskins to coach at his alma mater, Notre Dame. On this occasion Marshall allowed Kuharich to leave with nary a quibble.

"I didn't want the Catholics to get mad at me. I've got enough enemies," Marshall explained.

"Every one of my coaches has gone peacefully with the exception of Curly Lambeau, who was my biggest mistake. He and I parted amid a loud and raucous scene in a Sacramento hotel lobby.

"It started when I discovered that some of our players were boozing on the third floor. I went down to tell Lambeau, 'We've got a drinking party upstairs.'

"He responded by telling me off. Then I told him off—and I had the last word."[10]

The Redskins were set to meet the Rams on August 11 for their annual exhibition game sponsored by the *Los Angeles Times*.

With Marshall's hiring policies headline fodder across the country, what had been just a handful of pickets for the last couple of summers had now blossomed into a well-organized protest for this meeting. Local civil rights groups called for a boycott of the game. The focus of the protest wasn't solely on the preseason contest, however. Unlike the modest campaigns from the past summer, the sponsor of the game also drew the ire of protesters. The *Los Angeles Times'* yearly support of the contest was a point of contention among activists. The game itself wasn't the only issue the demonstrators had with the *Times*. The newspaper had a poor reputation for hiring minorities. The minimal number of black persons hired usually filled only the most menial jobs at the newspaper.

More than 150 men and women, black and white, marched outside the Los Angeles Coliseum prior to the exhibition contest. Many carried signs denouncing George Marshall, the Redskins, and also the *Los Angeles Times*. Inside the coliseum boos drowned out the musical tribute played for the Washington Redskins and George Marshall. As it turned out, the game was little more than an afterthought. Marshall gave no consideration to the protesters outside the stadium. Pickets meant nothing to him. Not only did he not care what they believed or what their silly signs read, they did not affect his bottom line. The contract Marshall had signed with the *Los Angeles Times* allowed the Redskins a guaranteed $30,000 regardless of attendance.

In his *Los Angeles Herald* column Mel Durslag addressed the controversy. The *Herald* reporter, having apparently forgotten that the annual Rams versus Redskins exhibition had been met by civil rights picketers in previous years, bemoaned that "an evening whose purpose was fun" had been sullied by a picket, "the first of its kind for a major sporting event here."

"Marshall's a man in his 60s, has money, a keen intellect and a distinct awareness that second-class citizenship in this country is outmoded," Durslag wrote in his weak-penned, and obviously biased, defense of Marshall's independence. "Marshall, to start with, is no bigot, as an acquaintance of his suggests. He's a peculiar individualist who will not be told how to run his business."[11]

12

"We Mean Business"

In the weeks prior to the exhibition game in Los Angeles there had been speculation circulating around Washington, as well as NFL circles, that George Marshall was more than ready to unburden himself of his beloved Redskins. Secretary of the Interior Stewart Udall's demands certainly played a considerable part in the gossip. Surely Marshall would not permit himself to stick around to witness the secretary's petulant demands being met.

Interest in purchasing the club was considerable. On his desk Marshall had an abundant number of offers to buy the team should he wish to sell. But he would have none of this talk of selling. The Redskins were his team, and he wasn't going anywhere.

"What would I do without football? Marshall asked. "I wouldn't know what to do with myself."[1]

George Preston Marshall and his Washington Redskins were entering a new season with a rookie head coach and a very youthful roster. Not surprisingly the consensus among football prognosticators was that the Redskins would finish last in the East (the East Division is what it was referred to at the time, as the American and National Football Conferences did not come about until the merger with the AFL). These predictions, educated though they may have been, fell on deaf ears at the Redskins camp. Understandably such forecasts had Washington as a two-touchdown underdog going into their inaugural contest against the 49ers in San Francisco.

Before the season's opening kickoff patrons of Kezar Stadium were met outside the park by protesters representing the Congress on Racial Equality (CORE).

Another game, another picket. CORE's protest had no effect on Marshall.

Just prior to the contest Marshall spoke with Curley Grieve of the *San Francisco Examiner*.

Referring to Washington's new sports complex, Marshall said, "This is the apex of my whole sports career. It's the biggest milestone of my life. It is a tremendous thing to get this most beautiful stadium in the world for Washington."

"Not a single bench in the park," Marshall bragged, "even arm chairs in the bleachers. Not a post to obstruct the view. Sixty percent of the seats are under cover. Parking for 12,000 . . . It will be the last word," he said. "I've never felt so exhilarated about anything."[2]

Grieve asked Marshall if he had any concerns about the proposed protests outside the stadium by members of CORE and the NAACP.

Ever truculent, Marshall responded, "Yes, tell them if they do as well as they did in Los Angeles, we ought to sell out Kezar."[3]

The new stadium had an enclosed press box; that sportswriters would be provided protection from the elements mattered not a bit to Marshall.

"It's like watching a game on television with the sound turned off. It takes a lot out of the game. I like to hear the crowd. Without it you miss half the enjoyment of the game," the Redskins owner said to the *Star*'s Lewis Atchison.[4]

The Redskins began their season with a 35–3 shellacking at the hands of the 49ers, followed by a week-two loss to the Eagles at Franklin Field. Despite the 0-2 start to the season, Marshall's optimism would not be stifled.

"Discouraged?" Marshall responded to a reporter's inquiry. "Hell no! Why should I be?"[5]

Marshall may have waved off the humiliation of the Redskins' opening losses because he was looking ahead to the first game at his gleaming new stadium.

At the Touchdown Club's annual Welcome Home reception Bill McPeak told attendees, "This is a young team and [the city] is going to be proud of it before the season is over."

After the Redskins' new head coach spoke to the group Marshall stepped to the podium and thanked all in attendance.

"This is my day of gratitude," Marshall acknowledged. "I might even forget, or forgive Harry Wismer. But at least he's gone and that's a blessing."[6]

Marshall had plans—big plans.

He had long been at the forefront of the showbiz aspect of professional football. Indeed Marshall, more than any other figure, had developed and nurtured the entertainment element of the National Football League. But with the construction of a new, modern stadium Marshall was taking things up a notch. No longer would the theatrical portion of a Sunday afternoon be confined to pregame activities and halftime. Inside the shiny new building Redskins fans would be seeing even more marching and hearing more brass horns than ever before.

Ten days before the opening of DC Stadium Marshall decided to alter his routine. Instead of summoning only the city's sportswriters to his office for lunch and a chat Marshall changed things up and invited several drama and entertainment critics to the Redskins' offices for one of his notorious monologues. Football wasn't the subject of the day this afternoon. Instead Marshall wanted to emphasize his plans for more color, more marching, and more music.

"This time-out show, or shows," Marshall explained, "is going to demand precision of a caliber you don't find in show business, except at its very best. We're going to be largely musical this year, you see, with a one-hundred-thirty member band and a singing chorus of seventy-five, and one or both groups will work to the split second for one minute and one half of each two minute timeout."[7]

Marshall looked sharp for the Redskins' home opener against the New York Giants. Over a sport shirt he wore his monogrammed Redskins blazer bearing the familiar GPM initials. On the mezzanine of the stadium the owner's box was filled with a variety of VIP guests. Commissioner Rozelle was on hand, as was Happy Chandler, the former baseball commissioner and governor of Kentucky. Also seated with Marshall were his minority partners in the Redskins, Bill Shea and Jack Kent Cooke.

Marshall and his guests watched the game in style and comfort while seated in plush red velvet theater chairs. A folding door closed off the owner's box, sealing its occupants off from the riffraff. Refreshments for the privileged were available in a cooler located in the back of the box.

Although not unexpectedly, one person was notably missing from the festivities: Secretary Udall. He had vowed to honor any pickets, and there indeed were dueling demonstrations marching outside the stadium, each group politicking to push its particular point of view. Early in the morning a number of protesters gathered and began parading in front of five of the park's seven entrances. The group of 150 comprised children as well as adults, both black and white, many of them carrying signs emblazoned with the now familiar slogans decrying Marshall and the Redskins' hiring practices.

"We Carry the Rifle," one of the placards read, with the follow-up query, "Why Can't We Carry the Ball?"

The majority of the marchers were members of the NAACP and the Congress for Racial Equality, but there was another, much smaller group in attendance showing support for Marshall. Several members of George Lincoln Rockwell's American Nazi Party were joined by six men representing the Fighting American Nationalists.

"Keep the Redskins White!" read one of the organization's placards.

Rockwell's Nazi counterprotest was surrounded by several police officers as the demonstrators occupied a knoll above the stadium's main entrance.

Like all previous demonstrations directed at Marshall personally, the proceedings outside the ballpark had no effect on him. He had never been intimidated by civil rights organizations, and Marshall was beyond being embarrassed by the endorsement of hate groups. Nothing was going to soil this day, this special afternoon that he had worked so hard to see come to fruition.

There were 36,767 fans present to witness the Redskins jump out to a 21–7 first-quarter lead behind rookie signal caller Norm Snead. Unfortunately the visiting Giants, directed by thirty-five-year-old quarterback Y. A. Tittle, stormed back to win the game 24–21.

"No excuses. No alibis," Bill McPeak said afterward. "We had the game in our hip pocket and blew it."[8]

Although it was difficult to discern from reading the *Post*'s sports page, Udall's concerns were more wide-ranging and more important than the roster of a professional football team. Four days after the Redskins fell to the Giants Udall presided over a regularly scheduled meeting with the press. Since the previous March these get-togethers had garnered more attention than a typical Interior presser would. Although Udall did not regret issuing his ultimatum to Marshall, the secretary was frustrated that the many matters his department focused on could not gather a fraction of the attention that his showdown with Marshall did.

One way to grab the attention of a roomful of male journalists was to introduce a parade of attractive young women.

To begin the news conference, seven young women came out in front of Udall. The models, all employees of the Interior Department, were wearing coats fashioned from sealskin obtained from the annual harvest of seals on Alaska's Pribilof Islands.

Having captured the attention of the occasionally staid corps of writers covering Interior, Udall began laying out his agenda. If George Preston Marshall and the Washington Redskins were on his mind, Udall gave no hint. The issues before his department were wide-ranging, from controlling the Alaskan seal population, to reviving the Military Advisory Board on Oil, to expanding the country's parks system.

"If this nation would earmark a sum equal to one percent of the $20 billion it spends each year on horse race betting, liquor, tobacco, and cosmetics, it could win its race for green space in one barrage," Udall informed the gathered press.[9]

This press conference was a pretty good one considering it was the Interior Department holding it. One scribe even rated it the very best of the Kennedy administration to date, comparing it to one held during the spring when the press was served rolls and coffee while Udall discussed parks, transmission lines, and water salinity. This most recent conference was indeed good stuff, important stuff, and those sealskin coats were certainly eye-catching, but what about George Marshall?

The Q and A predictably began with a question about Udall's adversary.

"Mr. Secretary, what floor are we in, between you and the Redskins?"

A perplexed Udall tersely responded, "What?"

The reporter tried again. "What floor are we in between you and the Redskins—what is the status between you and George Marshall?"

"We are in status quo as far as the arrangement I made in August," Udall explained, adamantly denying that he had backed down from his March ultimatum. "I accept his statement in good faith. I hope a satisfactory solution has been engineered. We never did want him to hire some Negro as token integration—put him on the bench and play him a couple of minutes a game."

Udall added that he would "respect" the NAACP's picket line. "They feel aggrieved and they will be aggrieved until he [Marshall] has Negro players."[10]

The week following the Redskins' home opener the team fell to the Browns in Cleveland, 31–7. After the lopsided loss McPeak revealed to reporters that a friend had sent him a bottle of fine Champagne to celebrate his yet-to-come first victory as the coach of the Redskins.

"One thing [is] sure," a humble McPeak told reporters. "It'll be well aged."[11]

The shellacking at the hands of Paul Brown's Cleveland squad was followed by a 20–0 loss to Pittsburgh, leaving the Redskins at 0-5.

On October 18 Lewis Atchison of the *Star* broke a story that asserted Marshall was negotiating with the Cleveland Browns to acquire the services of Bobby Mitchell.

Mitchell was a spectacularly talented halfback who unfortunately was stuck behind Jim Brown on Cleveland's depth chart. The Browns' legendary coach, Paul Brown, looked for any weather variant as an excuse not to utilize Mitchell.

Too much rain?

"The field is too slick for Bobby." Or the field was too muddy. After all, "Mitchell needed a fast track to flourish."

A frozen surface?

"Mitchell needs firm footing," Brown insisted.

Mitchell suffered silently as his talents were squandered under Brown's leadership. That's not to say he didn't thrive when given the opportunity. Mitchell had a canny knack for shining when performing against the Redskins. In the most recent meeting between Washington and Cleveland, on October 8, Mitchell had scored three touchdowns on runs of 52, 64, and 31 yards.

Bobby Mitchell and the Redskins were seemingly a good fit. Marshall would honor his word to Rozelle to desegregate his team while also adding a very good football player to his club's roster. However, Marshall and Paul

Brown were not exactly bosom buddies. In fact Brown couldn't stand Marshall and all his pomposity. That he and Brown did not get along didn't prevent Marshall from trying to swing a deal with the Cleveland coach, however. Marshall wanted Mitchell, who ironically was in the U.S. Army reserves and serving at Fort Meade, a military instillation located just twenty-three miles from the nation's capital. Marshall couldn't help but use that coincidence to tweak Brown in the telegram he sent offering a trade.

In his wire to the Browns coach Marshall wrote, "Knowing your great interest in having your players paid while they are in the service, the Redskins offer you their No. 2 pick in the 1961–62 selection meeting for the rights to half back Bobby Mitchell. The Redskins will assume the responsibility of Mitchell being able to obtain his commanding officer's permission to play in the remaining 1961 National Football League games. Since we are last in the league standings, this deal can be made by your simply asking waivers on Mitchell and us claiming him."[12]

The deadline for nonwaiver trading transactions ended following the third game of the season. However, a deal could still be consummated if a player passed through waivers. For the nominal fee of $100 the Redskins, with the league's worst record, had first claim on any player placed on waivers.

Paul Brown was widely considered the most innovative coach in pro football annuals; he was also one of the most accomplished. Brown came to Cleveland via Ohio State University and Massillon High School, and at each stop he won championships. He was a taskmaster and a perfectionist; he was obsessive when it came to game preparation. What Brown had no truck for were people he considered "nonfootball" men, and George Marshall was not a football man, certainly not by Paul Brown's measure. In Brown's mind Marshall was a bellicose showman, a huckster, and a boor. While other team executives shrugged off Marshall's eccentricities as "that's just George," Brown was revolted by some of his antics. Brown was a stickler for being on time for appointments, as well as a bit of a prude. At one league meeting in Florida eleven team executives waited for a tardy Marshall so that they could begin their proceedings. When Marshall arrived, nearly an hour late, he was informed that he would be fined $500 for his tardiness.

Marshall shrugged off the castigation. "Well she was worth every penny."[13]

The enmity could be traced back to 1950, the first season Cleveland played in the NFL. During the week leading up to a late-season Browns-Redskins matchup, Marshall attempted to activate an assistant coach, Tommy Mont, to back up his only healthy quarterback, Harry Gilmer. Paul Brown protested and did not allow Marshall's personnel move to stand.

And George Marshall had a long memory.

More recently the two men had had a run-in over a rather routine roster designation, and a very similar scene had played out early in the 1961 season. Prior to their October 8 contest Cleveland head coach Paul Brown tried to obtain permission from the league to use Dick Schafrath when the Browns went up against Washington. At the time Schafrath was in the U.S. Air Force reserves. A "gentleman's agreement" usually covered such circumstances, but in this instance Marshall blocked the request.

"All George has done is prevent a boy in the service from getting a payday of several hundred dollars," Brown said in reaction to the news.[14]

Marshall responded to Brown's criticism with a terse comment.

"The reason we put in the rule in the first place was to avoid the label of being a weekend football league during the war."

He then went on to explain that the commissioner's second survey on the subject presented a different question than the original poll and carried a rider to bring up the matter at the league's annual meeting.

"And there he [Brown] sits, and here I sit," Marshall said, while sizing up the stalemate.[15]

Upon receiving Marshall's message Brown immediately denied that a trade was in the works. Through Harold Sauerbrei, the Browns' business manager, Brown released a statement to the press.

"As of now, the deal is definitely not being considered. . . . I have a feeling Mr. Marshall is trying to project me into his racial problems. This is unfair to the player who still has some games to play for us."[16]

Marshall responded to Brown's critique of his trade proposal with characteristic candor: "[It is] pretty unfair to Mitchell to say that I only want him because he is a Negro."

The offer for Mitchell, Marshall added, wasn't "phony," and he lambasted Paul Brown for not responding to the offer "like a man."

"Mr. Brown has been projecting himself into racial problems for a good many years and should be an expert on that subject.

"In this case, however, we are not interested in settling the Negro problem. We are interested in winning a football game. Mitchell's color has nothing to do with our offer. We think it is a fair one both to the player and to our team or we wouldn't have made it."

Marshall ensured that his telegram to Brown was made public by slipping a copy of the text to Lew Atchison. He also wanted to make it known to the *Star* reporter that Commissioner Rozelle had given his approval on the proposed deal.

Marshall added that if his bid to obtain Mitchell failed he wouldn't necessarily draft a Negro at the league's December meeting just to have a Negro on the Redskins.

"I made no commitment to Udall," Marshall responded. "I only told Rozelle I would draft a good Negro player if I could get one."[17]

The following day Shirley Povich devoted his column to dissecting Marshall's motive in making such a trade proposal. The *Post*'s columnist pointed out that Marshall had placed himself in a no-lose position. If Brown accepted the offer, the Redskins would acquire a great player at a very good price. If Brown declined, Marshall's color line would remain intact.

"The Redskins' end zone has frequently been integrated by Negro players, but never their lineup," Povich quipped, paraphrasing himself from an earlier column.

"Marshall does have a racial problem," Povich continued. "Not only is Secretary Udall threatening literally to run his team out of their new park unless they integrate, but in their thirteen straight defeats his Redskins have been beset by very pushy Negroes on other teams on the other clubs, perhaps in the awareness of what has been Marshall's aversion to living color on his own team."[18]

"The Washington Redskins keep losing ballgames," began an October 27 letter to the editor printed in the *Evening Star*.

> The NAACP keeps informing management the reason they don't win is because there isn't a Negro on the club.
>
> Perhaps the NAACP, America's number one policy framer in all matters, could set us straight on why the Washington Senators baseball team made such a poor showing during the past season. There are several Negroes on that team.
>
> The NAACP, Commissioner Torbiner, and Secretary Udall threatened to boycott the Redskins until Marshall signs a Negro player. I wonder if Torbiner and Udall would support the Skins if the team were integrated or would they demand free passes and transportations for their honorable presence at the stadium.[19]
>
> Nick Showers

As the season wore on, things were getting no better for Marshall's club on the field.

The St. Louis Cardinals visited Washington on October 22. When the Cardinal Prentice Gautt crossed the goal line to give St. Louis a 17–0 lead, a fan was overheard to say, "I wonder what George Marshall's doing now?"

A man sitting nearby replied. "He's up there," he said, pointing to Marshall's private box, "counting your money."[20]

A 24–0 shutout loss to the Cardinals was followed up the next week with the Redskins' most competitive game since the opening of the new stadium. McPeak's charges scored their first touchdown in three weeks when they faced the Eagles at home on October 29. The Redskins even threatened to win their first game of the season, as they led 24–20 with forty seconds remaining in the contest. Washington's record remained unblemished by victory when Sonny Jurgensen quickly took the Eagles down the field in a drive that culminated with a 41-yard touchdown pass to Tommy McDonald. The Redskins' winless streak reached seven with the defeat.

"It's been a helluva lesson for a young team," Bill McPeak said to reporters following the game. "It showed them that a game is never over in the National Football League until the final whistle. It was a heartbreaking lesson, but I hope they learned from it."[21]

Ernie Davis of Syracuse University possessed all of the attributes found in the best halfbacks. He ran with power as well as great agility and speed. Many compared Davis to former Syracuse icon Jimmy Brown. The comparison made the shy and soft-spoken Davis appreciative of the compliments, but "guys like Jimmy Brown come along once in a lifetime," Davis said. "I just want to play like Ernie Davis."[22]

He was indisputably the finest talent available in the upcoming draft, and among experts the consensus opinion was that Davis would be the first player selected. As the Redskins' season slipped deep into the month of November the club seemed destined to have the honor of choosing Davis. Washington possessed a 0-9 record when Bill McPeak sent assistant coach Ted Marchibroda on a scouting mission to South Bend, where the Orangemen were scheduled to play Notre Dame. Prior to the November 18 game he asked Syracuse coach Ben Schwartzwalder for permission to speak with the senior halfback.

Following a 17–15 Notre Dame victory in the game Marchibroda was allowed access to Davis. Marchibroda had previously seen Davis and Syracuse play against Penn State and Maryland, but he had not yet spoken with the Heisman hopeful. Although the rules prohibited Marchibroda from making any contractual proposals to the collegiate star, he was permitted to "say hello" and spend a few moments with Davis. The encounter was brief, but Marchibroda came away deeply impressed with the young man. His skills on the gridiron were obvious, but Davis possessed intelligence that went beyond the playing field. Yes, he was certainly the finest prospect in college football, but Davis was also black—a fact that wouldn't affect his draft status with thirteen NFL teams. It was the fourteenth franchise, however, that evaluated players by a different standard.

"Ernie has everything," Marchibroda reported. "He has all the attributes to be a top pro."[23]

In the midst of the trade and draft conjecture and despite a terrible season on the field by his football club, Marshall found time to pen an article for the *Saturday Evening Post*. The piece, titled "Pro Football Is Better Football," appeared in the December 12 issue of the magazine.

Yes, Marshall argued via his ghostwriter Mel Durslag, pro football, the NFL in particular, was on the cusp of becoming the country's most popular sport.

Baseball?

Recently Marshall had witnessed relief pitchers riding from the bullpen to the mound in a golf cart.

"If a sport desperate for a speed up and gasping for pep becomes dependent upon gasoline power, it is no challenge to football," Marshall stated.

As for bowling, which many experts placed as the number-one participant sport in the United States, Marshall was predictably dismissive, though he reasoned the game could be brought into question.

"Bowling is a stupid game in which the participants wear the shabbiest clothing in sports.

"Showmanship was a big factor in causing the turnstiles to click a pleasant profit for us last year, and in convincing our Washington sports public that football is our national game," he noted. "Showmanship, the showmanship of Sammy Baugh on the gridiron and the showmanship of management in offering the Sunday afternoon crowds plenty of added attractions made Washingtonians feel that the Redskins are 'their team.' And I believe that the professional showman's touch could not only be added to baseball teams mostly colorless with profit, but to college football teams as well, with more pleasure and profit, too, for everybody."[24]

In early November the Philadelphia Eagles turned down the opportunity to play the 'Skins in the fall of 1962 at Norfolk's Kiwanis Bowl. The Eagles cited the segregated seating as the club's reason for turning down the offer.

Changing times, evolving viewpoints—these things meant nothing to Marshall. In typical fashion he shrugged off the rebuff, saying, "Well we'll get the Chicago Bears. I think they'll draw more people."

A reporter asked Marshall if the Bears might resist for the same reason as

Philadelphia. "They'll play," Marshall said with confidence. "George Halas is not running for office."[25]

Months before the Dallas expansion franchise took the field for the first time, Clint Murchison, so as not to confuse his outfit with the city's minor league baseball team, opted to change the name of his Rangers team. After some deliberation Murchison settled on the perfectly fitting name of "Cowboys."

Several days before the Redskins traveled to Texas for their November 19 game against the Cowboys, Marshall spoke with Dallas reporters via speaker phone.

"The Redskins have been in the NFL for thirty years and we're a flop," Marshall told the gathered journalists. "Dallas is successful this year in my book. But we're drawing more people and more money than you are."

Marshall couldn't deny the futility of the Redskins' 0-9 start to the season.

"Our youth movement is doing about as well as Kennedy's Peace Corps," Marshall quipped.

Would Marshall be present that Sunday at the Cotton Bowl?

No, he replied, because the trip via train was too long, and he wasn't about to set foot on an airplane. He would be viewing the game on television from the comfort of his home.

Besides, Marshall added, "I'm plugged into the bench. I can call the coach from my living room and tell him what to do. Sometimes the coach doesn't do it, and that's how we lose."[26]

Without doubt the 1961 Redskins were bad, all kinds of bad. Following a 28–28 stalemate with the Cowboys, the Redskins' 27–6 loss to the Colts in the eleventh week of the season assured the Redskins the first overall selection in the draft. The day after the game in Dallas Marshall greeted a group of writers invited to his weekly luncheon.

"Well, we won the booby prize," Marshall said upon entering the room. "We get the first pick. We're sure of it now."[27]

The topic of the college draft was on the minds of every writer present at Marshall's Tuesday luncheon for the press.

Someone casually asked Bill McPeak if the team was interested in drafting Ernie Davis.

Marshall interrupted before his coach could reply. Lest anyone present forget who the boss was, Marshall would remind the room.

"That question should be directed to me because I'm responsible for this team," he said. "But I will defer to the coach. He may make the deal or he may not. It's up to him. Naturally, as owner, I would insist upon being consulted before any final decision is made."

Marshall was asked if it was likely the Redskins would select a Negro in the draft despite the club having traded away their fifth and sixth picks.

"If we take a Negro, it will be because we think he's the best pick," Marshall replied. "It won't be because a player is a Negro."[28]

McPeak interjected that he might exchange the selection for a couple of proven players. "I've got my ears open," he said. "We'll entertain offers."

But the coach wouldn't deny that Davis was a very talented young man who excelled at a position where the team was deficient.

"Teams have no respect for our running game and defense us accordingly. . . . We have to get Davis or a back of similar ability."[29]

During the luncheon McPeak fielded a phone call from Steelers head coach Raymond "Buddy" Parker. Pittsburgh was interested in dealing for the Redskins' pick, and they weren't alone. Eight different clubs had reached out to McPeak.

Lewis Atchison pointed out that Harry Wismer had hinted that he just might take Ernie Davis with the New York Titans' first pick in the AFL's draft. If Wismer followed through, Atchison continued, he might induce Davis to join the new league. A healthy financial offer coupled with the reminder that the Redskins had a well-established history of never employing a Negro—well, the Heisman Trophy winner just might be hesitant to play in Washington.

Marshall dismissed Atchison's hypothetical scenario. "If he signs with Wismer, he's not the kind of player we want," Marshall flatly stated.[30]

The Department of the Interior called a press conference on November 30, four days before the NFL's collegiate draft. Normally these events were sparsely attended by members of the press, but on this afternoon the room was packed with reporters eager to question the secretary of the interior. The journalists were primarily interested in George Marshall and the Redskins. It was a subject that had begun to wear on Stewart Udall, and this annoyance was evident in his demeanor as the press conference began.

"I don't think there is any thought other than that the draft is a showdown," a stern-faced Udall said. "We have been proceeding on the basis that Mr. Marshall's representations of some time ago were made in good faith. We mean business and believe he knows we mean business."[31]

The first query centered on a recent interview during which Marshall claimed that he made no pledge to Udall. All he had committed to, Marshall maintained, was to promise the commissioner that he would sign a "good Negro," but only "if he could find one."

"Well through no fault of mine, he has the first choice in the draft," the secretary said as the room erupted in laughter, "and it has been customary I think . . . the Heisman winner is usually pretty close to the top."

"I am no football expert," Udall continued. "Unfortunately, I haven't been able to go to many games locally this year."

"How many games have you been to this year?" a writer called out.

"I attended one of the Baltimore Colts' games in Baltimore," Udall replied.

The questions continued, all of which centered on the Marshall controversy.

What if Marshall drafted one or more Negro players but failed to sign them?

"If, if, if," Udall replied, brushing aside conjectural questions.

Why is George Washington University permitted to play in DC Stadium when the school fields no Negro players?

"They're not professional," Udall replied.

A reporter chimed in, "What difference does that make?"

Before Udall could respond, Orren Beaty, assistant to the secretary, stepped forward.

"Employment practices are the issue," Beaty said. "Colleges do not employ players. The pros do."[32]

Of course it would go against Marshall's nature to remain silent, especially when the term "showdown" was used in connection with him. His reply to

Udall's press conference came through Dick McCann, who delivered Marshall's statement.

"I have nothing to say to what the Secretary of the Interior says. He doesn't work for me. He works for the President."

One thing was for certain, Marshall emphasized. "Mr. Udall will not be drafting for the Redskins."[33]

13

"I'm Still Running This Team"

At 10:10 a.m. on Tuesday, December 4, Pete Rozelle called the college draft meeting to order.

Spread throughout the Chicago Sheraton's Grand Ballroom were green-draped tables, each equipped with a private telephone and stacks of note-books filled with individual team scouting reports. Marshall was not on the premises, but he was hooked into the proceedings via telephone and receiving information from Bill McPeak, who was ready with the Redskins' selection. Before things got going, however, the Redskins coach had a request.

"Got any blanks this year," he asked the commissioner, "or are we using these little white pads?"[1]

At 10:12, satisfied about which form he should use to list the Redskins' selection and the player's school, McPeak made the announcement.

"Washington selects Ernie Davis, halfback, Syracuse University."

All the debate, arguments, and guessing games over the past nine months now had a resolution.

Or did they?

Almost immediately speculation ran rampant throughout the ballroom that the Redskins were trading Davis to the Browns, most likely for their first choice, receiver Gary Collins. These rumors were shot down by officials of both Washington and Cleveland, but such gossip fueled the industry.

"We drafted Collins because we want a good pass receiver," Paul Brown explained. "We have no intention of trading him."

Brown would neither deny that Bobby Mitchell was part of a transaction that would jettison the back and send him to the Redskins nor would the coach confirm any such deal.

"Mitchell is scheduled to be in the army until the middle of October and that means we can't count on him," Brown said. "It might be to his advantage to be traded seeing he is stationed so close to Washington."[2]

"We picked Ernie Davis number one," McPeak told Jack Walsh of the *Post*. "That's the story. We're not responsible for wild speculation obviously. We like Davis. I have high hopes we will sign him."[3]

A member of the local press pushed Marshall for clarity. Would the Redskins be able to sign Davis?

"I think it's no problem," Marshall stiffly replied.

The reporter pressed further. Had a deal been made to send Davis to Cleveland?

"I wouldn't say so," Marshall answered.

At a late hour the evening before the draft Baltimore Colts owner Carroll Rosenbloom complained on the record to reporters that the Redskins had already made a trade with Cleveland for Ernie Davis.

"I should think the repercussions in Washington would be considered when the Redskins trade Davis to a team in its own division," Rosenbloom said. "I'd bet anything I have, the deal is done."[4]

Two days after he became the first pick in the National Football League's college draft, Ernie Davis was in New York to receive the Heisman Trophy. Davis was peppered with the same questions that he'd been inundated with throughout the previous week. The queries varied little, though each succeeding reporter found a slightly different way to ask the Heisman winner, "Who are you going to sign with?"

"I'm going where I get the best deal," Davis said. "I want good money, sure, but I also want happiness and a guarantee of a future. I want to be able to do something constructive in the off-season so ten or fifteen years from now I can step out of pro football and into business."

"What do you think about being the first Negro on the Redskins?" Davis was asked.

"I wish they would quit bringing up this racial stuff," Davis was quoted as saying by an Associated Press reporter. "I don't want to be another Jackie Robinson. I just want to play football and I'll go where I can get the best offer."[5]

Mo Siegel of the *Washington Daily News* was one of the many reporters present in New York. He had time for one question. Predictably Mo had to ask the Heisman winner about his potential employer.

"What have you heard about George Marshall?"

"I have heard many things," Davis replied. "I hear Mr. Marshall is quite a business man and is out to make the best deal possible for himself. That's the way I feel about it, too. I have also read that he is prejudiced. Frankly I'm not interested."[6]

Davis was at the Downtown Athletic Club in the midst of a media session for newsreel and still photographers when word came that President Kennedy was in the city and wanted to meet him. Davis and a small entourage, which included the Syracuse University publicist and a couple of athletic club officials, grabbed a cab and headed for the Carlyle Hotel, where Kennedy was staying. The party was delayed by security as they approached the hotel. By the time they received consent to proceed the president was in a limousine leaving the Carlyle.

Back to the athletic club Davis went. He was just about to take a bite of roast chicken when another call came. President Kennedy was at the Waldorf Astoria and still wanted to meet Davis. The same scene played out again. Into a taxi the group went, though on this occasion Davis and company made it past security before the president was gone.

The introductions were made in the West Foyer of the Waldorf.

"What are your future plans, Ernie?" Kennedy asked as he shook Davis's hand.

"I play at the Liberty Bowl at Philadelphia, December 16. After that, I haven't made up my mind."[7]

Sometimes even the president of the United States couldn't get a straight answer.

"I missed my lunch, but it doesn't matter," Davis said with a hint of wonder in his voice. "Imagine a President wanting to shake hands with me."[8]

Davis remained noncommittal, but the Redskins were expecting a group of draftees to come to town for the weekend. The hope was to get the prospects under contract before the other league started throwing money at the young men. While the selection of Ernie Davis dominated the news cycle, there was another story flying under the radar: the Redskins' eighth-round selection, Ron Hatcher of Michigan State.

Hatcher was a six-foot, 215-pound halfback from Carnegie, Pennsylvania. Mild-mannered and articulate, Hatcher was married and the father of a four-month-old son. He was also black. He expected to be drafted, but the thought of being selected by the Washington Redskins had never crossed Hatcher's mind. He knew the reputation of the organization; most black athletes were aware of George Marshall's prejudice, and when the Michigan State athletic director called to inform Hatcher that he had been selected by Washington, Hatcher was surprised.

He knew of Marshall's reputation, but Hatcher's ambition was to play professional football. The AFL's New York Titans had also picked him, but Hatcher first wanted to hear what the Redskins would put on the table. Hatcher flew to Washington on December 8 for a noon meeting the following day at the Redskins' office. The negotiations were completed in under an hour—less time than Hatcher had spent waiting for the arrival of Bill McPeak, who was late returning from a midwestern scouting trip.

The talks were indeed brief as Hatcher quickly came to terms with McPeak. A minimum salary and a modest $1,000 bonus, and the Washington Redskins had signed their first black player. A half dozen members of the media were shuffled into the head coach's office for the contract signing.

The reporters then began peppering Hatcher with questions.

Jack Walsh of the *Post* began by pointing out that Hatcher looked unruffled by all the hype.

"Maybe I don't show it," he replied with a broad smile. "This is my first trip to Washington and the first time I've seen the Capitol. I was thrilled but everything looked so familiar, I felt as if I'd been here before."[9]

The elephant in the room, so to speak, wasn't in McPeak's office at all. Conspicuous by his absence was George Preston Marshall, who remained a floor away from the proceedings. Marshall did take a few moments to meet with his team's eighth-round pick. He spoke with Hatcher, but Marshall would not shake the young man's hand.

"I was impressed with him," Hatcher said in response to a question about the encounter. "He told me he'd be happy if I'd consider playing for the Redskins."

Hatcher then paused. For a moment he seemed as if he wished he hadn't spoken so freely.

"That's just my recollection of the conversation," he added. "I don't want to step on anyone's toes. And I don't want to get off on the wrong foot here."

What kind of speed do you have?

"I don't know exactly how fast I am. Fast enough, I guess."

How does it feel coming to the Redskins?

"It's just like signing with any other football team."

What do you think about being the first Negro to sign with the Redskins?

"I'm here to play football," Hatcher quietly responded.[10]

For the better part of nine months George Marshall had been under fire. The federal government had boxed him into a corner, and despite all his defiant rhetoric George Marshall succumbed. What was he thinking at this historic moment? Several reporters made their way back upstairs in the hope of grabbing a few quotes from him. As usual Marshall did not disappoint, though the normally verbose Redskins owner was a little less expansive on this occasion.

"This boy was signed as a player," Marshall said, downplaying the significance of the day. "His name was put on our draft list by Bill McPeak last August as one of the top football players available. He was signed on his football ability and not for racial exploitation. I don't want him handicapped on the Redskins because of his race."[11]

A *Post* photographer requested a shot of Marshall with his newest Redskin.

"Let's keep this at a football level," Marshall said. "You have the coach and the player. We're not seeking any exploitation of this thing."

Exactly how Marshall would be "exploiting" Hatcher by sitting for a photograph with him was unknown and unasked. "George being George" was old hat to the Washington press corps. Marshall's statement was not questioned by the reporters, and the only photograph printed in the next day's newspapers had a smiling Ron Hatcher seated next to Bill McPeak. A second snapshot was taken with Hatcher decked out in an oversized Indian headdress, just the type of "nonexploitive" publicity Marshall sought for his team.

"I had a long talk with the boy," Marshall told reporters. "And I was very much impressed with his intelligence, his size, and general build.

"I explained to him he would be the first Negro in our 25-year history here and told him he had a real responsibility."[12]

In his column the next morning Shirley Povich couldn't resist poking at Marshall's reluctance to "exploit" the situation.

"For Marshall, a promoter all his life, this is a sudden attack of tender concern lest an act of his be viewed as keyed to his own advantage of profit," Povich wrote. "Marshall has exploited laundries, auto races, basketball teams, state fairs, radio-TV, and even the Southern Confederacy, none of them shyly."

Yes, there was a chance that the Redskins would not be able to sign Ernie Davis and might lose the Heisman Trophy winner to the AFL's Buffalo Bills. But if that were to happen, Povich reasoned, it would be for financial reasons and not racial bias.

"No longer are colored players born ineligible for the Redskins," Povich observed. "That is a gain."[13]

In the aftermath of the draft Marshall surprisingly agreed to an interview with Sam Lacy, his most virulent critic in the black press.

Upon Lacy's arrival at the Redskins' headquarters Marshall offered him a chair and extended his hand to the reporter.

"It has been a long time—fifteen, twenty, twenty-five years."

"All of twenty," Lacy replied, "possibly the twenty-five. I couldn't afford to be seen in your company.

"I had no reason to see you before today. You made your policy clear to me the last time we discussed the matter. And since I recognized you as a man of conviction, there was no point in coming here," Lacy said.

"You have shown good faith in drafting three colored athletes and inviting two of them [Ron Hatcher and Joe Hernandez] to come in for contract talks.

"I wish to be an honest reporter, so I plan to show good faith, too. We intend to go along with you until we have reason to suspect that your organization is not acting in good faith."

Marshall then offered, "This is something you can write that hasn't been written before. For years, I was one of this city's largest employers of colored people.

"I was the first laundry operator to use all colored route men. How many do you see on laundry trucks today?

"I was the first to use colored ushers and vendors at Griffith Stadium athletic contests and at one time there were nearly five hundred colored persons employed in this very building when the (Palace) laundry plant was situated here."

"But you must admit there is quite a difference between menial work and a professional job," Lacy said.

"For years," Lacy continued, "colored people have been able to do laboring work and to find employment as washers of clothes and dishes and floors. But like everyone else, the colored man has no desire to make that his ceiling.

"The complaint is that you have shown evidence that you think this which you gave him in the past, is his level."

"This complaint comes from my refusal to exploit the colored athlete," Marshall responded.

"But you have exploited Jim Crow," Lacy shot back. "Exploitation, as I understand it, means to use an individual or an issue in such a way as to derive benefits from it, financial or otherwise. You've been capitalizing on discrimination."

Marshall was hearing none of this argument.

"Photographers want me to pose for a picture with Hatcher," he told the *Baltimore Afro-American* reporter. "I won't do it. I won't do it because I don't intend to exploit the boy.

"Why take pictures with Hatcher when we have scores of rookies to sign Redskins contracts each year. I don't pose with them. Let the boy be a football player like the rest of them. That is what I want him to be."[14]

On December 10 Ron Hatcher was invited, along with several other draft picks, to view that week's game from the Redskins bench. During pregame warm-ups Steelers defensive back Johnny Sample made his way across the playing field. Sample approached Hatcher and stuck out his hand.

"It's about time they got some black players around here," he said.[15]

The Steelers won the contest, 30–14, dragging the Redskins to a 0-12-1 record, but the defeat wasn't the worst degradation of the day for Marshall. A steady Sunday downpour in Washington revealed a number of leaks in the roof of Marshall's $24 million playground. Stadium attendants removed seven buckets full of water from Marshall's private box, and the source of the leaks had to be mended before he and his friends could spend time in the box.

One week later the Redskins closed out their historic and tumultuous season with a home contest against the Cowboys.

The final home game of the year always held special meaning to Marshall. He took as much pride in the annual halftime show, which included the arrival of Santa Claus, as he did in his players on the field. Through the years Santa had arrived at Marshall's yearly Christmas show by nearly every transport imaginable.

Kris Kringle had entered by helicopter, Mississippi steamboat, dogsled, Brink's truck, fire engine, and canoe. Just a couple of years earlier Santa had been scheduled to arrive via parachute. Unfortunately the jolly fat man missed Griffith Stadium altogether and instead landed on top of a house situated beyond the right-field fence. Marshall, however, was prepared for such a mishap. A back-up Santa was at the ready, and the stand-in strolled onto the field from offstage waving heartily to the crowd as he walked to midfield.

On another occasion Marshall had the genius idea of having Santa enter atop an elephant. To hedge his bet Marshall had three elephants on site to transport Santa should a bout of stubbornness overtake any of the trio. As it turned out all three elephants weren't feeling the holiday spirit, and each refused to budge with the red-clad stranger on its back. So the crowd (and Marshall) had to settle on Santa sauntering out with the three obstinate elephants trailing a few steps behind.

What Marshall didn't realize as he watched the Cowboys and Redskins battle during the first half of the game was that a prank had been planned to embarrass him and spoil the appearance of Saint Nick.

Prior to the game two "unidentified Dallas rooters" had surreptitiously made their way to the field. Once there they proceeded to spread chicken feed all over the playing surface. At nearly the same time two bellboys from the Cowboys' hotel arrived at DC Stadium with two large crates covered with tarp. Questioned by security, the bellboys explained that the crates, and the numerous chickens inside the coops, were part of the halftime show. Marshall had put on many an eclectic extravaganza, but chickens? But the two young men, supplied with field badges provided by a Dallas official, passed the security checkpoint, took the crates to the baseball dugout, and left the chickens there.

Dick McCann not only served as the Redskins' general manager but also played the role of producer for the halftime shows. As the clock ticked toward the end of the second quarter McCann made his way from the field and walked through the dugout. The clatter of the birds stopped McCann in his tracks. He walked over and lifted up the tarp covering the coop; beneath the canvas McCann saw dozens of clucking chickens.

"What the hell is this?" he asked a guard who was standing nearby.

With a shrug of his shoulders the guard replied, "Part of the halftime show."[16]

McCann, being in charge of production, knew better.

It was a prank prevented. A catastrophe averted. An embarrassment forestalled.

An inventory of the contraband revealed seventy-five white chickens and a single black chick.

Despite the 34–24 Redskins victory, McCann was furious following the game.

"It was a deliberate attempt to humiliate and degrade the Redskins as an organization and Mr. Marshall personally," McCann huffed. "Did you ever see how much trouble they have catching a small dog who runs across a field? How do you think they would have done trying to run down the scared birds?"[17]

For his part Marshall called the abortive prank "childish and immature." Had it been successful the chickens would have ruined his Santa Claus halftime show. "It costs us thousands of dollars to put that show together," he said, "not to mention the fact that an awful lot of kids were at the stadium more for the halftime show than the game itself."[18]

The star of the show made his annual appearance on a sleigh pulled by a dogsled team of eight huskies that were apparently suffering from malnutrition. When he arrived at midfield Santa disembarked from his ride and began doing the popular dance of the day, the Twist.

Edward Bennett Williams, a noted Washington attorney and friend of Representative Adam Clayton Powell, reached out to that influential New York congressman and asked him to try and persuade Ernie Davis to sign with the Redskins. In recent weeks Powell had become something of a mentor to Davis, and Williams hoped a good word from Powell would be the difference between Davis signing with Washington or going with the rival league.

"I don't know how influential Adam will be with Davis," Williams said, "but it would be a good thing for Davis as well as the Redskins. It would be a beautiful wedding."[19]

All the talk and speculation concerning Ernie Davis's future took another turn when the Associated Press broke a story on the morning of December 14 suggesting that the Browns and Redskins had actually come to an agreement prior to the college draft. It turned out that Marshall wanted Bobby Mitchell wearing the burgundy and gold bad enough to go back to Paul Brown and try once again.

The Redskins did not initially comment on the Associated Press release, choosing to neither confirm nor deny the report. Lew Atchison decided to go directly to Marshall for an answer.

"Nobody's told me anything about it," he told the *Evening Star* reporter. "My name's Marshall and I'm still running this team. Paul Brown hasn't talked to me."[20]

They were a mismatched pair, Marshall and Brown.

Marshall's shenanigans annoyed Brown, who avoided the Redskins owner whenever possible, but the Cleveland coach also coveted Ernie Davis, the prototype for his offensive strategy. Brown didn't believe that Bobby Mitchell, at 6 feet and 190 pounds, could withstand the weekly pummeling a primary back received on a weekly basis in the NFL. Davis was nearly the mirror image physically of Cleveland's best player, Jim Brown. The thought of Jim Brown and Ernie Davis as a one-two punch for the Browns certainly intrigued the Cleveland coach.

With Marshall's reluctant blessing McPeak reached out to Paul Brown a second time.

The offer was unorthodox. With the first choice the Redskins would select any player Cleveland wished. In exchange the Browns would give Washington Bobby Mitchell as well as the third overall pick, which the Browns had obtained in a preseason trade with Dallas. Paul Brown turned down the offer, leading the Redskins to make a similar proposal to the Los Angeles Rams. The Rams, however, had their sights set on quarterback Roman Gabriel, and they also refused the offer.

With time running short McPeak decided to make one more run at the Browns. The proposition was similar to the previous one except this time the Redskins asked for Mitchell and the eighth pick overall, Cleveland's original first-round choice. An agreement was reached, but Paul Brown didn't immediately tell McPeak who he wanted with the first choice, Davis or Gabriel.

Moments after Pete Rozelle pounded the gavel bringing the session to order Brown sent word of his choice: Ernie Davis.

About an hour later the Redskins told the Browns to select Leroy Jackson. Why the subterfuge?

The secrecy obscured the fact that Paul Brown wanted to retain the services of Mitchell for the rest of the season. Cleveland, in fact, still had a game to play against the Giants when news of the trade was leaked. And Mitchell's name wasn't officially in the press release. It simply mentioned a "veteran player from the active 1961 roster to be mutually decided upon on or before February 1, 1962."

The deal would stand even if Davis opted to sign with the AFL.

One day after the Associated Press story was published Marshall changed his mind and wholeheartedly endorsed the deal.

He posed a rhetorical question to Atchison: "Who would you take between a runner like Mitchell and an untested boy like Davis? We know Mitchell is a game breaker. He can go all the way. The other boy must prove himself."[21]

To Jack Walsh of the *Post* Marshall said, "We think we've solved immediate problems confronting us. The coach thinks it's a great deal for the immediate future[.] I'm inclined to agree."[22]

Although born Robert Cornelius Mitchell, to his closest friends he was known as "Neal," and it wasn't until his sophomore season at Illinois that Mitchell became "Bobby."

His birthplace was Hot Springs, Arkansas, a town that drew countless visitors who wished to bathe in the geothermal springs. Despite Mitchell's having been nurtured in a southern town, his memory excused his hometown of racism.

"I don't ever remember sitting on the back of the bus in my town," Mitchell recalled years later. "Twenty miles down the road, I'd get hanged if I sat in the front of the bus. I actually was told to get off the bus in Louisiana. Another place they pulled a curtain in front of us. Some crazy stuff. But my town was unique, a resort area of about forty thousand permanent residents that would swell to half a million at times."[23]

Mitchell came from a family of athletes. His father, a minister in the Church of God, was a standout athlete.

"My father was an all-conference star in football in high school and so were my brothers," Bobby explained. "All my older brothers could outrun me until I got into junior high school."[24]

The warm springwaters found in Mitchell's hometown did draw visitors from all over. The waters had properties that were reputed to treat any number of maladies. Hot Springs was not a typical southern town, and with visitors coming in from all across the country the Jim Crow regulations were not enforced to the same extent as they were in most parts of Dixie.

Before entering high school Bobby Mitchell was a bit of a recluse. He was prone to keep his head down, eyes facing the ground, rather than make contact with someone passing by.

"When I was a kid," Mitchell later explained, "I guess I spent three-quarters of the time by myself. I'd take long walks and if I saw someone I knew, I'd cross the street. I never understood it except sometimes I needed to be alone."

Following a thoughtful pause Mitchell continued. "I guess I used to think that everything and everybody was against me. You know? I mean I was anti-everything and anti-everybody."

Something clicked inside the young Mitchell, though. He stopped hanging with a crowd that could be described as a "bad element." Although he still was not outgoing, Mitchell began to interact more, and he became fully focused on sports as a means to get ahead.

"If somebody was a fast runner, I had to be faster," he explained. "If someone hit a ball far in a game, I had to hit it further."[25]

In high school Mitchell began to excel at baseball, track, and football. His grades also improved, resulting in a scholarship to the University of Illinois.

When he first entered the University of Illinois, Bobby ran the 100 in 9.5 seconds. A nice time certainly, but not quite good enough to be among the elite. The Illinois track coach thought Mitchell should try the hurdles. Bobby didn't jump at the suggestion, so to speak. He never did care for the hurdles, but Mitchell was willing to try whatever would give him a chance to compete.

At one of his first meets Mitchell approached Ohio State's Glenn Davis, the Big 10's best hurdler.

"I'm going to beat you," Mitchell told Davis, who just smiled at his new rival. Mitchell then proceeded to win the race.

The same scene was repeated at four consecutive meets.

"I'm going to beat you," Mitchell promised.

On his fifth attempt Mitchell not only won but also broke a sixteen-year-old world record for the low hurdles. Mitchell's record was broken just six days later by Hayes Jones, but for six days he was a world record holder. Mitchell's ambition was to make the 1956 Olympic team; pro football was not a priority. Also while at college Bobby Mitchell met and later married his sweetheart, Gwen, who was a prelaw student at Illinois.

The prospect of a steady paycheck now took precedence over Olympic dreams.

Bobby Mitchell was in the U.S. Army reserves and stationed at Fort Meade when he learned of his trade to the Redskins in December 1961. Mitchell made the short trip to Washington and paid a visit to the Redskins office, where he met George Marshall for the first time. There the newest Redskin was greeted with three pieces of advice from Marshall.

"Bobby, I'm glad to see you," Marshall said. "I'm going to take you out of the shadow of Jimmy Brown. Put you out front. But, Bobby, we don't have no money."[26]

"Bob, I have three things I want to say to you," Marshall counseled. "First, you must remember you're in a political town and I want you to stay out of politics. Secondly, I just want you to be a good guy. And third, I don't want you to ask for too much money."[27]

Mitchell was pleased with the trade. He could be counted among the growing number of Cleveland players who had become disenchanted with the predictable play calling of Paul Brown. The legendary coach was coming under fire from critics both inside the locker room and out.

"I was elated at the trade," Mitchell admitted later. "Paul Brown knew for two or three years that I wanted out. He waited until he thought he got somebody to take my position. At Cleveland [Brown] called all the plays. When you keep running the same pattern and it doesn't work, after a while maybe you stop running it to the best of your ability."[28]

In late January Sam Lacy caught up with Ernie Davis for a twenty-minute interview in the Washington Sheraton's Continental Room. Davis had already been the first black player to win the Heisman, and just a week earlier he was the first black athlete to be given the Touchdown Club's Walter Camp trophy. Now Ernie was back in the capital to attend the twenty-seventh annual Distinguished Persons Honors event at the Sheraton.

"I have never compared myself to Jackie Robinson," Davis said to begin the conversation.

It seems that Davis was quite bothered by newspaper stories, published a couple of months earlier, in which he was quoted as saying, "I don't want to be another Jackie Robinson."

"There has been a great deal of discussion about this, most of it based on the assumption that I was quoted correctly in the newspaper articles concerning myself and the Washington Redskins.

"I have denied making the statement attributed to me, but for some reason the denial never received the publicity that was given the original story.

"I've never compared myself to Jackie for the simple reason that I think it would be absurd for me to do so.

"Our situations are quite different. Jackie was the pioneer; I'm no more than one of a number of athletes who were fortunate enough to have the way made easier by him.

"You can't imagine how many letters I received from people all over the country, criticizing me for the statement attributed to me. I answered a few of them personally, but with postseason football trips for personal appearances, and school making demands on my time, it was just impossible for me to reply to all the letters.

"Several times in subsequent interviews, I told newspaper reporters that I never said I wanted to be another Jackie Robinson. I thought this would serve to correct the impression, but apparently it wasn't important enough to them to write it."

Davis then responded to a Lacy question. Was he disappointed when he learned that the Redskins had drafted him?

"No . . . I would not be compelled to sign with the Redskins, or any other team if I preferred not to do so.

"And this brings up another point I'd like to clarify. I'd have had no objection to playing with the Redskins. In fact, I like Washington. I think I would have enjoyed playing here.

"If things had not worked out as they did, it would have been purely a matter of money. If the offer made me by Mr. Marshall compared favorably with those I received from other clubs, I would have played here, and I'm sure I would have enjoyed it."[29]

14

"Is That All?"

On January 8, 1962, NFL owners ripped up the three-year contract that they had given Pete Rozelle just two years earlier. In its place Rozelle was given a five-year deal that paid him $50,000 annually. Rozelle, who came by his position as something of an afterthought following twenty-five ballots, had rapidly become the league's indispensable man. The two-year, $9.3 million television contract that was consummated with CBS cemented Rozelle's worth and endeared the commissioner to his employers.

The deal with CBS guaranteed each NFL franchise $332,000 annually. For some teams this figure provided a significant boost from their previous broadcast agreements. The Redskins, despite their network that covered a large swath of the American South, had previously earned only $178,000 from televising games. The Giants, in the nation's largest market, received but $210,000 from their television package. Chicago was at $200,000 and Cleveland, $185,000. The new contract did offer a substantial increase for nearly every team, but there were a couple of outliers. The Steelers would take a small cut from their $355,000 arrangement, and Baltimore would take a substantial loss relative to their prior $445,000 deal.

Persuading the Colts and Steelers to abandon their previous pacts demonstrated Rozelle's value as a leader and visionary. With great foresight the commissioner was able to recognize that if the league members were unified, if they agreed to share television revenue equally, the growth of the National Football League knew no boundaries.

What was perhaps more important was that he was capable of persuading the fourteen disparate team owners to follow his lead and get on board with the deal.

The Cowboys lost an estimated $600,000 after one season of sharing the city of Dallas with the AFL's Texans. The large deficit was startling. No NFL team had produced so much red ink since the conclusion of World War II. Corrective measures needed to be taken, and Marshall believed the first step should be moving the Cowboys into the same division as the Redskins.

In mid-January Marshall found an avenue to present his agenda: Jack Walsh of the *Washington Post*. A complete overhaul of the league's divisional structure needed to be made, Marshall argued.

"Minnesota belongs in the division with the Chicago Bears and Green Bay Packers," Marshall told Walsh. "For the future of the league, the East needs a team with a big stadium. Dallas seats 70,000 to Minnesota's 40,000. Too, the East needs a warm-weather port.

"With the exception of Philadelphia, we all play in parks used by major league baseball teams. With our season opening at least a week earlier to get in fourteen games, this poses some real tough scheduling problems."

Marshall was absolute in his reasoning that Baltimore and Washington should be placed in separate conferences.

"Baltimore has built strong rivalries by now and wouldn't want to change," he said, before mentioning his old landlord at Griffith Stadium. The Senators had left Washington following the 1960 season and relocated to Minnesota.

"Before he left town, Calvin Griffith often regretted that Baltimore and Washington were in the same baseball league," Marshall said. "He said then, that he'd be happy to go to the National League or have the Orioles do it.

"It's no good when you're playing a team less than forty miles away. It complicated the television set up of both."

Marshall acknowledged to Walsh that he had already tried to persuade his fellow owners to move Dallas to the Eastern Conference.

"Nobody's against it," he said, before confessing, "but I have to admit, I don't have any commitments, either."[1]

A couple of days after his conversation with Walsh, Marshall appeared as a guest on a weekly sports panel show, which aired on WLBM radio in Miami. Tommy Devine, the sports editor of the *Miami News*, and Jimmy Burns, the sports editor of the *Miami Herald*, were serving as interviewers. The two men peppered Marshall with a variety of queries, the first of which questioned the Redskins' owner about the Ernie Davis trade. Did he still think it was the right move?

"We've only won two football games in the last two years," Marshall explained. "I want to win games next year, not five years from now. . . . What caused the Redskins to lose twelve games was lack of speed. . . . Davis is going to be a great football player; Mitchell is right now."

Devine then asked about a recent news story that quoted Bill McPeak as saying that the Redskins had allowed their scouting system to collapse.

"It had been grossly neglected," Marshall admitted. "It had gone down, died. McPeak was hired to do something about it—and has started the rehabilitation."

Well, Burns asked, when do you think the Redskins will be contenders?

"That's an easy question to answer," Marshall replied. "I expect to be in contention next season. I'll predict we'll win a minimum of seven games, maybe eight or nine. We think we'll have the best quarterback in pro football next season."

"With this new, bigger stadium, you'll have to sell more tickets, right?" Devine asked.

"I've never had a problem selling tickets," Marshall responded. "We won one game last season, but it was the biggest year in our history financially.

"We're loaded with money," Marshall boasted. "Money's no problem. I can't keep it forever. The government will step in and take it anyway."[2]

Two and a half weeks later Lew Atchison used his *Evening Star* column to write an open letter to George Marshall at the Kenilworth Hotel in Miami Beach, Florida.

"Dear George," Atchison began. "Just a line to let you know everything is okay and hope you are the same. After that exhausting football season with the Redskins you deserve a rest. Two in a row like that really takes a lot out of a guy and I'm surprised you're cutting your stay to two months. That will hardly give you time to look over the baseball camps and get them straightened out.

"As I said, everything's ok here, except that Bill McPeak is making noise like he's running the team. Anyone who heard him at the last luncheon and didn't know the situation would have thought you weren't going to be back this year. Honest, George, he was talking about moving Bob Toneff to offensive tackle, putting Bobby Mitchell out on a flank and even making a deal for another fullback. If I didn't know you'll be back, I might have thought he will coach the team."[3]

Marshall did indeed return to Washington earlier than he usually did, although Atchison's tongue-in-cheek column was not the reason Marshall shortened his winter getaway. The primary reason Marshall cut short his stay in Florida was the AFL's antitrust suit, which was due to kick off on February 26 in the Baltimore courthouse of federal judge Roszel Cathcart Thomsen.

The AFL's suit accused the NFL of a monopoly and asked for more than $10 million in damages. Chief among the many charges was that the established league had expanded into Dallas only as an attempt to destroy the new, competing circuit.

Roszel Thomsen, who was appointed to the federal bench by President Eisenhower on May 12, 1959, decided against seating a jury in the case. Rather, it would be a bench trial, and the lawyers would be presenting their case directly to the judge.

To start things off the AFL's attorney, Warren E. Baker, rattled off a litany of requests to the court.

He asked for injunction relief: for the judge to remove the Cowboys from Dallas.

The NFL had locked up two television networks, CBS and NBC, thus stripping the new league of its negotiating power with the American Broadcasting Company (ABC), the sole remaining network, resulting in the AFL receiving a comparatively paltry sum of just under $1.65 million from their ABC agreement.

At one time NBC had revealed its interest in obtaining rights to air AFL games, but the network abandoned its pursuit when it signed the Pittsburgh and Baltimore franchises.

Baker then requested that the court not permit any National Football League team to be placed in any AFL city for at least five years. Baker further wanted the NFL enjoined from referring to its year-end title game as the "world championship" unless an AFL club was played for the right to such a designation.

Baker also offered a timeline, which he believed proved the NFL's culpability in trying to monopolize pro football.

Next up was Gerhard A. Gesell, the NFL's counsel, who told Judge Thomsen that "we're trying a dead man here," in reference to the late commissioner Bell's crusade to expand the NFL.

Gesell then refuted Baker's basic premise, arguing that the fledgling league's attorney had offered an incomplete and erroneous account of past events.

"The dates are crucial," Gesell said. The NFL had formed its expansion committee in January 1958, before the new guys "even had a team or even a player."[4]

Gesell contended that George Halas, in his role as chairman of the NFL's expansion committee, had announced in January 1958 plans to venture into Dallas, Houston, and Minneapolis "before the American Football League was even a dream."[5]

The first witness sent to the stand by the plaintiffs was Lamar Hunt, the man behind the formation of the rival league and the owner of the Dallas Texans.

Hunt's testimony began by imparting the information that on June 29, 1959, Bert Bell had informed him that the NFL "was not interested in expansion."

"If you owned an NFL franchise and had lost money," Hunt quoted Bell as saying, "(and) fought and scrapped to keep it going . . . would you be interested in expansion?

"There will be no expansion at the next NFL meeting," Hunt testified that Bell had said to him. "If you say this, I will have to deny it. I'm sure you understand my position on this."[6]

Hunt then recounted his saga of trying to purchase a team in the NFL. In 1957 the young Texan made a $3 million offer to purchase the Chicago Cardinals outright. The money was right, but Cardinals owner Violet Bidwill did not want her team relocated to Dallas.

A year later Hunt had approached Bell and inquired into the possibility of being granted an expansion franchise. The commissioner dismissed the idea, telling Hunt that the failure of the 1952 Dallas Texans had soured the league on the city.

A decade earlier the New York Yankees had relocated to Dallas following the 1951 season and had taken the name "Texans." The Dallas outfit played in the Cotton Bowl before a large quantity of empty seats. The franchise fared so poorly that it did not even finish out the season in Dallas. The club picked up and moved again. This time they were a team without a home, though they were based in Hershey, Pennsylvania.

So a Dallas franchise in the NFL was out, but Hunt was not one to give up easily. In March 1959 he spoke with George Halas, who was serving as chairman of the National Football League's expansion committee. Once again Hunt was turned away empty-handed. The NFL had no plans to expand for "several years," Halas informed the young Texan.[7]

Rebuffed three times, Hunt decided to try a different path. If the NFL wouldn't have him, he would start his own damn league. Hunt began recruiting like-minded men across the country, men of wealth with an itch to inflate their self-esteem by dabbling in professional sports.

One of the men Hunt recruited for his new league was George Marshall's nemesis, Harry Wismer.

Having corralled and coerced enough men to fund his vision, Hunt once again met with Bell and notified the NFL's commissioner that he had begun to form the foundation of a new pro football league. Hunt asked Bell if he would be receptive to the notion of serving as commissioner of both leagues. Perhaps pro football could have a structure similar to Major League Baseball's setup with American and National Leagues.

Bell politely declined the offer. He was already overworked as the commissioner of one league; two just might spell the end for him. During the three-hour discussion with Bell, Hunt put forth a few other proposals, including a joint player draft between the two leagues and television blackouts involving both leagues. Bell rejected each pitch. This new league was not going to ride the coattails of the National Football League.

On his first day of testimony, during which he spent four hours on the stand, Hunt stated that officials in the NFL had repeatedly told him that he stood to lose "a great deal of money" if he pursued his ambition of forming a new pro football circuit. In addition Hunt testified that he had had a telephone conversation with Colts owner Carroll Rosenbloom in which Rosenbloom vowed that he "would do everything he could, 'to fight the American Football League.'"[8]

An unconfirmed rumor made the rounds: the AFL's Texans had supposedly lost even more in their initial season than the Cowboys had in theirs. The word was out that Lamar Hunt had absorbed a deficit of a million dollars.

"At that rate," Hunt's father was quoted as commenting, "Junior will be broke in a hundred and fifty years."

The younger Hunt was well aware of the financial losses he had endured during the Texans' initial season, but he was still steadfast in his determination to pursue his desire to own and operate a professional football team, without the impediment of the National Football League.

Four hours on the stand wasn't enough.

Lamar Hunt was asked to return the following day to continue his testimony. On the second day of the trial George Preston Marshall's name was brought up for the first time. This stuff was headline material: Hunt informed the court that Marshall had told him that the only reason for (NFL) expansion was to kill the new league.

"Mr. Marshall told me," Hunt testified inside Judge Thomsen's courtroom, "that there was no possible way that we could succeed."

His second day of testifying was exhausting. As he neared the eight-hour mark under oath Hunt could not conceal his weariness. Occasionally Hunt would hold his head in his hands between questions to fight off fatigue; still he continued to make his argument.

Hunt recalled numerous telephone calls and conversations with NFL officials. Rosenbloom and Marshall weren't the only NFL owners who had informed Hunt that failure would be the only outcome of his effort to build a new pro football circuit. The Giants' Tim Mara, Tony Morabito of the 49ers, and Ed Pauley Sr. with the Rams had all told Hunt his prospective league would fail. The Cowboys' Clint Murchison, Hunt said, offered him a significant percentage of the Dallas franchise should the lawsuit against the NFL be dropped.

He dismissed Murchison's offer, Hunt explained, because of the commitments he had made, "not only to individuals, but cities."[9]

The message was always the same: don't waste your money, because all your designs will crash and burn.

The NFL did not announce its intention to expand until he had locked up seven commitments for an AFL team, Hunt asserted.

The question was posed to Hunt about exactly what would induce the scion of an oil tycoon to venture into the unsteady world of professional football.

"Why am I 'bothering' with a risky business like a new pro football team?" Hunt responded, "when I would be assured of profits in oil? I think it was George Preston Marshall of the Redskins who said people get into sports to get their names in the papers."

Hunt had played some football at Southern Methodist University. Among his Mustangs teammates he counted Raymond Berry, who had joined the Colts, and Forrest Gregg, now a Packer. The truth of the matter was that Hunt enjoyed the challenge and competition that came with professional sports.

"Though it may sound corny, I got into pro football because of civic pride in Dallas," Hunt continued from the stand. "You know Big D . . . it wants to be big league in everything."

Hunt recalled the days when Kyle Rote and Doak Walker starred at SMU. Back then the Mustangs had played eight home games a year at the Cotton Bowl, averaging sixty-three thousand spectators a contest. The healthy attendance at SMU games had influenced the NFL to relocate the New York Yankees of the All-American Football Conference to Dallas as the Texans in 1952. The original Texans' failure, Hunt argued, wasn't a fair measure of the Dallas market.

"They didn't have it," Hunt said of the previous Texans. "I'm confident one good pro team can succeed in Dallas.

"We wanted an arrangement with the NFL to protect each other from telecasts," he said, "and to have a common player draft. We really weren't ready for a title game with the NFL at first."[10]

During his testimony Hunt informed the judge that the AFL had been formally organized at a conference held in Dallas on August 22, 1959. Six

$25,000 checks gathered from the participants were deposited in a local bank, thus formally establishing the American Football League.

Just one week later George Halas announced that the NFL would field teams in Houston and Dallas for the 1961 season.

The NFL's San Francisco and Los Angeles franchises were excluded from the lawsuit and trial because each team had requested that the suit be heard by a jury. Minnesota was exempt because it was not in operation when the complaint was filed back in 1960. And thanks to Marshall's earlier statements—made while speaking under oath to Congress—that he had been opposed to expansion from the get-go, the Redskins were also dropped from the suit.

During his testimony of March 5 AFL commissioner Joe Foss introduced into evidence a letter, dated January 6, 1960, he had penned to all NFL owners.

It read in part, "I am writing to ask your help and cooperation in preventing your National Football League from taking action to destroy our league.

"The AFL was organized . . . [and] following the untimely death of (Bert) Bell, it now appears that no stone was left unturned to certain members of your league to repudiate Bell's assertions," Foss wrote, as a reminder of Bert Bell's 1959 testimony before the antitrust subcommittee chaired by Senator C. E. Kefauver.

"To follow your present 'scorched earth' policy is heresy to the cities involved, the American sporting public and especially to the Senate anti-trust committee," Foss continued.[11]

In the midst of the antitrust suit, Judge Thomsen ruled on another football matter. The ownership of the fight song of Thomsen's beloved Baltimore Colts was brought before the judge. The composers of the tune claimed the rights to the song had reverted to them after the original Colts folded in 1950.

Thomsen ruled against the composers and affirmed that the current Colts maintained the privilege to call the fight song their own.

On March 13 Gesell presented a three-page motion contending that after two weeks of testimony the AFL had failed to prove its allegation that the NFL was a monopoly. He had good reason to believe that Judge Thomsen might dismiss the suit. The judge had earlier said, "I would think the evidence is very thin" to prove a monopoly.

Thomsen was referring to what he termed the "coached answers of [AFL] witnesses who made bare statements with no supporting evidence."[12]

"Rather, the proof affirmatively shows there are sufficient cities, facilities, players, television outlets and financial and other resources available to enable competing leagues to enter and continue in the field."

Furthermore, the motion read, the plaintiffs had established that there was a conspiracy in restraint of trade or "to demonstrate that any illegal act was the proximate cause of any specific loss."[13]

The NFL's attorney sensed which way the wind was blowing, and while addressing the court directly Gerhard Gesell argued, "Evidence of injury to the AFL had been wholly speculative and highly conjectural." He asked Judge Thomsen to dismiss the suit.[14]

Gesell offered several points as grounds for dismissal of the suit.

No relevant market was monopolized, and no attempt to monopolize a relevant market had been proven.

Furthermore, no conspiracy in restraint of trade or to monopolize had been established.

Finally, Gesell maintained, no injury had been shown.

The attorney for the National Football League argued that since the AFL had continued to operate for two seasons, that fact alone should be grounds to dismiss any claim that the NFL had tried to obliterate its rival.

Warren Baker then offered in response, "It is not necessary for the AFL to wait until it is dead to bring this suit."[15]

Judge Thomsen listened to Gesell's arguments, but he wanted to hear more. Three days after hearing Gesell's motion Thomsen ordered on March 16 that the trial continue, though he had failed to conceal his leanings toward the NFL's argument.

The fourth week of the trial began on March 19. On that day Judge Thomsen dismissed the Redskins as a part of the conspiracy aspect of the suit. Marshall was on record, Thomsen explained, repeatedly decrying the prospect of expansion.

On March 27 George Preston Marshall made the forty-mile trip to Baltimore in the passenger seat of his chauffeur-driven limo.[16] The courtroom was not filled to capacity, despite anticipation of Marshall's appearance; the reason for the lower than expected attendance was explained by an NFL official.

"It was packed Monday," the unnamed official told the *Evening Star*. "Everybody thought George was going to testify then, and there was plenty of grumbling when he didn't show. They wanted ticket refunds," he joked.[17]

Accompanied by his attorney, Edward Bennett Williams, Marshall finally appeared in Judge Thomsen's court, but his testimony did not live up to the hype preceding his arrival.

When asked under oath by Gerhard A. Gesell to identify himself, Marshall responded, "President of Pro Football, Inc."

That would be Marshall's most coherent answer of the day.

Asked by Gesell if he had ever said, "The only reason any member of this league [the NFL] has ever given me for expanding into Dallas, is to ruin the other league," Marshall demurred, then obfuscated.

"I cannot remember specifically what I said, but I did state I was opposed to our going into Dallas," Marshall replied.

As usual, he was impeccably dressed in an eye-catching suit, accented with a handkerchief folded perfectly to a point in his suit pocket.

"That, if anybody had used the expansion or made the statements in talking to him that the theory was to head off another league," Marshall continued, "I said I would not change my opinion about the thing. I thought it was impractical and unsound and not good for our league."

He hedged and dodged, darted and ducked.

Marshall produced little more than a free flow of double-talk, a muddied testimony that added up to a tangled mess, a jumbled declaration of a whole lot of nothing.

"I did not make any general assumption of the question of the anti-trust version of it, because I had always felt that the NFL was not in violation of anti-trust in spite of the decision that was made, and I had always opposed the NFL's expanding to stop any other league, and introduced—it got passed into the constitution which you will read, some years ago, preventing the NFL from ever having any association with minor leagues which they had

had before, or getting involved in any of the phases which the baseball people have been involved in."

Marshall took advantage of the opportunity to levy the charge that Clinton Hester, a Capitol Hill lobbyist, had "hounded" the league on the question of expansion. According to Marshall, Hester had promised that if the NFL added new franchises he would help push through the Judiciary Committee a bill that would remove the government's threatened antitrust suit against the NFL.

And so it continued as Marshall weakly explained away his previously uttered, highly publicized words and opinions—thoughts that just a short time earlier had predicted antitrust action should the NFL expand into Dallas.

At the conclusion of Gesell's direct examination the AFL's attorney, Warren E. Baker, stood up and told the court, "I have no questions."

After a mere eleven minutes Marshall was dismissed from the witness stand.

During a recess Baker explained to reporters why he had passed on his opportunity to cross-examine the double-talking witness; he explained that Marshall had already said enough in his pretrial deposition.

Outside the courtroom Marshall spoke briefly with reporters.

"Is that all?" he asked incredulously, seemingly disappointed that he did not have the chance to spar with Baker from the stand. "You wasted your trip over from Washington," he told the assembled journalists.[18]

A few days after his appearance in Judge Thomsen's court Marshall spoke with Cal Jacox of the *Norfolk New Journal and Guide*.

"The signing of Mitchell should erase all doubts as to the future of the Redskins," Marshall stated.

Kennedy? Udall? Those liberal punks had nothing to do with the Redskins signing Bobby Mitchell, scoffed Marshall.

"Our lawyers, and for that matter some of the Secretary's own legal talent[,] told him he could not keep us out of the stadium."[19]

And then on May 22 Judge Roszel Thomsen released his much-anticipated decision. Thomsen ruled that the NFL had expanded into Minnesota and Dallas prior to the new, renegade league announcing its intention of moving into those territories. Thus the established league did not constitute a monopoly nor had it engaged in "a conspiracy in unreasonable restraint of trade or commerce."[20]

Thomsen had rejected the AFL's argument. He declared that for the plaintiffs to prove their point they were required to establish that the NFL had possessed a monopoly power and that the established league had taken a course of action to prevent competition. In his judgment Thomsen explained that he could not find culpability on the two key issues, and he also pointed out that the NFL should not be compelled "to forgo normal competitive business methods."

Furthermore, "neither rough competition nor unethical business conduct is sufficient [to prove a monopoly]. The requisite intent to monopolize must be present and predominant."[21]

The AFL lawyers, Thomsen determined, had not established proof of the original charge that the NFL sought to dominate in the televising of games or acquiring of rights to college players through its draft. With these issues decided Thomsen had only to rule on the question of monopoly and damages caused by the established league's move into Minnesota and Dallas.

"None of the defendants has attempted to monopolize or [has] combined or conspired with any other persons to monopolize major league professional football," Thomsen wrote in his decision. "None of the plaintiffs is entitled to relief in this case.

"Defendants did not have the power to prevent or unreasonably to restrict competition."

Judge Thomsen did concede that the NFL, if so inclined, could force the AFL franchises out of nearly every city with the exception of New York and perhaps "Dallas and Houston, where rich owners are determined to fight it out."[22]

Yes, Thomsen acknowledged, the existence of the NFL's Cowboys had proved costly to the AFL's Texans. However, Thomsen wrote, "attendance was also poor at the NFL games."

The fact that each league's Dallas franchise had lost a substantial amount, Thomsen clarified, "may indicate that the city is not as good a location for a professional football team as was generally believed."

The judge explained that the claim for damages in lieu of the NFL's decision to locate a franchise in Minnesota "was based on an inferior Oakland franchise."

The AFL had retreated from Minnesota after discovering the NFL's determination to move into a city there. Instead the new league had placed a franchise in Oakland, California, where the new club struggled at the gate.

"The first of these propositions is doubtful," the judge stated. "Whatever injury there may have been was contributed by unskilled handling of the Oakland arrangements."[23]

Thomsen had arrived at the conclusion that it was indeed "true that Hunt was not entirely candid and was devious in his dealings" with NFL officials.[24] However, Thomsen continued, it was not sufficient to legally bar Hunt and the AFL from recovering damages if the court found they were entitled to them.

"This has been a costly lesson," Harry Wismer said upon hearing the verdict. "I was against the suit from the beginning. Once it began, I was highly critical of the way it was being conducted. I feel that football should be played on the fields and not in the courts. Now that it is over, our clubs can settle down to playing football."[25]

Upon hearing Judge Thomsen's ruling, the NFL issued a statement.

"Representatives of the new league have publicly vilified the National Football League for two and one half years. They have blamed the NFL's illegal conduct for their lack of success. It is now apparent as we have known all along, that the American Football League was badly misleading the public."

According to an obviously pleased George Halas, "The decision is most gratifying as a vindication of the National Football League's efforts to maintain its operation on a high level of integrity."

For the better part of two years Halas's league had been under attack in the press and disparaged by members of the new league. "And it was pretty hard to take at times after forty years of devotion to an idea and an ideal," the Chicago Bears founding father acknowledged. "This decision makes it all worthwhile."[26]

15

Out of the Shadows

On his first day at the Washington Redskins' 1962 training camp Bobby Mitchell took a look at his new teammates.

This group was a far cry from the Cleveland squads he'd been with for the previous five years. Those teams had been led by Coach Paul Brown and had enjoyed a grand winning tradition on the shores of Lake Erie. Although several years had passed since their last championship, the Browns team Mitchell knew so well had remained a professional outfit through and through. This Redskins crew was something else completely.

"This is my team?" Mitchell asked Bill McPeak.

"Yeah," McPeak sheepishly admitted, "this is the team."[1]

Mitchell had arrived at Occidental College on July 24, three days later than the rest of his teammates due to his military obligations at Fort Meade, where he had stayed in shape by serving as the army post's track coach. Despite prolonged lack of sleep Mitchell stepped on the practice field for the first time and impressed the Redskins' coaching staff, as well as his new teammates, with an electrifying performance.

"Our passing ought to be a lot better," Norm Snead said following Mitchell's first workout with the club. "Mitchell's so fast they've got to respect him. They won't be able to cover him with one man and concentrate on our running game."[2]

A few months earlier, during the first week of April, the Redskins had traded offensive guard Ray Lemek to Pittsburgh for lineman John Nisby. In a year of firsts this transaction was the first time in team history that Washington had exchanged a white player for a black player.

Although a native of California, Nisby had made a home in Pittsburgh.

Drafted by the Packers in 1957, Nisby was traded to the Steelers before playing a single game in Green Bay. His young wife was a Pittsburgh girl, and Dolores Nisby wasn't too happy when news of the trade to Washington reached her. Moving away from her home certainly held little appeal to Mrs. Nisby, but being transplanted to Washington and having John play on *that* team all seemed like a cruel joke to Dolores. For his part Nisby was surprised to be traded to the Redskins, but he understood the business. He, along with every other black player in the league, understood the history in Washington. He knew the reputation of George Marshall, but Marshall wasn't alone in his bigotry. On several occasions Nisby and Steelers head coach Buddy Parker had butted heads. Nisby, a bright and outgoing person, was prone to speak his mind, and this trait didn't exactly endear Nisby to his coach. The tension between player and coach came to a head on a team flight when Parker unleashed an alcohol-fueled torrent of racial epithets at Nisby.

It wasn't the first time Parker had had too much to drink on a team trip; he was well known to get half lit. On this occasion, however, Parker was particularly inebriated.

"Nigger" was just one ugly term Parker spewed at Nisby. A wide variety of abusive terms came forth—"black son of a bitch" and "black ass" were just a couple of the combinations Parker directed toward his lineman, who sat dumbfounded. The diatribe caught the attention of Pittsburgh owner Art Rooney, who banned drinking on all team flights thereafter. Offenders would be subject to a $10,000 fine, this in a day when a starting player took home $13,000 a year.

The threat of a ten-grand fine was all well and good, but that didn't change what was in a man's heart. Nisby knew it, and he also understood that Marshall was no different than Parker.

For the most part the newest members of the Redskins were each made to feel welcome by their new teammates. There were a couple of exceptions, to be certain, though the offenders were greatly outnumbered by the men in the Redskins locker room who accepted their new black teammates. Those in opposition to change revealed their hostility through body language and murmured comments meant to demean.

As the club made its annual exhibition trek through the South after training camp in California, the newest Redskins were faced with the cultural mores of the region. The black members of the squad were sequestered in an army barracks while the rest of the team stayed in a hotel. The gratis tickets given each player for family and friends were some of the choicest seats available. Rather than being able to watch the games from the 50-yard line, as the tickets called for, the friends of the black players were relocated to the Jim Crow seating in the end zone.

Indeed, Bobby Mitchell, Ron Hatcher, John Nisby, and Leroy Jackson were something apart from the rest of their Redskins teammates.

At one point during the training season the entire team stood in unison as "Dixie" began to play in the hall. An incredulous Mitchell took in the scene in silence. Suddenly he felt a tap on his shoulder.

"Bobby Mitchell, sing!" Marshall commanded.[3]

Along with the rest of his teammates Mitchell was expected to sing the sacred pairing of songs played prior to each home contest. The indignation of mouthing the lyrics of "Dixie" grated on the newest member of the Redskins. Mitchell and Nisby in particular seethed as they stood on the sideline while Marshall's band blared out the insufferable tune.

The B&O Capitol Limited pulled into Union Station on a sweleringly hot morning. The day was August 16, and George Preston Marshall had just concluded his seventeenth round-trip to California for his football club's annual training camp. He stepped off the train seemingly the picture of health and ego, in full command of his faculties as well as his Washington Redskins. The image was deceiving, however. Marshall had not been himself in California. Marshall's impediment had been noticeable enough that his discomfort was mentioned by the Redskins beat writers in their daily reports for the city's newspapers. He needed surgery for a hernia, and Marshall was waiting until he returned home from California to undergo the necessary procedure. But before that he had some business to tend to. Following a brief nap Marshall reported to his office, and there he addressed a variety of unsettled business interests.

A commercial photographer stopped by the team's headquarters. For a few moments Marshall posed with a can of Redskins-brand kidney beans. When that obligation was concluded, a television crew from Philadelphia arrived.

The group had taken the train to Washington in order to film Marshall for a CBS special titled *The Rise of Pro Football*. With the cameras rolling Marshall was asked about the pioneering rule changes he had proposed back in 1933.

With great flourish Marshall offered his recollections of tales often told, of alterations to the league that had changed professional football for good. And, just as quick as that, the interview was concluded.

"We're going next to Chicago to film George Halas," the producer informed Marshall.

"Halas?" Marshall dismissively replied. "He's too old, too. Don't give him any more time than you gave me."[4]

Halas and Marshall—their antagonistic love affair could be traced back more than three decades. There was nobody Marshall enjoyed beating on the playing field more than George Halas, and eight days after his August 23 surgery at Doctors' Hospital Marshall's Redskins defeated the terrible Chicago Bears in Norfolk, Virginia. The nail-biting 29–28 Washington victory was the Redskins' first exhibition victory since their 1959 triumph over the Rams. Eighteen consecutive preseason defeats grated on Marshall, and the fact that the losses were meaningless for the standings mattered not one bit.

Just a few hours after the Redskins' splendid victory, Mo Siegel paid a visit to his friend at Doctors' Hospital, where Marshall continued to recuperate from his surgery. Siegel stepped into Marshall's room and was spellbound by what he saw.

"On one wall, opposite the bed, was a tattered Confederate flag," Siegel described in an *Evening Star* piece. "Above the bed was a portrait of George Washington. The furniture was early American, *real* early American. The only concession to the 20th Century was a telephone."[5]

The telephone! One of God's greatest gifts to mankind.

Throughout Siegel's visit Marshall was working the phone. He called the hotel in Norfolk where his team had stayed prior to their gloriously meaningless victory over Halas's Bears. Marshall just wanted to let the innkeeper know that he was doing a crackerjack job.

"He told me that he was glad to see the team leave," Marshall told Siegel. "They [the Redskins players] were so happy they were about to wreck his hotel, and he was going to join them."

Other calls came in from friends and associates—some to wish George well, some to congratulate him on the Redskins' triumph over that awful Halas. One caller even had the gall to not know the outcome of the game and asked Marshall to provide him with some details of the contest.

"Tell him I'm sick or something," Marshall demanded of an attendant. "I've got no time for anybody who doesn't know we won. Can you imagine someone not knowing about the game?"

Yet another call came in, this one from a new friend, a fellow named Ben who just happened to own the Beverly Hills Hotel.

"Fine place," Marshall remarked to Siegel upon hanging up, "but like I told him, he's got to put telephones [in] those cabanas."[6]

The Cleveland Browns had selected Bobby Mitchell in the seventh round of the 1958 draft, the eighty-fourth pick overall.

Mitchell's reading material spanned the typical favorites of athletes—the *Sporting News*, *Sport Magazine*, and the like—but Bobby's intellectual curiosity also led him to works by the likes of James Baldwin and C. Wright Mills.

Some in Washington's black community criticized Mitchell for not being more politically committed. Those detractors wanted a firebrand willing to take anger to the streets, a vocal proponent in the fight against social inequities. His bride, Gwen, was active in several civil rights groups, organizing and coordinating various events. Although Bobby was not apolitical, he preferred to approach racial matters in a different manner. Having made his way into pro football automatically made him a proponent of racial equality. Running downfield on a Sunday afternoon could do more than marching in protest down a street. Black athletes had repeatedly shown that they were capable of excelling, if only given the chance.

"I think the Negro athlete can say, 'I'm doing as much as the next man,'" Mitchell explained. "I don't have to apologize to anybody. Every time I run down the field, I am doing something tremendous for the Negro race."[7]

Mitchell had a real commitment to the education of children. He often spoke to groups made up of both black and white kids. Such engagements went a long way toward promoting racial tolerance and understanding. Speaking to white groups exposed those children to the fact that black men were not the great bogeymen they had been portrayed as by so many bigots.

To black youth the message that came through was that they could succeed, too; there are no barriers.

In its September 9 issue *Sports Illustrated* magazine previewed the coming NFL season.

"Washington supports failure spectacularly," the football reporter Hamilton "Tex" Maule wrote. "The ticket prices last fall were the highest in the team's history and so were the attendance figures—even though the Redskins have won but two games in two years. Now it appears the Redskins are willing to risk that allegiance by getting good."

Maule's brief preview presented a viable argument for a drastically improved Redskins team during the 1962 campaign. Personnel additions, chief among them Bobby Mitchell and Leroy Jackson, plus the emergence of Norm Snead as an effective pro quarterback allowed for optimism among football fans in the nation's capital.

But, Maule wondered, "Will Washington support a winner?"[8]

On September 16, 1962, the Cowboys and Redskins ushered in a new era in Washington football.

It was a stifling late-summer afternoon, with the thermometer reading 88 degrees, but the Texas humidity made the temperature feel more like 110 degrees inside the Cotton Bowl. A sparse crowd numbering 15,730 spectators was treated to a sloppy but exciting affair. The scoreboard operator had his hands full as the two clubs piled up 70 points, 35 per side. Despite the ambiguous outcome, few left the stadium unsatisfied thanks to the jaw-dropping exploits of Bobby Mitchell.

The next day the *Star's* game story carried a headline declaring, "One Man Show Saves the Redskins."

Mitchell crossed into the Dallas end zone on three occasions, and only a pass interference penalty at the goal line prevented Bobby from a fourth touchdown. His scores came on a 6-yard pass, a 92-yard kickoff return, and an 81-yard reception, with each play more spellbinding than the previous.

It was only a draw, but given recent Redskins history a tie was nearly as good as a victory.

Washington's next opponent held special meaning for Bobby Mitchell. His former Browns teammates would play the Redskins on September 23 in Cleveland. For journalists on the sports beat this "homecoming" was hard to resist.

"Mitchell vs. Browns Will Provide Drama" was the headline above a Jack Walsh piece in the *Post*. Walsh wondered, could Mitchell repeat the previous Sunday's heroics against his old club? What could he possibly do for an encore?

Do you have anything to prove to Coach Brown? Mitchell was asked.

"I'm not interested so much in impressing Paul Brown. . . . He knows what I can do," Mitchell answered. "But I have many fans in Cleveland and throughout Ohio. I want them to know I'm still a good ballplayer."[9]

Mitchell was stymied through much of the game. Paul Brown had developed a brilliant game to slow his former player. Cleveland put an "inside out" zone on Mitchell, a scheme that had two, sometimes three men covering Bobby. Brown's plan worked to perfection for nearly sixty minutes, until Washington had possession of the ball at midfield with two minutes remaining in the game and Cleveland up by a score of 16–10.

"I wanted it so bad," Mitchell admitted. "But the more a receiver goes without touching the ball the more he tightens up."[10]

He still had a chance to alter the game's score, but time was running short.

Mitchell, lined up as a halfback, was called on to run a post pattern. However, Cleveland linebacker Galen Fiss bumped him at the line of scrimmage, throwing off the timing of the play call. Mitchell spun around and saw Norm Snead encircled by Cleveland pass rushers. Somehow Snead managed to get off a dart in Mitchell's direction. He grabbed the bullet pass at the Cleveland 40-yard line and took off for the sideline. To the spectators it seemed that Mitchell was hemmed in by Cleveland defenders; he appeared to be running out of bounds and into the Browns' bench. At the last instant, however, Mitchell turned the corner and sliced through a cluster of Cleveland defenders. He then split two Browns safeties and darted toward the Cleveland end zone and the game-winning score.

"It was an impossible run," Mitchell acknowledged. "I had nowhere to go, but I found somewhere. I don't think that many individuals could have done that. I don't think that I could do it again myself. . . . It was the greatest run I've ever made, and I've made many a run, and I've caught many a pass. And with all that pressure on me, that was confidence personified."[11]

At the sound of the final gun Mitchell could not contain his glee. He happily trotted off the field, waving his burgundy helmet high in the air, unable to suppress a wide grin creasing his handsome face.

Across the field Paul Brown lowered his head and strode quickly to the Cleveland dressing room.

More than fifty-seven thousand fans had flocked to Municipal Stadium, the biggest crowd to ever see the Redskins perform in Cleveland. The large audience resulted in Marshall being handed a check for $64,323, the largest payout Marshall's Redskins had ever earned on the road. To what extent Mitchell could be credited with the great turnout Marshall couldn't say, but the Redskins' owner certainly liked what he'd seen in the season's first two weeks.

On September 21, the afternoon before Mitchell and company had departed for Cleveland, the team was honored at the first annual Redskins alumni luncheon held at the Statler Hilton. The affair primarily served as a welcome for new members of the team. A similar gathering had been held every year at the Touchdown Club, but some "internecine strife" between Marshall and club president George Neumann had brought an end to that annual event.[12] Apparently the Touchdown Club, which had honored Harry Wismer during the course of the offseason, had offended the Redskins' owner, and no one could hold a grudge quite like George Preston Marshall. Other sources said that Neumann got angry with Marshall over something, or perhaps it was the other way around. Either way, a tradition had gone by the wayside because of petty bickering, but a new ritual was born in its stead.

The venue for the fete wasn't the only thing that was different. Dick McCann had moved on from his position as Redskins general manager to become the director of the new Pro Football Hall of Fame in Canton, Ohio. McCann was present at the luncheon, however, and he spoke to the players present in the Statler ballroom. In addition to those on the current roster of Washington players a number of Redskins from the past were seated throughout the room. They included Cliff Battles, John "Tree" Adams, Wilbur Moore, and Casimir "Slug" Witucki. Approximately five hundred of the Redskins faithful filled the ballroom and saved their biggest cheers of the afternoon for Bobby Mitchell, the hero of the previous Sunday's 35–35 stalemate with Dallas.

McCann, however, wasn't speaking to the old-timers when he took the dais.

"You're playing in a great town for great fans," McCann said. "We—and I still speak of the Redskins as we—have finished last a few times[,] but the fans of Washington have never been last in loyalty.

"I think I can speak freely because I'm out of Mr. Marshall's will and I'm out of the way. But you Redskins will never play for a man more dedicated to football and to the fans.

"When I had ulcers, somebody asked Mr. Marshall how come he had given them to me. Mr. Marshall answered, 'I didn't give Dick McCann ulcers. Anything he's got, he worked for.'"[13]

The 1962 Redskins were then presented one by one to the assembled crowd, and the Hecht Company announced the selection of Richard "Dickie" James as the team's outstanding player for the 1961 season. He was awarded a gold wristwatch and presented with a trophy on which his name would later be inscribed.

It all played out like so many Welcome Home luncheons of the past. Something was amiss, however.

Marshall arrived at the affair late, looking tired and worn. This man, who had always walked with cocksure confidence, stepped gingerly into the ballroom. His entrance triggered a spontaneous reaction from the crowd—a standing ovation in appreciation for Marshall.

Many had heard that Marshall had been stricken by illness over the summer, but few had seen him in person in months. The change in Marshall's appearance was dramatic. He seemed to have aged a decade in just a few weeks. Bob Addie wrote, "[Marshall] walked with the cautious temerity of a man with spiked shoes stepping into a room full of eggs."[14]

The affair marked Marshall's first official public appearance since his operation a month earlier. He had missed being out of the limelight and was more than ready to answer any question posed to him by the reporters attending the event.

Commenting on the procedure that had laid him up for several weeks, Marshall said, "We hope to cut out a few defeats and really get into action this year."

The double-talk was gone when Marshall was asked about his coach.

"McPeak never made better moves as a coach than he did yesterday. . . . It was a good one to win. Now we can live another week."

Marshall shared with reporters a few congratulatory messages he had received following Sunday's game. A phone call from the Giants' Jack Mara was given special attention.

"He said it was good for the league," Marshall relayed. "I used to call his father when they'd beat a team the Redskins were interested in and tell him that."

Marshall also had something to say about Bobby Mitchell.

"I like that boy. He's intelligent, clean cut, modest and a great player. The way he cuts reminds me of Steve Bagarus. I had a long talk with him before he signed and I was impressed. The thing he likes most about being in Washington is the opportunity he's getting in business here. That's the thing uppermost in his mind. Jimmy Brown once said Mitchell would be a bigger sensation than Brown is in Cleveland, and he's right."[15]

As the ceremonies came to a close Marshall again, in a labored shuffle, proceeded to the podium. A hush came over the ballroom as the legendary Redskins owner began to speak.

With his voice trembling Marshall asked the crowd, "Will you please stand and join me in my favorite hymn, 'Hail to the Redskins'?"

Businessmen united with journalists, and players, both former and current, all rose as one and began singing the familiar tune. As the notes echoed throughout the Statler ballroom tears flowed freely down Marshall's jowly face.

Several days prior to the alumni luncheon Bill Shea had spoken with Dave Brady of the *Washington Post*. Along with Jack Kent Cooke, Shea had become a minority shareholder in the Redskins earlier in the year. According to Shea's telling of the tale it was he and Cooke who had persuaded the stubborn Marshall to adhere to Secretary Udall's edict. That issue, however, wasn't the reason Shea sought out Brady. Shea wanted to make public Marshall's deteriorating health and its subsequent effect on the team's affairs. Without mentioning Marshall's recent surgery Shea advanced the notion that perhaps the time had come for Marshall to step aside from his decision-making role with the Redskins.

"Marshall is the best promoter I've ever known," Shea admitted, "but running the team and promoting it have been getting too much for him."

However, Shea added, "I'd always want him for his know how."[16]

Following their victory in Cleveland the Redskins continued their newfound winning ways with defeats of the St. Louis Cardinals and Los Angeles Rams at DC Stadium. The surprising Washington squad, now 3-0-1, had captured the interest of the national media. After the Rams game a piece penned by Tex Maule appeared in *Sports Illustrated* under the title, "The Redskins Find a New Kick: Winning."

"They think they can lick any team in football," Bill McPeak told Maule, "and some of this is due to Bobby Mitchell because the kids know he can break up a ball game at any time from any spot on the field.

"The original squad I took over two years ago had only fifteen or sixteen players. The club had to be rebuilt with grade A football players, and we started with the 1960 draft."

Maule didn't ignore the most important piece to Washington's surprising start, but Bobby Mitchell's contribution to the team's turnaround was somewhat downplayed in the article.

"I was very happy to be traded to the Redskins," Mitchell admitted. "That Mr. [Paul] Brown is a nice man in many ways, but he is very difficult to get along with when he is coaching."

Mitchell may have been the catalyst for the Redskins' revival, but it was quarterback Norm Snead who received the most attention in the *Sports Illustrated* piece.

"They taught us something we needed," the second-year player said. "They are used to winning. I mean guys like [Bob] Pellegrini and Billy Barnes we got from the Eagles. They talk about it all the time, about how little difference there is between a winning effort and a losing one. I mean in this league it takes maybe just a little bit more to win. This year we've had a little bit more and last year we didn't."

Snead explained that it was in the final games of the exhibition season that he and his teammates began to gain confidence in one another. A 29–20 victory over Chicago and a close defeat to Green Bay were the turning point, according to Snead.

"Then Pellegrini and Barnes and the other guys who know began saying we were as good as any club in the league, and we got to believing it," Snead said. "Now everyone on the club believes it."[17]

In late October Bobby Mitchell sat down with Shirley Povich in the Redskins' locker room. Mitchell had just come off the practice field, where he and his teammates were preparing for their October 28 game against the Giants. The conversation quickly focused on Mitchell's previous trip to New York, when he had played in the final game of the Cleveland Browns' 1961 season. A New York loss to Cleveland would have forced a playoff between the Giants and Eagles.

"I never could figure out why the man didn't use me," Bobby Mitchell said of Paul Brown. "He knew that I knew I already had been traded to Washington, but that didn't make any difference to me.

"Oh, I played the whole game," Mitchell acknowledged, "but I never got my hands on the ball until the very end."

Although Mitchell effectively returned kickoffs and punts throughout the contest, he rushed the ball from scrimmage only three times and had one reception.

"I went up to New York from Fort Meade, where I was still with the Army, with only one thought in my mind," Mitchell explained. "I wanted to give a great effort for my teammates. I had a lot of friends on that Cleveland club; they meant the world to me.

"I know the guys were doing a lot of grousing during the game. Jim Brown even went up to Paul and said, 'Give the ball to Mitchell.' Paul just said, 'Yes, yes.' But nothing happened."

With the game knotted at 7–7 and the clock quickly running down late in the fourth quarter Paul Brown opted to punt, all but conceding the division championship to the Giants. Brown's lack of competitive fire, as well as his submission to a deadlock, grated on Mitchell and his teammates.

"I'll never forget how bad I felt after that game. I sat there in a daze in front of my locker. I was terribly hurt. I might not have been fond of the Cleveland Browns organization, but I wanted so much to do some good for the fellows."[18]

In the seventh week of play the Redskins suffered their first defeat of the season, falling to the Giants 49–34. Following the game Mitchell did not travel back home with the rest of his teammates. Instead he stayed behind in New York to speak before the Pro Quarterbacks' Club, a group that gathered together every Monday following a Giants home game.

The "opening" act for Mitchell's appearance at the club was the comedian Buddy Hackett. The stocky comedian had once played guard at Brooklyn's Utrecht High School.

"In my time," Hackett recalled, "football players were very stupid and maybe they ain't changed as much as I thought."

Hackett may have been a professional funny man, but Mitchell took offense at his pigeonholing of all football players as unintelligent. Obviously the comedian had never met Bobby Mitchell.

Mitchell's talk surprised his audience by its breadth and honesty. He spoke of Paul Brown, issued a not so veiled threat to George Marshall, chastised the New York media, and offered tribute to his current coach, during which Mitchell even managed to pat himself on the back.

"You wrote us off for dead yesterday," Mitchell said to members of the

New York media in attendance, "but you'll be in Washington two more times this year, once when the Giants come down to play us, and again for the championship."

Asked about his former coach in Cleveland, Mitchell answered, "He knew I wanted out for three years, but it was a matter of me waiting until he could get somebody to fill my position. We were opposed to his calling all the plays, although sometimes we were happy he did. . . . He was hard-headed and convinced the plays he called were right. We had to keep running them even if we knew they weren't working. Frankly, there were a few times when I didn't run to the best of my ability when I was convinced the play wasn't working."

Mitchell had nothing but admiration for his new coach.

"He knows the game, and he knows the players," Mitchell said of Bill McPeak. "He knows our feelings and emotions and he spends many hours demonstrating this. He'll listen to suggestions. He doesn't send you the same way all the time when you're getting hit on the head and a play doesn't work.

"The happiest day of my pro career came when McPeak told me I was going to play flanker back. I was getting tired of fellows like Sam Huff hitting me in the mouth. I wanted to get outside where I could scare someone."

On George Marshall: "He welcomed me to the Redskins and told me they were taking me out of the shadows of Jimmy Brown. In Washington I'd be a star in my own right. He said he was glad to have me. He then added, 'But we don't have that much money.'

"I don't want to have them think I'm so intelligent," Mitchell said. "I know there are a lot of people in the stands. Sellouts every week. And that Mr. Marshall is walking around with fat checks in his pocket. I would imagine, well, being the dumb individual I am, I imagine I'll be the highest paid player in pro football next year."

Mitchell's prediction brought a broad smile to his face, prompting the audience to break out in laughter.

At the conclusion of Mitchell's appearance Buddy Hackett bounced from his seat back to the microphone. He wished to revise his opening remarks.

"I just want to say, Bobby, football players used to be stupid."[19]

Prior to leaving New York, Mitchell also sat down with John Devaney of *Sport Magazine*. Mitchell wasn't exactly being modest when he articulated the thought that he was the finest back in the game.

"I figure I wasted the first four years of my career," Mitchell said, dismissing the notion that he had accomplished much while in Cleveland. "When they spoke of the Jimmy Browns and the Sam Huffs, the greats, I wasn't mentioned in the group. I was the best running back in the league, but I wasn't among the greats in the league, and that hurt."

Mitchell paused and pounded his right fist into his left palm. "If I only had those years, I could be the greatest."[20]

Mitchell hadn't completely exorcised the demons that had made him a loner in his younger days. Gwen Mitchell acknowledged that her husband occasionally still needed to be left alone, totally alone.

"Sometimes he'll go off by himself for four or five days without talking to anybody," Gwen explained. "It used to bother me, but it doesn't anymore. I don't care really. I tell him I'm going to put a bed down in the rec room in the basement, and he can just stay there while he gets over it."[21]

A couple of days after Mitchell sat with Povich, George Marshall acquiesced to an interview with Frank Boggs of the *Dallas Times Herald*. The Cowboys were coming to town for a November 4 date with the Redskins. The talk covered a wide range of topics, including the possibility of the NFL merging with the upstart American Football League.

Such a proposal was preposterous to Marshall. "The other league has nothing to offer," he exclaimed.

Turning the topic to Marshall's club, Boggs asked how Redskins fans were responding to the integration of the team.

"They haven't paid any attention to it," Marshall responded. "Only thing that interests them, is can they play football. That's the important thing."

Boggs also mentioned to him that at one time the Redskins were picketed because of Marshall's refusal to sign a Negro. Did the protests bother him?

"No."

Boggs continued with a similar line of questioning. Had Secretary Udall forced Marshall to integrate his team?

"No! No! No!" Marshall bellowed emphatically. "He had nothing to do with it!"[22]

The Redskins' October 28 loss to the Giants at Yankee Stadium brought their record to 4-1-2 at the halfway point of the season. For the moment the Redskins were sitting atop the Eastern Conference of the NFL, and there was no denying the fact that Bobby Mitchell was the spark that had turned around the moribund franchise.

Performing between the lines, Mitchell could handle that. He always knew that if given the opportunity he possessed the talent to excel. In Cleveland Mitchell had rarely been allowed the chance to demonstrate his capabilities. Ironic though it may have been, the Washington Redskins supplied Mitchell with the platform to display his wide-ranging abilities and innate football intellect. Mitchell was also very active in DC's black community; he was a frequent visitor to district schools. Sometimes the appearance was to hand out awards, while on other occasions he gave a talk. The message was always the same. Stay in school. Get an education. You can make a difference in this world, but first you need an education.

He was a star, even a savior to some, but to others Bobby Mitchell was something *other*, something beneath contempt. This truth was something Mitchell could not possibly have been prepared for when he came to Washington. Although he was joined by Nisby, Hatcher, and Jackson, Mitchell was the man credited with integrating the Redskins. He and he alone was the man at the forefront.

At one point during the fall the Mitchells went out to dinner at Rive Gauche, a prominent French restaurant in Georgetown. While Bobby and Gwen were in the midst of a quiet dinner a man came by their table.

"Are you Bobby Mitchell?" he asked.

"Yes, I am," Bobby replied.

Without another word the man spat at Mitchell.[23]

The vile act shook Mitchell. To be confronted with such hatred was not easy to overcome.

Mitchell's spectacular play on the field made headlines and had certainly turned around the Redskins' fortunes, and though he drew the most attention, both praise and repulsion, he wasn't the only Redskins player breaking ground in 1962.

Officially Leroy Jackson was the first black player to take the field for the Redskins when he stepped between the lines to take the season-opening kickoff against Dallas. As Mitchell's backup at halfback, Jackson had limited playing time. He was a poor receiver out of the backfield, and when he carried the ball Jackson's average per attempt was just barely above 2 yards.[24] Jackson's primary role was as a kick returner.

Jackson's teammates Nisby and Mitchell were both married, and their wives offered support, a sounding board, and some solace from the indignities they endured. Jackson, Nisby, and Mitchell were friendly on and off the field. Each member of the trio, along with Ron Hatcher, was individually suffering a variety of indignations, but the bigotry they faced they did not discuss among themselves. While the Mitchells and Nisbys enjoyed a stable and loving home life, Jackson, as a single man, carried his burdens silently.

Ron Hatcher held the distinction of being the first black player signed to a contract by the Redskins. Although he possessed a fraction of Mitchell's playing skills, Hatcher still was confronted with prejudice as he tried to make his way into the NFL. He noticed a particular coolness from some of his Redskins teammates.

Bobby Mitchell also served as a mentor and roommate to the rookie. The veteran took Hatcher under his wing and provided much-appreciated advice, including counsel extending beyond football.

Throughout the five-game preseason schedule Hatcher, wearing No. 33 in honor of his hero Ollie Matson, carried the ball only once, for 6 yards. The few times he was in the exhibition games Hatcher's main duty was to serve as a blocking back, a function he performed well.

McPeak, however, needed more versatility with his roster, and Hatcher's contribution to the team would be limited if his only role was as a blocking back. Hatcher was waived September 11, along with lineman Don Lawrence, a maneuver that brought the Redskins' roster down to thirty-six.

As the Redskins' season wound to a close, Hatcher, who had served as a one-man taxi squad, was activated by McPeak prior to the December 6 game against the Eagles.

John Nisby was a halfback in an offensive lineman's body.

Nisby badly wanted to carry the ball, and despite playing a nondescript position he wished to be a star. While he may not have had the physical attributes and skill sets of his good friend and Pittsburgh teammate John Henry Johnson, Nisby was a quality lineman. He was the "quarterback" of the offensive line. He called defenses and signaled his line-mates their assignments.

Truth be told John Nisby and Bobby Mitchell were two contrasting personalities. Although a proud man, Mitchell kept his own counsel and bore the numerous racial affronts with quiet dignity. Nisby, however, boisterously made his discontent known. He was a free spirit. He was independent and outspoken, two attributes that did not endear Nisby to team management. Nor did John ingratiate himself to all of his Steelers teammates in Pittsburgh, thanks mostly to his blunt demeanor.

Mitchell was insular and intelligent, while Nisby was outgoing and intelligent. The two men got along well, though, with each man's personality complementing the other's.

Nisby found little difference between the fans of Pittsburgh and those in Washington; working-class whites in both cities displayed bigotry openly. What Nisby didn't have in DC was a hard-drinking, foul-mouthed coach. McPeak was appreciated by his new players for his fairness. But there was a shared history between Nisby and his new coach, as well as a bit of tension. Back in the summer of '57, in Allegany, New York, when both men were trying to catch on with the Pittsburgh Steelers, Nisby beat out McPeak. The events that September at St. Bonaventure University led to the end of Bill McPeak's playing career and the beginning of John Nisby's life in pro football.

Did McPeak hold a grudge five years later? Whether he did or not is immaterial. What mattered was that Nisby believed his coach did, and he in turn held a grudge against the Redskins' front office, not necessarily for how he had been treated but for what had occurred before his arrival in Washington.

Nisby, like every other black player in the league, was fully aware of George Marshall's unabashed bigotry.

The presence of Mitchell and Nisby certainly had a beneficial impact on Marshall's wallet. For the 1962 season the Redskins had approximately six hundred black season-ticket holders compared to the twenty they had had just one year earlier. Chances are, Norm Snead wasn't the reason for the drastic change.

"Well, it was fun while it lasted," Francis Stann of the *Washington Star* began his November 5 column.

One day earlier, following a week of anticipation and hype, the Redskins came out and laid an egg against the Cowboys before a record crowd of 49,888 fans at DC Stadium. The loss dropped the Redskins to a 4-2-2 record.

"It was the flattest game we've played since our first exhibition against the Rams," McPeak said of the 38–10 loss. "We never got untracked. We couldn't get going."[25]

The Redskins rebounded the following week with a 17–9 win over Cleveland, but things quickly unraveled over the course of the next few weeks. A defeat at Pittsburgh was followed by a home loss to the Giants. Washington's record stood at 5-4-1 when Philadelphia came to DC Stadium for a December 2 date.

Throughout the fall Mitchell had surprised local reporters with his candor. In an era of unrevealing and uninteresting postgame quotes and canned interviews Mitchell was a breath of fresh air. Despite his eight receptions for 114 yards the Redskins fell to the Eagles, 37–14. In the locker room afterward Mitchell had some critical words for Philadelphia defensive back Ben Scott.

"He's nothing," Mitchell said. "When he's in there I'm sure of a catch. When [Mike] McClellan's in there I've got to work. He's a rookie, but he's cool and he plays it smart. You don't fool him too often. I respect him."

A reporter informed Mitchell that he had broken a couple of Washington team records, having surpassed Fred Dugan's single-season receiving record for catches and Hugh "Bones" Taylor's mark for receiving yardage.

"Yeah," Mitchell snapped, "and we lost the game.

"I'm getting tired of this," he said. "Tired of getting beat up. It's not only this team—it happens throughout the entire league. A lot of punches come this way, but when you're on top you've got to expect it. I don't mind getting hit. I can take a blow. I got hit as a half-back, but it's extra-curricular activities that bother me."

Mitchell added, however, "It won't keep me from catching passes. I'm gonna catch it if they kill me."[26]

The Philadelphia game marked the debut of Ron Hatcher, who performed on special teams.

"I only changed my seat from the grandstand to the bench," Hatcher said. "To tell the truth, you see better from the grandstand."[27]

After their impressive start the Redskins finished the season with a 5-7-2 record. The end results were disappointing, but Washington fans had been treated to a talent the likes of which they had never had on their side before.

Mitchell finished third in the 1962 Player of the Year voting behind Jim Taylor and Y. A. Tittle. He was also named to his first Pro Bowl, which was scheduled to be played January 14, 1963, at the Los Angeles Coliseum.

"My wife and I are going to take a vacation," Mitchell said, "but I want to play in that Pro Bowl. We'll interrupt it for that."[28]

Epilogue | "Sit Down for Nobody"

Art Rooney Jr. was attending the 1961 winter league meetings in Miami Beach with his father and brothers.

Rooney was in the lobby of the Kenilworth Hotel awaiting an elevator with his younger brother Tim when an immaculately dressed George Marshall brushed passed him with a showgirl on each arm. The doors to the elevator opened, and before the Rooney brothers could enter, Marshall and his companions boarded, leaving the young men behind.

The two Rooneys looked at each other in silent wonder and admiration of the old man.

Eleven months later the Steelers were at DC Stadium for a game against the Redskins. Art Jr. was shocked when the press box elevator opened and revealed a feeble Marshall seated in a wheelchair, his lap covered with a blanket and an attendant at his side.

Rooney took one look at his brother Tim. The two shared the same unspoken thought: *did the showgirls cause that?*

It wasn't the women who were the cause of his decline but complications from hernia surgery that Marshall underwent in the summer of 1962. It was an illness from which Marshall never fully recovered. Initial concerns about Marshall's health came while the Redskins were training at Occidental College earlier in the summer, when he missed a number of practices. He passed up most of the exhibition games, and then, following his procedure to remove the hernia, Marshall skipped all of the Redskins' road games. Prior to his illness Marshall had rarely missed a practice of any kind, let alone a game.

A few days after the Redskins concluded their 1962 season with a 27–24 loss to the Steelers, Marshall boarded a train for Florida. This trip south had been an annual ritual for Marshall, who would spend a couple of months in the warmth and sunshine to rejuvenate the bones before heading back to work. While in Florida Marshall was informed that he had been selected as member of the first class of the Pro Football Hall of Fame. When told of the news Marshall opted not to pat himself on the back. Instead he focused on potential troubles that might lie ahead for his team and the league.

"The clubs should be more active in keeping an eye on their players and helping them to avoid questionable associates. I've done it with my Redskins," Marshall said.

"You have to pay the price of eternal watchfulness. The players get careless. They join a team and are new in town. They are easily picked up and carried to dinner. Their hosts may not even mention gambling, but the association is bad. The players must remember their responsibility to the game and the public, and not ever attract suspicion."[1]

In January 1963 the winter league meetings were held in Miami. Even though Marshall was nearby at his Miami Beach hideaway the gathering proceeded without him.

Pete Rozelle told the attending owners of Marshall's poor health, asking them to "please make arrangements to go over and see George and wish him well."[2]

The commissioner's request was met by nearly every attending owner, who recognized the importance of Marshall's contributions to the league's success.

Mo Siegel, too, paid a visit to Marshall in late March and found that he was still not himself.

"I feel plain lousy," he told Siegel.[3]

To see George Marshall wasting away in this manner seemed a cruel fate to those who knew him well. One of his closest friends remarked with sadness, "Marshall always envisioned his demise coming at the hand of some broad's husband."[4]

Unlike all his other trips to Florida through the years, this time Marshall remained in Miami until long after the cherry trees along the Tidal Basin had blossomed. When he finally did return to Washington, Marshall looked noticeably older. His once sharp memory was now foggy. His sharp tongue was now tamed. His confident gait had slowed to a shuffle.

A return to the Redskins' offices appeared to have a positive effect on

Marshall. For the first time since World War II the Redskins were not training in California. The team's new home away from home was Dickinson College in Carlisle, Pennsylvania. Although not as glamorous as the West Coast, Carlisle was certainly a more practical locale. Marshall, however, wouldn't be present when his team arrived. Just days before the Redskins reported to camp he suffered a severe setback.

"He needed rest" was the word out of Georgetown Hospital, where Marshall was admitted on July 13.

Eleven days later an announcement came from the team's offices that Leo De Orsey would temporarily have the authority to make any major decisions that confronted the team.

Nearly a month after Marshall was admitted to Georgetown Hospital he displayed no sign of recovery. On August 15 the Redskins were set to play Chicago in an exhibition contest at DC Stadium. "Papa Bear" Halas certainly couldn't come to Washington without paying his respects to his old pal and antagonist. Accompanied by Pete Rozelle and Mo Siegel, George Halas stopped by Georgetown Hospital for a brief visit with Marshall.

Halas was visibly shaken when he saw Marshall in his weakened state, but he quickly composed himself.

"Hello, Dynamite," Halas said, extending his hand to Marshall. "Good to see you again."

Marshall struggled to smile. "Sit down, George," he replied in a hoarse whisper.

"You brought the commish, eh? You never change, Georgie; still trying to get the edge."

Halas had to laugh at that. "This guy over here," he said, pointing to Marshall, "between the two of us we really did something for the league back in '33. We got the goal posts moved to the goal line. That was Marshall's idea. We allowed them to pass from anywhere behind the line of scrimmage—Marshall did that too. And we also moved the ball in fifteen yards from the sidelines.

"I told Marshall it would open up the game. That didn't interest him as much as he thought it would attract spectators." Halas paused for a moment. "We got those rule changes through by a 3–2 vote, remember, George?"

The young commissioner was transfixed by the history lesson. "Who voted against them?" Rozelle asked.

"You'd never guess," Marshall explained. "Two damn good passers, Benny Friedman and Curly Lambeau."

Lambeau Rozelle knew, but Friedman?

"Benny Friedman?" a puzzled Rozelle asked.

The conversation sparked something in Marshall. He perked up for the first time in months. "Friedman with Brooklyn, the Brooklyn Dodgers," Marshall explained.

Joe Kuharich then entered the crowded hospital room and spoke a few quiet words with his old boss.

"Got enough here for a rules meeting," Siegel thought out loud.

Halas jumped in. "Yeah, and Marshall will have a few proposals to make, won't you George?"

This time there was no reply. The guests realized it was time to head out.

As Halas was leaving Marshall thanked the old coach for the flowers he'd recently sent. "Nice of you," Marshall said. "The girl doesn't forget the man who doesn't forget."

"See you at the game tonight," Halas said.

Against the advice of his doctors Marshall did attend the contest that evening. Confined to a wheelchair, he sat silently in his private box and watched the game being played out before him. The Bears versus the Redskins— nothing stirred the blood in Marshall's veins more. All those bitter Sunday afternoons. Battling the Bears or fighting Halas, Marshall had savored every moment of each encounter. But on this night the spark just wasn't there. Indeed the embers were now nearly extinguished. Try as he might Marshall struggled to make it to halftime before retreating back to the hospital.

A few weeks later the Pro Football Hall of Fame inducted its inaugural class in Canton, Ohio. The Hall of Fame was in its infancy and in fact had not yet opened its doors. Discussion of such a museum had first been bandied about in the late 1940s, and the location tentatively chosen for such an establishment was Latrobe, Pennsylvania. The proposal quietly died, though, and plans were tabled for more than a decade. The idea was resurrected after the *Canton Repository* ran an article headlined "Pro Football Needs a Hall of Fame and the Logical Site Is Here" on December 6, 1959.

The *Repository*'s pitch had an impact. From there the idea caught fire. A substantial amount of money was raised to bring the museum to "the birthplace of professional football," and in 1961 NFL owners decreed that Canton would be home to the league's Hall of Fame.

Marshall had been informed months earlier that he was among those to be honored for their contributions to professional football. The first class of inductees included some of the greatest names in the history of the game. Marshall's nemesis, George Halas, was on the list, as was his favorite player, Sammy Baugh. Bert Bell, Jim Thorpe, Red Grange, and Curly Lambeau were a few of the other influential greats to be a part of the inaugural Hall of Fame class.[5] In the past nothing could have precluded Marshall's attendance at such an event, but Marshall's deteriorating health prevented him from being present at the September 7 induction ceremonies. He was the only one of twelve living honorees not present in Canton.

Milton King accepted the honor on Marshall's behalf. His longtime friend made the most of the opportunity. Along with all the other inductees King rode in the three-hour parade. King was so caught up in the swirl of events that he signed autographs—writing Marshall's name.

Stewart Udall

Following the death of President Kennedy the Johnson administration asked Stewart Udall to continue in his role as secretary of the interior. During his eight years in the department Udall presided over sixty additions to the national park system, including the creation of four national parks—Redwood, Canyonlands, Guadalupe Mountains, and North Cascades. He also supervised the acquisition of 3.85 million acres of new federal lands, six national monuments, twenty historic sites, fifty wildlife refuges, eight national seashores, and nine national recreational areas. All along the way Udall fought opposition from both local and corporate interests.

He left a lasting legacy. His litany of accomplishments included the Wilderness Act of 1964, the Water Quality Act of 1965, the National Historic Preservation Act of 1966, the Endangered Species Preservation Act of 1966, and the Wild and Scenic Rivers Act of 1968.

Stewart Udall passed away on March 21, 2010. His was a vibrant voice for conservationism until his dying days, and he was a shining example of a public servant.

Upon his death Udall was eulogized by President Barack Obama, who said, "Whether in the skies above Italy in World War II, in Congress, or as Secretary of the Interior, Stewart Udall left an indelible mark on this nation and inspired countless Americans who will continue his fight for clean air, clean water and to maintain our many natural treasures."[6]

Udall's own words, written in his 1963 best-selling book *The Quiet Crisis*, still seem prophetic: "We cannot afford an America where expedience tramples upon esthetics and development decisions are made with an eye only on the present."[7]

Bobby Mitchell

Statistics tell only part of the story.

With Bobby Mitchell's arrival in Washington the Redskins immediately became charged with a new spirit. Prior to his appearance in the capital the Redskins' struggles on the field had reached an epic scale. Over the previous decade the club had steadily regressed, and the once proud franchise had become a laughingstock. Mitchell's presence changed everything. His transcendence, his genius between the lines brought a new attitude and enthusiasm to a moribund franchise. During Mitchell's time in Washington the Redskins won no championships, but the team had reinvigorated the city.

Nearly five decades following his retirement Bobby Mitchell reflected back to the day he met Marshall inside the Redskins' Ninth Street offices.

"I barely heard a word he said," Mitchell recalled, "because I was so impressed that all around the room were portraits of Indian chiefs. He had every Indian chief that you could name. Big portraits. He was talking and I was just looking. I was so impressed."[8]

Mitchell stepped away from the playing field during training camp in the summer of 1969 after realizing that he could no longer perform at the same level as he had in his prime. At that moment he held the mark as second on the NFL's all-time list for combined yards. Despite those stats it still took ten years for Bobby Mitchell to be recognized by the Pro Football Hall of Fame.

Mitchell stood at the vanguard of the fight for civil rights in pro sports. He was there on the front lines, standing alongside Muhammad Ali with a group of prominent black athletes when the heavyweight champion of the world refused to step forward for induction into the U.S. Army. Ali objected to the Vietnam War on religious grounds, and standing with the champ was something that could have had significant ramifications for Mitchell.

"A lot of people don't understand," Mitchell explained, "that when we decided to have a meeting with Muhammad Ali about going into the service . . . it could have cost us our jobs."[9]

In the years that followed Mitchell rarely spoke of the terrible affronts he endured during those initial years as the "first" black man to play for the Redskins. His reluctance to speak of the indignities betrayed a hurt that Mitchell chose not to acknowledge, but the wound inflicted by hatred and bigotry was deep.

"He had to suffer for being black more than any person that I know, during the time I played," Jim Brown said upon reflection. "With that kind of ability, if he were white, everybody on this earth would know who he was."[10]

"I had to deal with white and black," Mitchell said to Ken Denlinger of the *Washington Post* on the eve of his induction into the Hall of Fame. "The whites didn't want me there, and the blacks got mad if I'd drop a ball. To the blacks, I had to be perfect, 'cause I was their banner. All this pressure, and I had to perform."[11]

On that special occasion Mitchell's memory ran free.

"I remember the years we'd come in here [the Cleveland Browns'] Jim and I used to be sitting on the bus driving through the city saying, 'Man, the first guy that comes to Washington as a player is gonna have it made.' 'Course you never think of being the guy."[12]

After Edward Bennett Williams introduced him at the Hall of Fame ceremony Mitchell delivered a heartfelt and reflective speech.

"It doesn't seem so long ago that I was playing on the fields of the city of Hot Springs, Arkansas. . . . How do you write a speech for this? How can a speech do justice to this Hall?

"My reaction [to the Hall of Fame honor] is one of joy, excitement, delight, and wonderment. . . . This makes you wonder if you are worthy. I've always wanted to be recognized and respected. My enshrinement today tells me that I am recognized. The love of my family and all my friends tell me I am respected."

Mitchell's speech was emotional, but he stumbled only when he spoke of his wife.

"She has worked tirelessly for many a year," Bobby said of his bride, Gwen. "I think of the number of times that she would walk behind so I could shine. I had the glory, she had all the strength. I just hope that sometime through this lifetime that I can find the strength to say to her that I think she has been a great partner."[13]

Pete Rozelle

The initial years of the National Football League under the guidance of Pete Rozelle witnessed an ever-expanding sport.

Johnny Unitas, Jim Brown, Vince Lombardi—these were the major figures of the NFL when Pete Rozelle took the reins of the league.

As the decade of the sixties progressed the popularity of the NFL grew exponentially with each passing year.

Lombardi, a one-time offensive assistant with the New York Giants, had moved on to Green Bay, where he constructed one of the finest teams to ever ply their trade on Sundays. With their seemingly endless run of championships Lombardi's Packers made their mark as the greatest dynasty the game had yet seen.

Jim Brown, perhaps the finest player to ever to spend a Sunday playing the game of football, had retired following the 1965 season, but not before the record books had been sent back to the printer for a rewrite.

Behind the great "Johnny U" the Baltimore Colts repeated their World Championship ways in 1959, though in much less dramatic fashion. Following his team's second championship Unitas struggled to reach the same heights. But the Colts' quarterback continued to display his singular brilliance on the field, and he remained the most bankable and recognizable figure in the NFL.

Lombardi, Brown, Unitas. The names struck a chord with any true sports fan.

Lombardi, Brown, and Unitas were indeed the most familiar names of the NFL as the league continued its assault on Major League Baseball in an attempt to become the national pastime. But it was Pete Rozelle who, more than any other individual, propelled the league to the forefront of the nation's sporting consciousness.

On June 8, 1966, a merger agreement was announced between the NFL and the AFL. The covenant acknowledged that the two leagues would continue to play separate schedules during the regular season; however, the agreement stipulated that the champion of each league would meet the other in a title game. This arrangement would continue for four years before the two leagues would become fully unified beginning with the 1970 season.

During the first years of the American Football League's existence the NFL did its best to disregard the new league. Although Lamar Hunt's AFL continued to operate, its presence had made little impact on the NFL. But when New York Jets owner Sonny Werblin signed the University of Alabama's star quarterback, Joe Namath, to play for his club, all bets were off. Sure, there had been some bidding wars between the teams prior to this agreement, but the Namath contract, an unprecedented $427,000 deal, tossed everything out the window. Leaders from both leagues saw the writing on the wall. Contracts like this would bankrupt everyone. Lamar Hunt knew his league couldn't survive with such numbers being bandied about, and he clandestinely approached the NFL about a merger. Notwithstanding his antitrust suit from just a few years prior, Hunt decided that monopolies weren't all that bad. This time the established league took the bait; they, too, would rather join the enemy than meet on an even playing field.

The champion of each league met for the first time on January 15, 1967, at the Los Angeles Memorial Coliseum. Lombardi's Packers dominated Lamar Hunt's Kansas City Chiefs.[14] Green Bay won again the following season, defeating the Oakland Raiders in convincing fashion.

It was the third "Super Bowl," as the championship came to be called, that captured the public's imagination. This contest was the victory "guaranteed" by Joe Willie Namath; the brash Jets quarterback had backed up his pregame talk of a "guaranteed" victory and in the process won over an entirely new audience for professional football.

Behind the brazen Namath the AFL champion defeated the NFL's champions, the Baltimore Colts, in a shocking 16–7 upset.

In the weeks following the third incarnation of the Super Bowl, Marshall's health went from bad to worse, as he suffered a mild heart attack, a mild stroke, and a bout of pneumonia. Several years earlier, in his incapacitated state, Marshall had relinquished control of the Redskins to team president Leo De Orsey. When De Orsey died in April 1965, Edward Bennett Williams took over the day-to-day operations of the team. Although Williams's 5 percent stake in the club was dwarfed by Jack Kent Cooke's stock holdings of 25 percent, Cooke ceded his voting shares to Williams due to his business commitments on the West Coast.

An associate of Marshall's once remarked, "George is like a skyrocket. He's very brilliant, but you don't know what direction he's taking off in."[15]

Death came to George Preston Marshall on August 9, 1969, at 7:55 a.m.

He passed away in his sleep at his Georgetown home. The last years of his life were days of suffering for Marshall. Since his 1962 hernia operation Marshall's health had steadily deteriorated. Through the ensuing years Marshall was plagued with numerous physical ailments: a cerebral thrombosis, hemiplegia, diabetes, a heart condition, and arteriosclerosis.

His passing came nearly eight months to the day after the New York Jets' stunning victory over the Colts.

Eulogies flooded in from across the country.

Jerry Izenberg wrote in his *Newark Star-Ledger* remembrance of Marshall, "George Preston Marshall; he was an ego in search of a theater."[16]

Those nearest to home, however, knew Marshall best.

"A man of million ideas" was how Francis Stann recalled him.

"If anything [Marshall] was born too soon. A generation before there was a Houston Astrodome he foresaw a domed sports stadium. He was a practical dreamer, more right than wrong."

Marshall's finest hours, Stann recalled, were the years of Slingin' Sammy Baugh. But those days, like all days, eventually passed. What we are left with, Stann acknowledged, were memories.

"All his life Marshall was controversial," Stann admitted. "He reveled in controversy. He was difficult for his coaches, whom he changed regularly. He feuded with newsmen, congressmen, Cabinet members, fellow stockholders."[17]

Had more column space been provided to him, Stann could have continued that list. Whether it was players, league commissioners, or fellow team owners, Marshall never backed away from a quarrel if he believed in his position, and he always believed in whatever position he took.

Obstinate, indeed.

An editorial in the *Washington Daily News* recognized the influence Marshall had had on the game.

"More than anyone else, he changed professional football from a somewhat dull, irrelevant imitation of the college game to the highly efficient, exciting razzle-dazzle scheme we know today," the editorial stated.[18]

Marshall's genius at promotion was also extolled. His many ideas and his numerous innovations had helped usher the NFL into the forefront of the nation's sporting conscience.

His legacy was secure years before his passing; Marshall was eulogized in print while he was still actively running the Redskins.

"At worst he can rest comfortably on his press clippings," Harold Weissman of the *New York Mirror* wrote in 1961. "These do not include the worst— the deflating notices he received as a frustrated World War I actor in a New Orleans stock company. George prudently abandoned [a] footlight career when his sense of frustration was transmitted to the audience. However, he need never apologize, except perhaps to the NAACP, for his accomplishments on the more realistic stage of day to day survival in sports."[19]

Marshall's primary antagonist in print, Shirley Povich, remained dignifiedly silent. The *Post* columnist chose not to resurrect past grievances. Rather than appear a hypocrite Povich refrained from submitting a column in the days following Marshall's passing.

The funeral was held August 13 at the National Cathedral. Services began at ten o'clock in the morning. The National Football League was represented by at least one envoy from every club. Halas, of course, was there. So were Art Rooney and his son Dan. Tex Schramm and Art Modell, representing the league's new generation, served as honorary pallbearers along with

John Chevalier and Milton King, as well as Gene Archer, the soloist who had performed the "Star-Spangled Banner" before numerous Redskins home games.

Members of the 1969 Redskins remained at training camp in Carlisle, where they attended a special memorial service at the Dickinson College campus's chapel. The team Marshall loved so dearly was represented at the funeral by head coach Vince Lombardi.

Marshall's old drinking pal and occasional sparring partner, Mo Siegel, read a brief Bible passage. Pete Rozelle also offered a few words on the memory and legacy of George Preston Marshall:

"George Preston Marshall's interests spanned a broad spectrum; the theater, government, business world and sports. Intimate friends ranged from Jimmy Walker and James Farley in the early years to Senator Warren Magnusson and Morrie Siegel later in his lifetime.

"But professional football was his main interest and where he left an indelible mark. So, I speak for those who were best able to appreciate his personal qualities and the contributions he made to the game he loved, people like the Rooney, Bidwill, Halas, and Mara families.

"Mr. Marshall was an outspoken foe of status quo when most were content with it. He had the courage of his convictions and energetically fought for his views. His powerful voice was heard and heeded and his fertile imagination and vision brought vital improvements to the structure and presentation of the game.

"He had a fierce commitment to keep the sport clear and above reproach—a position that strongly influenced commissioners past and present.

"The game of professional football does in many ways reflect his personality. It has his imagination, style, zest, dedication, openness, dry humor, brashness, strength and courage.

"All of us who participated in some form of the game and those millions who enjoy viewing it are beneficiaries of what his dynamic personality helped shape over more than three decades."[20]

The day following the funeral Marshall was taken home to Romney, West Virginia, where he was laid to rest in the family plot alongside his mother. A graveside service was conducted at Indian Mound Cemetery.

Marshall's last testament and will specified the creation of a foundation. The mission of the institution was the improvement of conditions for children in the Washington area. The will specified that the foundation "shall never use, contribute or apply its money or property which supports or employs the principle of racial integration in any form or which supports any principle of religious discrimination in any form."[21]

Notes

Prologue

1. *Baltimore Afro-American*, November 28, 1959.
2. *Washington Post*, December 1, 1959.
3. Griffith wrote the lyrics, and the music was composed by Barnee Breeskin, the leader of the Washington Redskins Marching Band.

1. "What's the Difference?"

1. Robert H. Boyle, "Horatio Harry," *Sports Illustrated*, October 31, 1960, 49–50.
2. *Los Angeles Times*, January 3, 1957.
3. *Baltimore Afro-American*, January 12, 1957.
4. *Pittsburgh Courier*, January 12, 1957.
5. *Baltimore Afro-American*, January 12, 1957.
6. *Baltimore Afro-American*, January 12, 1957.
7. *Washington Daily News*, January 4, 1957.
8. *Baltimore Afro-American*, January 26, 1957.
9. *Washington Post*, January 27, 1957.
10. *Atlanta Daily World*, January 18, 1957.
11. *Atlanta Daily World*, January 18, 1957.
12. *Atlanta Daily World*, January 18, 1957.
13. *Atlanta Daily World*, January 18, 1957.
14. *Philadelphia Inquirer*, February 1, 1957.
15. *Philadelphia Inquirer*, February 1, 1957.
16. *Washington Star*, January 31, 1957.
17. *Washington Star*, January 31, 1957.
18. *Washington Star*, February 2, 1957.
19. *New York Times*, February 2, 1957.
20. *Washington Star*, February 2, 1957.

21. *Washington Star*, February 2, 1957.

22. *Washington Post*, February 4, 1957.

2. Pomp and Pageantry

1. Arthur Daley, "George Preston Marshall: The Great Showboat," in *Pro Football's Hall of Fame: The Official Book* (Chicago: Quadrangle Books, 1963), 209–21, photocopied chapter obtained at the Pro Football Hall of Fame.

2. Daley, "George Preston Marshall."

3. Morris Siegel, "George Preston Marshall: Master Showman, Mastermind," *Pro Magazine*, October 28, 1973.

4. Siegel, "George Preston Marshall."

5. Siegel, "George Preston Marshall."

6. Howard Roberts, *The Story of Pro Football* (Chicago: Rand McNally, 1953).

7. *Washington Evening Star*, April 22, 1962.

8. Daley, "George Preston Marshall."

9. Siegel, "George Preston Marshall."

10. Daley, "George Preston Marshall."

11. Roberts, *Story of Pro Football*.

12. *Buffalo Evening News*, August 22, 1969. Marshall apparently made the comment in the early 1950s.

13. Roberts, *Story of Pro Football*.

14. *New York Telegram*, December 1, 1956.

15. This story was retold in many articles written about Marshall throughout his career. Each telling of the story is remarkably similar. This particular version is from Daley, "George Preston Marshall."

16. William Henry Paul, *The Gray-Flannel Pigskin: Movers and Shakers of Pro Football* (Philadelphia: Lippincott, 1974).

17. Following his release Kemp appealed to Rooney and asked to be reinstated to the team. The two men had known each other for several years. Though sympathetic, Rooney refused to override his head coach.

18. Daley, "George Preston Marshall."

19. Thomas Sugrue, "Soapsuds and Showmanship," *American Magazine*, December 1937.

20. *Washington Star*, December 17, 1936.

21. Paul, *Gray-Flannel Pigskin*.

22. Paul, *Gray-Flannel Pigskin*.

23. Paul, *Gray-Flannel Pigskin*.

24. Robert Boyle, "All Alone by the Telephone," *Sports Illustrated*, October 16, 1961.

25. Bob Curran, *Pro Football's Rag Days* (Englewood Cliffs NJ: Prentice Hall, 1969).

26. *Washington Post*, December 9, 1940.

27. *Washington Star*, December 9, 1940.

28. *Buffalo Evening News*, August 22, 1969.

29. Joe King, *Inside Pro Football* (Englewood Cliffs NJ: Prentice-Hall, 1958), 47.

30. Thom Loverro, *Hail Victory: An Oral History of the Washington Redskins* (Hoboken NJ: Wiley, 2008), 17.

31. *Washington Post*, September 17, 1937.

32. *Washington Post*, September 17, 1937.

33. *Washington Post*, August 24, 1954.

34. *Washington Star*, January 11, 1957.

35. *Washington Post*, August 24, 1954.

3. It Takes Ten to Tango

1. *New York Times*, undated clipping, 1958.

2. Phil Muscik, "A Football Man," probably from *Pro Magazine*, July 1976, from a photocopy of the article.

3. Muscik, "Football Man."

4. *Pittsburgh Press*, January 12, 1946.

5. *Pittsburgh Press*, January 12, 1946.

6. W. C. Heinz, "Boss of the Behemoths," *Saturday Evening Post*, December 3, 1955.

7. Muscik, "Football Man."

8. Al Hirshberg, "He Calls the Signals for Pro Football," *New York Times Magazine*, November 23, 1958.

9. Quoted in Hirshberg, "He Calls the Signals."

10. Myron Cope, *The Game That Was: The Early Days of Pro Football* (New York: World Publishing, 1970).

11. *Pittsburgh Press*, August 12, 1969.

12. Cope, *Game That Was*.

13. Curran, *Pro Football's Rag Days*.

14. Muscik, "Football Man."

15. Heinz, "Boss of the Behemoths."

16. Heinz, "Boss of the Behemoths."

17. Muscik, "Football Man."

18. Upton Bell, telephone interview by author, June 16, 2010.

19. *Washington Post*, October 9, 1956.

20. *Washington Post*, October 9, 1956.

21. *New York Times*, February 26, 1957.

22. *New York Times*, February 26, 1957.

23. *Los Angeles Times*, February 26, 1957.

24. *Washington Post*, February 28, 1957.

25. *Washington Post*, April 7, 1957.

26. Ed Linn, "Big Noise in Washington," *Sport Magazine*, November 1957.

27. *Washington Post*, February 27, 1957.

28. *Los Angeles Times*, March 6, 1957.

29. *Washington Star*, March 5, 1957.

30. *New York Times*, July 25, 1952.

31. *Washington Post*, July 25, 1957.

32. *Philadelphia Bulletin*, August 2, 1957.

33. *Washington Star*, August 1, 1957.

34. Hirshberg, "He Calls the Signals."

35. *Washington Star*, August 2, 1957.

36. *Washington Star*, August 2, 1957.

37. *Los Angeles Times*, August 2, 1957.

38. *Washington Star*, August 2, 1957.

39. Recalled by Victor Gold in interview by author, July 6, 2010.

40. *Washington Post*, September 20, 1958.

41. *Washington Post*, September 20, 1958.

42. *Los Angeles Sentinel*, September 19, 1957.

43. *Los Angeles Sentinel*, September 19, 1957.

44. *Washington Post*, October 17, 1957.

45. *Washington Post*, October 17, 1957.

46. Linn, "Big Noise in Washington."

47. Linn, "Big Noise in Washington."

48. *Washington Post*, September 25, 1958.

49. *Washington Post*, September 26, 1958.

50. *Washington Star*, August 14, 1957.
51. *Washington Star*, August 15, 1957.
52. *Baltimore Afro-American*, September 27, 1957.

4. There Was Interest
1. Recalled in Bell interview.

5. Fight for Old Dixie
1. *Washington Post*, July 26, 1959.
2. *Washington Post*, September 7, 1959.
3. Bill Gilbert, "A Forty Year Morning" (manuscript), folder 2, box 1, 1946 series, Shirley Povich Papers, Library of American Broadcasting, 3210 Hornbake Library, University of Maryland, College Park.
4. Gilbert, "Forty Year Morning."
5. Richard Nixon quoted in Gilbert, "Forty Year Morning."
6. Gilbert, "Forty Year Morning."
7. Gilbert, "Forty Year Morning."
8. *Washington Post*, September 26, 1942.
9. Gilbert, "Forty Year Morning."
10. *Washington Post*, February 13, 1953.
11. Gilbert, "Forty Year Morning."
12. Gilbert, "Forty Year Morning."
13. Gilbert, "Forty Year Morning."
14. Lynn Povich, ed., *All Those Mornings—at the Post: The Twentieth Century in Sports from Famed "Washington Post" Columnist Shirley Povich* (New York: Public Affairs, 2005).
15. *New York Mirror*, October 1, 1961.
16. Bill Peeler, interview by author, August 16, 2010.
17. Bob Alden, interview by and email exchange with author, October 25, 2010.
18. Siegel, "George Preston Marshall."
19. Tom Hurney, interview by author, July 12, 2010.
20. Hurney interview.
21. Siegel, "George Preston Marshall."
22. Peeler interview.
23. *Washington Post*, November 9, 1959.

24. Washington Redskins media guide (1959).

25. *Washington Post*, December 1, 1959.

26. *Washington Post*, December 1, 1959.

6. The Last Word

1. Gordon Parks, *Voices in the Mirror: An Autobiography* (1990; repr., New York: Three Rivers Press, 2005), 105.

2. Quoted in Constance Green, *The Secret City: A History of Race Relations in the Nation's Capital* (Princeton NJ: Princeton University Press, 1967), 278.

3. Kenesaw M. Landis, "Segregation in Washington: A Report of the National Committee on Segregation in the Nation's Capital," Chicago, November 1948.

4. Pauli Murray, ed., *States' Laws on Race and Color* (Athens GA: Women's Division of Christian Service, 1950), 73.

5. *Baltimore Afro-American*, January 21, 1961.

6. *Washington Post*, September 20, 1940.

7. Paul B. Miller and David K. Wiggins, *Sport and the Color Line: Black Athletes and Race Relations in Twentieth Century America* (New York: Routledge, 2004), 306.

8. *Baltimore Afro-American*, January 10, 1961.

9. *Washington Post*, January 27, 1958.

10. *Washington Post*, July 28, 1956.

11. *Washington Post*, October 6, 1956.

12. *Washington Post*, January 6, 1957.

13. *Washington Post*, July 26, 1956.

14. *Washington Post*, April 22, 1958.

15. *Washington Evening Star*, April 25, 1962.

16. *Washington Post*, April 23, 1958.

17. *Washington Post*, April 23, 1958.

18. *Washington Post*, July 8, 1958.

19. *Baltimore Afro-American*, November 28, 1959.

20. *Washington Post*, December 25, 1959.

21. Stewart Udall, memo to President Kennedy, March 21, 1961, Stewart Udall Papers, Special Collections, University of Arizona, Tucson.

22. *Washington Star*, November 4, 1959.

7. "It's Not That Important"

1. *Los Angeles Times*, July 29, 1959.
2. *Chicago Tribune*, July 21, 1959.
3. *Chicago Tribune*, July 21, 1959.
4. *Chicago Tribune*, August 30, 1959.
5. *Chicago Tribune*, August 30, 1959.
6. *New York Times*, August 30, 1959.
7. *Chicago Tribune*, August 31, 1959.
8. *New York Times*, August 31, 1959.
9. *Rome News Times*, October 12, 1959.
10. *Washington Post*, October 12, 1959.
11. *Washington Post*, October 12, 1959.
12. *Washington Post*, October 17, 1959.
13. *Washington Post*, October 21, 1959.
14. Associated Press, October 17, 1959.
15. *Milwaukee Sentinel*, January 8, 1960.
16. *Christian Science Monitor*, January 8, 1960.
17. *Atlanta Daily World,* January 8, 1960.
18. *Washington Post*, February 7, 1960.
19. *Washington Star*, July 15, 1979.
20. *Los Angeles Times*, August 29, 1958.
21. *Newark Star-Ledger*, August 11, 1969.
22. *Washington Post*, January 22, 1960.
23. *Washington Post*, January 27, 1960.
24. *Hartford Courant*, January 29, 1960.
25. *Washington Post*, January 29, 1960.
26. *New York Times*, January 29, 1960; *Chicago Tribune*, January 29, 1960.
27. *Christian Science Monitor*, January 29, 1960.
28. *Los Angeles Sentinel*, February 18, 1960.
29. *Washington Star*, January 12, 1961.
30. *Washington Star*, January 12, 1961.

8. The Last Citadel of Segregation

1. *Washington Star*, October 1, 1960.

2. *Washington Post*, October 10, 1960.

3. *Washington Star*, November 1, 1960.

4. *Washington Post*, October 31, 1960.

5. *Washington Evening Star*, October 23, 1960.

6. *Washington Post*, December 29, 1960.

7. *Washington Post*, December 29, 1960.

8. *Washington Star*, February 14, 1961.

9. *Chattanoogan*, January 24, 2010.

10. *New York Times*, March 7, 1961.

11. Udall memo to President Kennedy, March 21, 1961, Udall Papers.

12. Recalled by Senator Tom Udall in interview by author, July 15, 2011.

13. Recalled in Udall interview.

14. The Udall family had a long and storied history of fighting prejudice and big-otry. One example is the story of Stewart and his brother Mo integrating the University of Arizona's lunchroom. Black students, not permitted inside, had to eat outside. The Udall brothers took a young black student by the name of Morgan Maxwell to the school's cafeteria. "He's our friend, serve him," Stewart said. This civil disobedience was in violation of the university's charter. Rather than expel the Udalls, however, university officials opted to change school policies.

9. States' Rights Football

1. *Washington Daily News*, March 25, 1961.

2. *Washington Evening Star*, March 25, 1961.

3. *Washington Evening Star*, March 25, 1961.

4. *Washington Daily News*, March 25, 1961.

5. Marshall letter to Udall, March 24, 1961, Udall Papers.

6. Siegel, "George Preston Marshall."

7. *Washington Star*, March 25, 1961.

8. James Reston was Washington Bureau chief for the *New York Times*.

9. *Washington Post*, March 25, 1961.

10. *Washington Evening Star*, March 25, 1961.

11. Curtis Williams to Secretary Udall, April 10, 1961, Udall Papers.

12. Secretary Udall to Curtis Williams, April 25, 1961, Udall Papers.

13. *Washington Evening Star*, March 28, 1961.

14. *Washington Evening Star*, March 28, 1961.

15. *Washington Post*, March 28, 1961; *Cleveland Call and Post*, April 8, 1961.

16. *Cleveland Call and Post*, April 8, 1961.

17. *Washington Post*, March 26, 1961.

18. *Washington Daily News*, March 25, 1961.

19. *Washington Post*, March 28, 1961.

20. *Washington Post*, March 26, 1961.

21. *Detroit News*, March 28, 1961.

22. *Washington Post*, March 28, 1961.

23. *Washington Evening Star*, March 29, 1961.

24. *Washington Evening Star*, April 3, 1961.

10. "This Isn't a League Affair"

1. *Washington Daily News*, April 4, 1961.

2. *Washington Daily News*, April 4, 1961.

3. *Augusta (GA) Chronicle*, March 2, 1961.

4. *Tulsa World*, March 31, 1961.

5. *Washington Post*, April 27, 1961.

6. *Christian Science Monitor*, April 27, 1961.

7. *Washington Daily News*, April 25, 1961.

8. *Washington Post*, April 27, 1961.

9. *Washington Evening Star*, April 27, 1961.

10. *Washington Post*, April 27, 1961.

11. *Pittsburgh Courier*, April 24, 1961.

12. Evan Thomas, *The Man to See: Edward Bennett Williams, Ultimate Insider, Legendary Trial Lawyer* (New York: Simon & Schuster, 1991), 168 (quotes); Martie Zad, interview by author, September 30, 2010.

13. *Washington Post*, December 14, 1960.

14. The Long Island Indians had once served as a minor league affiliate for the Redskins.

15. *Milwaukee Journal*, April 24, 1961.

16. *Milwaukee Journal*, April 24, 1961.

17. *Washington Evening Star*, May 5, 1961.

18. *Washington Evening Star*, May 2, 1961.

19. *Washington Daily News*, May 9, 1961.

11. In Good Faith

1. *Washington Post*, July 13, 1961.
2. *Washington Post*, July 13, 1961.
3. *New York Herald Tribune*, July 14, 1961.
4. George Marshall to Pete Rozelle, August 9, 1961, Udall Papers.
5. *Washington Evening Star*, August 15, 1961.
6. *Washington Star*, August 5, 1961.
7. *Washington Evening Star*, August 17, 1961.
8. *Washington Evening Star*, August 15, 1961.
9. *Washington Evening Star*, July 18, 1961.
10. *Los Angeles Examiner*, July 6, 1961.
11. *Los Angeles Herald*, August 15, 1961.

12. "We Mean Business"

1. *Washington Evening Star*, September 8, 1961.
2. *San Francisco Examiner*, September 19, 1961.
3. *San Francisco Examiner*, September 15, 1961.
4. *Washington Star*, January 12, 1961.
5. *Baltimore Sun*, September 19, 1961.
6. *Washington Evening Star*, September 30, 1961.
7. *Washington Evening Star*, September 22, 1961.
8. *Washington Post*, October 1, 1961.
9. *Washington Post*, October 5, 1961.
10. Transcript of October 5, 1961, news conference, *Baltimore Sun*, October 6, 1961; unidentified clipping, Udall Papers.
11. *Washington Evening Star*, October 10, 1961.
12. *Washington Evening Star*, October 18, 1961.
13. Recalled by Mike Brown in interview by author, March 5, 2010.
14. Following the October 8 game, all fourteen league team owners rescinded the rule that prohibited players in the service from participating in league contests.
15. *Washington Evening Star*, October 10, 1961.
16. *Washington Evening Star*, October 19, 1961.
17. *Washington Evening Star*, October 19, 1961.
18. *Washington Post*, October 20, 1961.

19. *Washington Evening Star*, October 27, 1961.

20. *Washington Evening Star*, October 24, 1961.

21. *Washington Evening Star*, November 3, 1961.

22. "Ernie Davis, Everybody's All-American," *Ebony*, December 1961.

23. *Washington Post*, December 5, 1961.

24. George Preston Marshall, with Melvin Durslag, "Pro Football Is Better Football," *Saturday Evening Post*, December 9, 1961.

25. *Baltimore Afro-American*, December 16, 1961.

26. *Dallas Morning News*, November 19, 1961.

27. *Washington Evening Star*, November 28, 1961.

28. *Washington Post*, November 21, 1961.

29. *Washington Post*, November 21, 1961.

30. *Washington Evening Star*, November 28, 1961.

31. *Washington Post*, December 1, 1961.

32. *Washington Post*, December 1, 1961.

33. *Washington Star*, December 4, 1961.

13. "I'm Still Running This Team"

1. *Washington Daily News*, December 7, 1961.

2. *Cleveland Plain Dealer*, December 5, 1961.

3. *Washington Post*, December 5, 1961.

4. *Washington Post*, December 6, 1961.

5. *Washington Evening Star*, December 7, 1961.

6. *Washington Daily News*, December 12, 1961.

7. *Baltimore Sun*, December 6, 1961.

8. *Baltimore Sun*, December 6, 1961.

9. *Washington Post*, December 10, 1961.

10. *Washington Star*, December 10, 1961.

11. *Washington Star*, December 10, 1961.

12. *Washington Post*, December 10, 1961.

13. *Washington Post*, December 11, 1961.

14. *Baltimore Afro-American*, December 16, 1961.

15. Recalled by Ron Hatcher in interview by author, August 5, 2010.

16. Recalled by Steve Guback in interview by author, August 26, 2010.

17. *Washington Daily News*, December 19, 1961.

18. *Washington Daily News*, December 19, 1961.

19. *Washington Evening Star*, December 13, 1961.

20. *Washington Evening Star*, December 14, 1961.

21. *Washington Evening Star*, December 14, 1961.

22. *Washington Post*, December 15, 1961.

23. *Washington Post*, July 24, 1983.

24. Quoted in Ken Denlinger and Paul Attner, *Redskin Country: From Baugh to the Super Bowl* (New York: Leisure Press, 1983), 94.

25. Quoted in Paul Fine, "Historically Speaking," *Black Sports Magazine*, January 1978.

26. *Hartford Courant*, October 30, 1962.

27. Quoted in Fine, "Historically Speaking."

28. *Hartford Courant*, October 30. 1962.

29. *Baltimore Afro-American*, January 27, 1962.

14. "Is That All?"

1. *Washington Post*, January 25, 1962.

2. *Washington Post*, January 25, 1962.

3. *Washington Evening Star*, February 15, 1962.

4. *Washington Post*, February 27, 1962.

5. *Washington Post*, February 27, 1962.

6. *Washington Post*, February 27, 1962.

7. *Washington Post*, February 27, 1962.

8. *Washington Post*, February 27, 1962.

9. *New York Times*, February 28, 1962.

10. *Washington Post*, March 4, 1962.

11. *Washington Post*, March 6, 1962.

12. *Washington Post*, March 15, 1962.

13. *Washington Post*, March 14, 1962.

14. *Washington Post*, March 15, 1962.

15. *New York Times*, March 16, 1962.

16. Marshall's chauffeur for a number of years was Marvin Cooper.

17. *Washington Evening Star*, March 28, 1962.

18. *Washington Post*, March 28, 1962.

19. *Norfolk New Journal and Guide*, April 28, 1962.

20. *New York Times*, May 22, 1962.

21. *New York Times*, May 22, 1962.

22. *Washington Post*, May 22, 1962.

23. *Chicago Tribune*, May 22, 1962.

24. *Chicago Tribune*, May 22, 1962.

25. *Washington Post*, May 5, 1962.

26. *Chicago Tribune*, May 28, 1962.

15. Out of the Shadows

1. Fine, "Historically Speaking."

2. *Washington Evening Star*, July 24, 1962.

3. Fine, "Historically Speaking."

4. *Washington Star*, August 16, 1962.

5. *Washington Evening Star*, September 4, 1962.

6. *Washington Evening Star*, September 4, 1962.

7. John Devaney, "Bobby Mitchell: The Power of Confidence," *Sport Magazine*, December 1963.

8. Tex Maule, "The Browns Break Through," *Sports Illustrated*, September 10, 1962.

9. *Washington Post*, September 19, 62.

10. Devaney, "Bobby Mitchell."

11. Devaney, "Bobby Mitchell."

12. *Washington Evening Star*, September 22, 1962.

13. *Washington Post*, September 23, 1962.

14. *Washington Post*, September 23, 1962.

15. *Washington Evening Star*, September 22, 1961.

16. *Washington Post*, September 12, 1962.

17. Tex Maule, "The Redskins Find a New Kick: Winning," *Sports Illustrated*, October 15, 1962.

18. *Washington Post*, October 27, 1962.

19. *Washington Evening Star*, October 30, 1962.

20. Devaney, "Bobby Mitchell."

21. Devaney, "Bobby Mitchell."

22. *Dallas Times Herald*, October 31, 1962.

23. Thomas, *Man to See*.

24. Jackson carried the ball forty-nine times, for 112 yards and one touchdown.
25. *Washington Evening Star*, November 5, 1962.
26. *Washington Evening Star*, November 3, 1962.
27. *Washington Evening Star*, November 3, 1962.
28. *Washington Evening Star*, December 17, 1962.

Epilogue

1. *Sporting News*, February 9, 1963.
2. Recalled by Art Rooney Jr. in interview by author, April 14, 2010.
3. *Washington Evening Star*, March 31, 1963.
4. *Washington Evening Star*, March 31, 1963.
5. The 1963 class of Hall of Fame inductees consisted of Sammy Baugh, Bert Bell, Joe Carr, Earl "Dutch" Clark, Harold "Red" Grange, George Halas, Mel Hein, Wilbur "Pete" Henry, Robert "Cal" Hubbard, Don Huston, Earl "Curly" Lambeau, Tim Mara, George Preston Marshall, John "Blood" McNally, Bronislau "Bronko" Nagurski, Ernie Nevers, and Jim Thorpe.
6. *Los Angeles Times*, March 21, 2010.
7. Philip L. Fradkin, *A River No More: The Colorado River and the West* (Berkeley: University of California Press, 1996), 232.
8. John Keim, "Bobby Mitchell Weighs in on Name Change" (blog entry), *NFL Nation*, ESPN.com, May 5, 2014, http://espn.go.com/blog/washington -redskins/post/_/id/7409/bobby-mitchell-weighs-in-on-name-change.
9. Keim, "Bobby Mitchell Weighs in on Name Change."
10. "Bobby Mitchell, the First Black Football Player for the Redskins," CBS 60 Minutes Sports Report, January 5, 2015, http://www.cbsnews.com/videos/bobby -mitchell-the-first-black-football-player-for-the-washington-redskins/.
11 *Washington Post*, July 31, 1983.
12. *Washington Post*, July 31, 1983.
13. *Washington Post*, July 31, 1983.
14. Following three years of battling the Cowboys for the loyalty of Dallas football fans, Hunt had thrown in the towel and relocated his Texans to Kansas City on May 22, 1963.
15. *Washington Star*, August 10, 1969.
16. *Newark Star-Ledger*, August 11, 1969.
17. *Washington Star*, August 10, 1969.

18. *Washington Daily News*, August 13, 1960.
19. *New York Mirror*, October 1, 1961.
20. *Washington Post*, August 14, 1969.
21. Marshall's surviving family was aghast at the odious stipulation in the will. Eventually his last act of bigotry was overturned by a judge, who deemed the clause to be illegal. In four decades the George Preston Marshall Foundation gave millions of dollars to DC area schools and charities.

Index

Bergman, Dutch, 17, 29
Berry, Raymond, 58, 175
Bidwill, Charles, 36, 58
Bidwill, Violet. *See* Wolfner, Violet
Blanchard, Doc, 6
Boggs, Frank, 196–97
Bostic, Joe, 81
Boston Braves, 18, 22–23
Boston Globe, 22
Brady, Dave, 55, 192
Brallier, John, 128
Breeskin, Barnee, 3
Brown, Hugh, 47
Brown, Jim, 8, 80, 103, 142, 147, 162, 191, 194, 208, 209
Brown, Paul, 43, 50, 103; Bobby Mitchell and, 166, 182, 188–89, 193–95, 197; consideration of, for commissioner, 92; 1961–62 draft and, 142–45, 153–54, 162. *See also* Cleveland Browns
Brown, Roosevelt, 80
Bryant, Paul, 30
Burns, Jimmy, 169–70

Canton Repository, 206
Capital Press Club, 5, 6–9
CBS television, 32, 39, 121, 122, 168, 171, 185
Celler, Emanuel, 45, 47
Chandler, Albert "Happy," 93, 139
Characters Social Club of DC, 52
Chevalier, John, 213
Chicago Bears, 23–26, 39, 64, 168. *See also* Halas, George "Papa Bear"
Chicago Cardinals, 9, 13, 21, 58–60, 89, 172

Chicago Defender, 7, 8, 81
Chicago Tribune, 89
Ciraolo, Frank, 40
Clark, Tom, 41–42, 63
Cleveland Browns, 43, 89; Bobby Mitchell and, 142–44, 162–63, 166, 182, 186, 188–89, 193–95, 197; integration of, 2, 8; and signing of Ernie Davis, 147, 150, 153–56, 162, 166–67, 170; television and, 39, 168. *See also* Brown, Paul
Collins, Gary, 153
Committee against Discrimination in Sports, 52
Conaty, John "Red," 24
Congress on Racial Equality (CORE), 137–38, 140
Conn, Billy, 65
Considine, Bob, 26
Cooke, Jack Kent, 126–27, 139, 192, 211
Coones, Rod, 24
Cooper, Chuck, 2
Custer, Rudy, 23

Dallas, expansion discussions and, 90, 95, 96, 99–100, 171–72, 179–80
Dallas Cowboys, 103, 104–5, 149, 160–61, 169, 171, 180, 190
Dallas Rangers, 98, 149
Dallas Texans, 169, 172–76, 178, 180, 228n14
Dallas Times Herald, 196–97
D'Andelet, John, 20
Davis, Ernie: Heisman Trophy and, 151, 154–55, 158, 166; mention of, in

letter to Stewart Udall, 132; signing
of, 147, 150, 153–56, 162, 166–67, 170
Davis, Glenn, 6, 165
DC Stadium: George Preston
Marshall on, 138; George Preston
Marshall's box at, 139, 160; halftime
shows at, 160–62; and need to
replace Griffith Stadium, 83–86,
128; and nondiscrimination clause
issues, 86–87, 106–10, 113, 117,
124, 129–30, 151. *See also* Griffith
Stadium
DeGroot, Dudley, 29
Denlinger, Ken, 208
De Orsey, Leo, 30, 86, 87, 204, 211
Devaney, John, 196
Devine, Tommy, 169–70
Dickinson College, 204, 213
Dietz, William "Lone Star," 20
"Dixie," 74, 184
Don, Ted, 105
Donoghue, Joseph A., 98
Donovan, Robert J., 131
Douds, Forrest "Jap," 21
Doyle, Larry, 18
Dugan, Fred, 200
Dumont Television Network, 37
Durslag, Mel, 136, 148
Dutton, Fred, 109

Edwards, Albert Turk, 29, 30
Eisenhower, Dwight D., 8, 13, 63, 72,
83, 86, 107, 171

Ferguson, Bob, 132
"Fight for Old Dixie," 4, 61

"Fight on Redskins," 3–4
Filchock, Frank, 28, 34
Fiss, Galen, 188
Flaherty, Ray, 16–17, 21, 29
Foss, Joe, 99, 100, 176
Friedman, Benny, 18, 205

Gabriel, Roman, 163
gambling, NFL and, 34–35, 38, 46
Gates, Frank, 109, 129
Gautt, Prentice, 146
Gesell, Gerhard A., 172, 176–78
Gibbons, Jim, 97
Gibron, Abe, 43
Gilmer, Harry, 144
Glen Echo Park, 77
Goldberg, Arthur, 63
Graham, Philip, 63
Grange, Harold "Red," 47, 206
Green, Elijah "Pumpsie," 61
Grieve, Curley, 138
Griffith, Calvin, 85, 169
Griffith, Clark, 63, 64
Griffith Stadium: black employees
at, 79, 159; neighborhood of, 76,
84; proposal to replace, 83–86, 128;
Sam Lacy and, 81–82. *See also* DC
Stadium
Guback, Steve, 123
Gunsel, Austin, 34, 92, 93

Hackett, Buddy, 194, 195
"Hail to the Redskins," 61, 66, 74, 96–
97, 103, 191
Halas, George "Papa Bear," 1, 96; and
AFL antitrust suit, 181; Bert Bell and,

Rooney, Art (*cont.*)
consideration of, for commissioner, 93; George Preston Marshall's death and, 212; league expansion and, 90, 94; on NFL game scheduling, 36
Rooney, Art, Jr., 202
Rooney, Dan, 212
Rooney, Tim, 202
Roosevelt, James, 13
Rosenbloom, Carroll, 93, 154, 174
Rote, Kyle, 175
Rozelle, Pete, 104, 106, 139; choice of, as NFL commissioner, 93; contract extension for, 168; George Preston Marshall and, 131–34, 142–43, 203, 205, 213; and Harry Wismer's share of Redskins, 125; impact of, on NFL, 209–10; league expansion and, 97–98, 99, 100; Los Angeles Rams and, 32, 51–52, 94, 100; 1961–62 draft and, 145, 153, 163; television contracts and, 121–22, 168

Sample, Johnny, 160
San Francisco Clippers, 40
San Francisco Examiner, 138
San Francisco 49ers, 37, 89, 176
Saturday Evening Post, 148
Sauerbrei, Harold, 144
Schafrath, Dick, 144
Schmelke, Gary, 24
Schramm, Tex, 212
Schwartzwalder, Ben, 147
Scott, Ben, 200
segregation in Washington DC, 76–78
Shaw, Robert Gould, 76

Shea, Bill, 126–27, 139, 192
Shea, George, 87
Showers, Nick, 146
Siegel, Mo, 69–73, 120, 155, 185–86, 203, 205
Slattery, Dave, 73
Smith, Alfred E., 7
Smith, Flavious "Nig," 72
Smith, Wendell, 81, 124–25
Snead, Norm, 104, 140, 182, 187, 188, 193
Sport Magazine, 1, 53–55, 186, 196
Sports Illustrated, 187, 192–93
sportswriters, 68–70, 73–74, 81. *See also specific writers*
Stann, Francis, 48, 49, 69, 73–74, 200, 211–12
Stein, Coleman, 126
Stimson, Henry, 64–65, 66
Sugrue, Thomas, 23
Super Bowls, 210
Supreme Court, x, 12, 40–42, 45, 78, 95
Swope, Tom, 82

Taylor, Hugh "Bones," 200
Taylor, Jim, 201
television contracts and revenue, 12, 31–32, 37–40, 44, 50, 52, 57–58, 74–75, 89, 94, 121–24, 168, 171, 173
Thomsen, Roszel Cathcart, 171–72, 174, 176–81
Thorpe, Jim, 206
Tittle, Y. A., 140, 201
Todd, Dick, 29
Toneff, Bob, 171
Torgeson, LaVern "Torgy," 55, 105

Touchdown Club, 70–71, 102, 138, 166, 189

Tulsa World, 121

Twelfth Street Y, 7. *See also* Capital Press Club

Udall, Stewart, 128, 196–97; antidiscrimination work of, 108–10, 111–19, 120–25, 127, 222n14; George Preston Marshall's letter to, 132–34, 140–42; legacy of, 206–7; 1961–62 draft and, 150–52; and picket lines at Redskins games, 140, 142; and proof of George Preston Marshall's discrimination, 129–31; *The Quiet Crisis*, 207

Unitas, Johnny, 57, 209

Van Brocklin, Norm, 55–56, 104

Vinson, Fred, 53

Walker, Doak, 175

Walsh, Jack, 118, 123, 130, 154, 156, 163, 169, 188

Ward, Arch, 32

Warren, Earl, 41, 63

Washington, Chet, 81

Washington Daily News, 68–69, 73, 120, 155, 212

Washington Evening Star, 133, 146, 162, 170, 178, 185, 200

Washington Post, 26, 52, 55, 68–69, 72, 80, 85, 126, 157, 192, 208. *See also* Povich, Shirley; Walsh, Jack

Washington Redskins, 75, 102–5; coaches of, 16–17, 20–21, 29–30, 105, 134–35; decline of, after Sammy Baugh's departure, 27–28; and draft of Ernie Davis, 147, 150, 153–56, 162, 166–67, 170; exclusion of, from AFL/NFL lawsuit, 176, 177; fight song of, 3–4, 61; after George Preston Marshall's death, 211; George Preston Marshall's refusal to integrate, 1–4, 9–14, 15, 51–56, 61, 122–25, 131; John Nisby and, 182–83; losing season and first draft pick of, 139, 142, 146–47; protests against discrimination policy of, 135–38, 140; and reception of first black players, 183–84; and recruiting from all-white colleges, 80–81, 129; signing of Ron Hatcher by, 156–59; television and, 39, 168

Washington Senators, 63, 64, 83–85, 146, 169

Washington Star, 48–49, 68–69, 73–74, 77, 123, 142, 145

Washington Times-Herald, 68

Washington Tribune, 8, 81

Weissman, Harold, 68

Werblin, Sonny, 210

Whelchel, John, 29

Williams, Curtis, 115

Williams, Edward Bennett, 63, 125–26, 162, 178, 208, 211

Wilson, Woodrow, 77

Winter, Max, 98

Wismer, Harry, 5, 53, 138, 189; on AFL antitrust suit, 181; on lack of integration of Redskins, 6–9, 14, 73; lawsuit of, against George Preston Marshall, 6–7, 13–14; and selling share of Redskins, 125–27; as "Voice of the Reskins," 5

Witucki, Casimir "Slug," 190